Religion in a
Free Market

MARKETING BOOKS FROM PMP

The Kids Market: *Myths & Realities*

Marketing to American Latinos, Part I

Marketing to American Latinos, Part II

The Whole Enchilada

Beyond Bogedas: *Developing a Retail Relationship
with Hispanic Customers*

The Mirrored Window: *Focus Groups
from a Moderator's Point of View*

The Great Tween Buying Machine

Marketing Insights to Help Your Business Grow

Why People Buy Things They Don't Need

A Knight's Code of Business: *How to Achieve
Character and Competence in the Corporate World*

India Business: *Finding Opportunities
in this Big Emerging Market*

Moderating to the Max! *A Full-tilt Guide to Creative
Focus Groups and Insightful Depth Interviews*

Marketing to Leading-Edge Baby Boomers

Clear Eye for Branding: *Straight Talk on
Today's Most Powerful Business Concept*

Advertising to Baby Boomers

What's Black About It? : *Insights to Increase Your Share of
a Changing African-American Market*

Marketing to the New Super Consumer: Mom & Kid

Hispanic Marketing Grows Up:
Exploring Perceptions and Facing Realities

Beyond the Mission Statement: *The Guide to Creating Truly Effective,
Cause-Based Communications*

Religion
in a
Free Market

Religious and Non-Religious Americans
WHO | WHAT | WHY | WHERE

BARRY A. KOSMIN AND **ARIELA KEYSAR**

PMP

PARAMOUNT MARKET PUBLISHING, INC.

Paramount Market Publishing, Inc.
301 South Geneva Street, Suite 109, Ithaca, NY 14850
www.paramountbooks.com
Phone: 607-275-8100; 888-787-8100 • Fax: 607-275-8101

Publisher: James Madden
Editorial Director: Doris Walsh

Cataloging in Publication Data available
ISBN 978-0-9766973-6-7

Contents

Figures

For Egon Mayer Ph. D. (1944–2004) Sociologist of Religion—

our good friend and colleague

●　　●　　●

THE AUTHORS would like to thank the following individuals for their help and advice with this project: Felix Posen and the Posen Foundation for their encouragement and support of the *American Religious Identification Survey* 2001; John De Wolfe of ICR for managing the survey fieldwork; Dale Kulp for his statistical expertise; Peter Coy for his editorial insights; and Doris Walsh for her vision of the potential market for our research.

Preface

FIVE YEARS AGO, Trinity College's Leonard E. Greenberg Center for the Study of Religion in Public Life embarked on a major project to assess the role of religion in the public life of each of eight regions of the United States. To do so, we needed to obtain the best picture we could of America's religious demography. And that meant we had to beat a path to Barry Kosmin and Ariela Keysar's door. As conductors of the 2001 *American Religious Identification Survey* (ARIS), Kosmin and Keysar had the best—really, the only sufficiently extensive—data showing how Americans identify themselves religiously. And against the background of the prior 1990 *National Survey of Religious Identification,* they were able to point to critical trends in the data. It is hard to overemphasize the importance of ARIS in enabling us to place our enterprise on a solid empirical footing.

Now, with this volume, we have the surveyors' own account of what they found. Without stealing their thunder, I would just note that much of what they have to say—about the growth of the secular segment of the population, about the character of religious switching, about the growth of non-Christian religions—is new and startling. No less important is how their findings can be used to sharpen and enrich other sources of information, both quantitative and qualitative, on religion in America.

Thus, in combination with membership data supplied by religious institutions, ARIS enables us to specify the size of a large and mysterious portion of the American population: those who claim a religious identity but are not members of any religious body. In the country as a whole, that represents over 25 percent of the population, and in those parts of the country where religious affiliation rates are low—the Western regions—ranges even more to nearly a third. Who are these people? How many of them are moving towards greater religious commitment, away from it, or standing still?

Beyond that, the ARIS data give us special insights into the character of our religious connections. Most Protestant denominations, for example, count as members significantly fewer people than claim to belong to these dominations; for example, less than half of those who identify themselves as some kind of mainline Protestant actually belong to a mainline Protestant church. By contrast, the number of individuals calling themselves Roman Catholics is only marginally greater than the number of members on the rolls of the Catholic Church, while the Church of Jesus Christ of Latter-day Saints actually claims more members than there are people who say they are Mormons. There is much to be made of such variations.

Finally, like any first-rate data set, ARIS permits us to interrogate theories that are based on it—including the meaning of America's religious free market. There can be little doubt that, as Kosmin and Keysar argue, this religion market has, nationwide, been amazingly productive of religious diversity and highly productive of religious commitment. But Kosmin and Keysar also insist on disaggregating the data by region, pointing out that regional religious cultures have, despite the mobility of the population, remained remarkably stable over time. And this suggests that the American religious marketplace may be considered as a series of different markets, each of which operates in somewhat different ways.

Thus, the Middle Atlantic States lend support to the idea that the more competing religious "firms" there are, the greater success religion will enjoy. But the same cannot be said of the West Coast, which has long been home to a remarkably varied and entrepreneurial array of religious groups, but which has significantly lower rates of religious participation than the rest of the country. And then there is the Mormon corridor of Utah and Idaho, where the Latter Day Saints church functions as a religious establishment—a virtual monopoly—and yet the religious commitment of the population is among the highest in the nation.

All this is to say that *Religion in a Free Market* belongs to that best of all species of social scientific literature: It makes provocative claims, gives the reader the wherewithal to evaluate them, and (last but not least) raises myriad new questions to answer. At a time when religion in American society is changing shape before our eyes, and when religious actors are taking a larger part in American politics than ever before, who could ask for anything more?

—Mark Silk
Trinity College, Hartford, Connecticut
2006

Introduction

GOD may be unchanging and heaven eternal, but religion in America is in constant ferment. New sects and faiths are born; others wither. People grow in devotion or become disillusioned. Religion both contributes to and is affected by the turbulence of modern society: war, economic growth, technological change, new ethical puzzles. While religion is about God, it is practiced by people. Those who offer up their prayers to the Almighty on the weekend (or don't) are the same people who buy cars and laundry detergent, watch sitcoms, and agonize over tax cuts, climate change and terrorism.

Reflecting that turbulence, *Religion in a Free Market* is not a book of eternal verities. It is the most complete statistical portrait available of religion as actually experienced in one country at one point in time: the United States in 2001, the dawn of the millennium. The statistical portrait covers religion from the perspective of politics, economics, gender, generation, and geography. The analysis is based largely on a resource of unrivaled richness and quality: the *American Religious Identification Survey* (ARIS) of 2001, which covered a random sample of more than 50,000 adults who identified themselves with dozens of religious groups, from Roman Catholics and Methodists to Sikhs, Rastafarians, and Druids.

Why read this book? First, because religious ferment is as strong as it has ever been, so whatever you learned about religion in the U.S. a generation ago is out of date. Second, because whether you are a political consultant, a marketer, a religious leader, or a social scientist, it is impossible to understand America without understanding religion in America. According to

ARIS, 75 percent of adults in 2001 said they are religious or somewhat religious, and 91 percent said they believe in God. Even those
who consider themselves secular—a rapidly growing portion of the
public—are acutely aware of and influenced by the religious milieu
surrounding them.

As its title indicates, *Religion in a Free Market* is built on one key
idea—that religion in America can best be understood as a product
on offer in the marketplace of ideas. It is no sacrilege to observe that
religious institutions craft sales messages, recruit "customers," and
focus intently on retention policies. The "customers," in turn, pick
from a smorgasbord of religious choices, including the choice of no
religion at all. What clergy have observed anecdotally, and other
researchers have speculated on, we document scientifically. Here are
the key findings of this book:

- America remains primarily a Christian society at the beginning of
  the 21st century. However, the share of the population that self-
  identified with a Christian faith tradition declined abruptly from
  86.2 percent in 1990 to 76.5 percent in 2001. Only a small part
  of the decrease in self-identified Christians can be attributed to a
  greater unwillingness among respondents to answer survey questions.

- The share of American adults who say they have no religion rose
  from 8 percent in 1990 to 14 percent in 2001, which amounts to
  approximately 30 million people.

- Somewhat surprisingly the minority non-Christian faiths' share
  of the national population rose only very slightly from 3.3 percent in 1990 to 3.7 percent in 2001.

- Sixteen percent of American adults had switched religious identification at some point in their lives as of 2001, with Catholicism
  as the biggest numerical loser and "no religion" as the biggest
  numerical gainer.

- The mobility of American society has done little or nothing to
  erode strong regional religious cultures such as those of the
  Catholics of the Northeast, the Lutherans of the Upper Midwest,

the Baptists of the South and the "Nones" of the Pacific Northwest.

- There is a huge generation gap emerging in religion. Despite popular impressions of religiously engaged youth, in general the old and middle-aged are far more likely than the young to believe in God and identify with a religious group.

For a subject of such intense interest, the religious identity and beliefs of the American people has been surprisingly under-researched. For constitutional reasons, the government does not ask questions about religious identification in the Census. Private surveys have inconsistent, conflicting, and incomplete information about membership in religious denominations. Religious bodies most often use their own membership lists as the basis of surveys, and given that the criteria for who counts as a member vary a great deal across religious bodies, religious statistics are a collection of "apples and oranges." The often cited source of religious data, the 2000 *Religious Congregations and Membership Survey* (RCMS) compiled by the Glenmary Research Center, assembled data based on the congregations' own criteria of adherents or participants. The 2000 RCMS did not include most historically African-American Protestant denominations. What is more, few private surveys include or adequately differentiate the large number of people who identify with religious traditions and groups but are not members of congregations. Finally, there has been little detailed comparative research on the religious beliefs of Americans in the smaller religious groups or among ethnic minorities.

Religion in a Free Market overcomes the failings of much prior research on American religion by drawing heavily on the findings of the landmark *American Religious Identification Survey* (ARIS) 2001. This survey covered a large, national, representative cross-section of the American public, and asked questions about religious identification, belief, and behavior. ARIS has been cited annually in the *Statistical Abstract of the United States*, a Census Bureau publication, as the primary data source for the religious identification of American adults.

Identifying people by their religion is fraught with potential controversy. Who decides who counts as a Roman Catholic, for example? Should it be the parish priest or the Pope in Rome? Who decides who's a Jehovah's Witness or Wicca? ARIS cuts this Gordian knot by relying on self-reporting. We opted for an open-ended question: *What is your religion, if any?* This approach takes away the power of classification from the religious institution—the supplier—and gives it to the individual respondent—the autonomous consumer. While some religious bodies might not agree with some self-classifications, the methodology of self-reporting has the essential merit of consistency across all religious traditions. It also has the merit of being respectful of our respondents. It is a democratic process where the public decide for themselves who and what they are, using their own words.

By casting a wide net, self-reporting catches a vast variety of self-descriptions: more than 100 categories of religious groups, faiths, denominations, and orientations. We realize that the large number of categories is challenging for analytical purposes. It would have been far simpler to create ahead of time a short list of religious groups, perhaps five to seven, as in some other surveys. Fortunately, we have the experience and statistical skills to analyze the vast quantities of data emanating from ARIS. The availability of 50,000 cases allowed us to create the sociodemographic and economic profiles of many religious groups usually not available in ordinary market, academic, or public opinion surveys with their limited sample sizes.

True, there are considerable problems involved in asking people in a telephone survey to self-identify their religion. Some people name their local church, rather than their denomination. Others give answers offering a generic "brand" or "tradition" such as "Baptist," leaving out the distinction between particular denominations such as American versus Southern Baptist. On the positive side, despite the personal nature of religion, we found that most people have no problem reporting on their belief in God, or religious preference. Indeed, the refusal rate to the particular question, *What is your religion, if any?* was just 5.4 percent. The fact that a great majority provided an answer ought to encourage social scientists to keep on asking such questions and to duplicate this approach of using open-ended self-reporting, even though it complicates the job of coding answers into categories.

Because ARIS essentially replicated the methodology of our previous study, the *National Survey of Religious Identification* (NSRI) 1990, we were able to generate trend data, something which has been scarce in the sociology and demography of U.S. religion. We are able to report on the shifts that occurred between 1990 and 2001, an important decade of societal and economic change. Waves of immigrants shaped the demography of the U.S. population, while major economic and political events, like the stock market's bull and bear markets and the Gulf War, influenced people's perceptions and world views. ARIS data collection was completed before the terrorist attacks of September 11, 2001.

The book is organized as follows: Chapter 1 develops the concept of the U.S. as a free marketplace for religion, drawing on the economic theory of Adam Smith and carrying the analysis forward to the present. Chapters 2 and 3 are detailed analyses of the ARIS results, including a national religious profile, detailed statistics on *belonging* to religious institutions, *believing* in God and *behavior*. Chapter 4 presents unique data on religious switching. Chapters 5 and 6 dwell on demographic variables such as gender, age, marital status and children in the various religious groups. Chapter 7 illustrates the relationship between geography and religion by providing details on regions and large states. Chapters 8 and 9 focus on socioeconomic status. They cover economic indicators such as educational attainment, employment status, household income, home ownership and attempt to rank the religious groups by socioeconomic indices. Chapter 10 is a case study that evaluates the religious factor in patterns of consumption of the new technologies. Chapters 11 and 12 look at reported religious affiliation and the pool of potential recruits. Namely, we compare the characteristics of members of religious congregations with those of the nominal adherents, i.e., those who self-identify with a particular religious group but do not belong to any of its religious institutions. Chapter 13 is devoted to an exceedingly topical issue—the interplay between religion and political party preferences in contemporary American society. Chapter 14 examines the race and ethnic factor in religious identification by taking advantage of the sheer size of ARIS to provide rare findings on a small minority, Native Americans, as well as the larger and fast-growing

Asian and Latino populations. Chapter 15 describes the profile of the American Muslim population. Chapter 16, the concluding chapter, distills the findings of the book and projects the trends forward.

Religion in a Free Market provides a statistical compendium on the current state of American religion. The reader may choose to read the entire book, or, alternatively, to consult the table of contents and list of charts and tables in order to focus on particular facts on a specific group, an individual age cohort, or a geographical area. We hope all readers will find this unique body of facts and figures useful in their work.

ONE

American Religion, Religious Brands, and Markets

The Link Between Religious and Economic Freedom

1776 WAS A banner year for freedom in America. It saw the publication of the two foundation documents of liberty, the rule of law and the idea of limited government that made the free world we now know: The American *Declaration of Independence,* authored by Virginian planter and politician Thomas Jefferson and *An Inquiry into the Nature and Causes of the Wealth of Nations,* authored by Scotsman Adam Smith, at one time Professor of Moral Science at the University of Glasgow. Both attacked mercantilism, meaning government control of economic life to enhance the wealth of the state.

These two true sons of the Enlightenment, Jefferson and Smith, were dedicated to upholding reason, liberty, and the possibility of progress in the belief that freedom can be achieved and societies enriched by the dynamism of economic growth and technical progress. Yet paradoxically their efforts probably benefited organized religion, especially in the United States, more than any other societal endeavor. The success of American religion, its amazing vitality and dynamism, is due to the free market–oriented regime it has operated under for over two centuries. Today America is an enclave of intense religious devotion and activity in the mostly secular club of advanced industrial democracies.

Most people are aware of Jefferson's contribution to the establishment of the *Novus ordo seclorum*[1]—the new world order—where for the first time no religious tests were to be demanded for public office and the state declared itself neutral or indifferent regarding religion. As third President of the United States (1801–09) he wrote of "the wall of separation between church and state."[2] It was James Madison, his fellow Virginian, protégé, and successor as President (1809–17) who in 1787 wrote the First Amendment to the United States Constitution creating "the wall." "Congress shall make no law respecting the establishment of religion, or prohibiting the free exercise thereof."

Less known is Adam Smith's contribution to these ideals that guaranteed free exercise of conscience and prohibited a state establishment of religion. Smith is famous for his economic thought and particularly his arguments in favor of free enterprise and his attack on government regulation and control of the economy. Put simply, he believed government intervention in the marketplace was inefficient and detrimental to growth and success of any enterprise. What is not so often recognized is that Smith dealt with religion in Book Five of *Wealth of Nations* and in his *Theory of Moral Sentiments* and that he applied the same market principles to religious enterprises with an attack on the laziness and inefficiency of highly subsidized state-run religious establishments such as the Church of England and the Lutheran and Catholic monopolies of continental Europe. These coercive monopolies relied on state support rather than popular appeal, he wrote. Their clergy had no incentive for "any vigorous exertion" since their parishioners could not defect to other faiths. Protected from competition by the state they had little incentive to minister to the needs of the population other than the upper or ruling classes.

Smith argued that a free market in religion was both good for religion itself and an important principle of liberty. A free society would produce a diversity of religious demand that in turn would produce pluralism. The more "religious firms" there were the better for society. Interestingly the practical example he pointed to of this system of "no ecclesiastical government" at work and where "the law in reality favours no one sect more than another" was the Colony of Pennsylvania. He also pointed out the great virtue of this free market system to Europeans who feared a recurrence of the religious warfare of the 16th and 17th centuries. Up to this time most philosophers, including his compatriots Thomas Hobbes and David Hume, recognized that the natural state of affairs was diversity of moral visions but they feared that this competitive situation would lead to religious strife and only an established church could prevent this undesirable result. Smith inverted this theory and postulated that:

> "sects . . . sufficiently numerous, and each of them consequently too small to disturb public tranquillity, the excessive zeal of each for its particular tenets could not well be productive of any very harmful effects, but, on the contrary, of several good ones: if the government was perfectly decided both to let them all alone, and to oblige them all to let alone one another . . ."[3]

This generation was animated by a belief that governments were potentially tyrannical and incompetent so it was unwise to have them looking after your spiritual needs or immortal soul. Indeed Smith asserted that politicians would inevitably debase or divert religion for their own ends. This skeptical attitude had a liberating effect as the principles of freedom were extended to non-Protestant religions. In 1790 in a letter to the Hebrew Congregation of Newport, Rhode Island, President George Washington assured America's Jews that "All possess alike liberty of conscience and immunities of citizenship. . . . For happily the Government of the United States gives to bigotry no sanction, to persecution no assistance."[4]

Smith and many of his contemporaries, especially the founders of the American republic, were undoubtedly unorthodox in their religious views, and often Deists or agnostics, but they saw religion as a public good and ally of their wider aspirations. They believed that religion, morals, and marriage were as important to society as political structures, economics, and markets and were closely bound up with them. Organized religion was useful to the nation and needed to be encouraged. Paradoxically a secular state needed a religious people because families and churches were the two main institutions that buttressed the intergenerational stability that a free society required. In terms of interpersonal relationships they recognized that religion was a moral enforcement mechanism that enhanced mutual trust and lowered levels of corruption, key requirements for the new society. They maintained that this utilitarian view of the political and social benefit supplied by religion did not demean it but actually suggested religion was essential to the welfare of mankind.

Smith's final argument for free-market religion was almost a prophetic account of the current American religious landscape. Without religious regulation or in circumstances of complete religious freedom, a religious market would be highly competitive because it allows for the promotion of multiple religious doctrines. "Specialized religious firms" would cater to the various spiritual niches in the religious market. As in the unregulated economic market each seller could set his own sale price and each buyer would be free to seek the lowest price acceptable. Yet religious strife would be minimal by historic standards. Religious groups would succeed and fail based on their own initiative and powers of persuasion. In this setting of active religious competition, no single group would corner the market and new movements that were best suited to the times and circumstances would grow and flourish. However, he warned that the outcome might not always favor reason and sophistication. "The new religions" could well be "led by popular and bold, though perhaps stupid and ignorant enthusiasts."

Religious Cost-Benefit Analysis

The description supplied by Smith is very close to the actuality of American religion, particularly in its most typical form, Protestantism. The market system allows different generations and groups to seek different responses to their spiritual and religious needs. Thus there has been a constant churning and change taking place with eras of "great awakening" and religious revivals. Sociologists Stark and Finke have claimed that individuals apply a "cost benefit analysis" framework to religious participation between this world and offers of goods in the world to come.[5] The lack of constraints on religious activity allows people to explore and celebrate beliefs and treasured values when, where and how they wish. It also allows the public to reject scandal-ridden institutions or theologies that no longer convince them. As Smith said, energy and enthusiasm may outweigh intellectual consistency and scholarship so there is no guarantee that American religion will go "up market."

Not only are established religious denominations and groups always mutating, new ones are constantly being born. Moreover, at the beginning of the 21st century there is as much religious flux as there has ever been. This is because of the way religious groups evolve from "sect" to "church." New movements tend to be ideologically and spiritually at odds with the surrounding society and seek an open "market niche." This is only possible in a political climate at least somewhat tolerant of religious unorthodoxy and a population open to new ideas. Most new groups on the religious scene define themselves in comparison with the status quo and command a sense of passion and community from their followers. Yet as these groups become successful they gradually develop an orthodox structure and an internal hierarchy and a relatively low-tension relationship with society. This in turn gives an opportunity for new entrants.

Adam Smith's insight was that in a "natural state" there is no fixed limit to the number of suppliers or their ability to formulate and offer religious culture and spiritual goods and services. Groups must evangelize and individuals must be free to shift loyalties accordingly—to go "religion shopping." Rational choice theory operating in a free-market religious economy[6] means there is plenty of choice (religious pluralism) which leads to intense competition and efficient supply (old and new movements operate). The theory also suggests that the more competition there is, the higher the level of consumption. This explains why the contemporary religious situation in the United States counteracts secularization theory, the notion that the more developed a country in terms of education, occupations, science, and technology the more its people move away from religion. The easiest measure of this "anomaly" in action is the national rate of church attendance, which today in the U.S. is 30 to 32 percent weekly, but in Western Europe only 5 to 15 percent.

Most studies of religion and faith involve theology and deal with serious and timeless transcendent concepts and mysteries such as the divine, truth, and salvation. While recognizing that a desire to explain the meaning and purpose of life underpins religious sentiments, this book will not venture into such territory. It will confine itself to aspects of religion's interaction with society and the economy. It will approach religious groups as social movements and communities of interest operating in the marketplace of ideas.

Religions and faith come in myriad forms but they rotate around a complex of doctrine, worship, ritual, and prayer. Key concepts for appreciating religion are notions of the sacred and the holy. For most religious groups a specific set of beliefs and values creates a certain lifestyle. Religion is also linked to a sense of identity and belonging in the personal dimension. Religious activity consists of more than praying or going to services once a week. It meets important human needs at emotional times. Illness and death are obvious moments. Thus most religious groups have clergy trained to provide solace and comfort. Chaplains are common in hospitals today and their presence is encouraged by the Joint Commission on Accreditation of Healthcare Organizations. It seems people want to talk after experiencing trauma, in fact most hospitalized Americans with serious illnesses request spiritual assistance.

Why marketing analysis?

Use of the term "market" and the application of marketing analysis to religion may be unsettling to many believers but it can be justified for three reasons. First, as Smith suggested, the use of the term market draws out the contrast between the contemporary situation of the United States, where there is competition for congregants, supporters, and funding and the historical "monopoly" of the Christian and Muslim religions in Europe and the Near East. Second, it indicates that religion operates in social space on economic principles so that patterns of production, exchange, and consumption apply to American religion. Third, religious goods and services circulate freely throughout the national economic system. Though privileged by certain tax exemptions on constitutional grounds religious institutions operate as businesses or firms. They employ staff (clergy) and even bid for staff. They both produce and offer or sell a variety services often for cash payment. Money is normally needed for a wedding or a funeral. Religious institutions are also major purchasers of goods and services, as we shall show.

Religion is a desirable and viable commodity in the contemporary United States. It offers consumers opportunities to address and alleviate material, physical, and metaphysical concerns. Yet religion is difficult to define both sociologically and legally. This has consequences even in the workplace. One of the protected categories of employment to which the Civil Rights statute's non-discrimination provisions were attached by Congress in 1972 is religion. Title VII legislation makes it a duty for employers to accommodate an employee's religious beliefs around issues such as scheduling conflicts, appearance standards, and religious conduct in the workplace. However labor lawyers and judges have had difficulty enforcing this provision because of the lack of certainty in this area due to the inherently subjective and personal nature of religion itself. The government has found it is not equipped or inclined to provide a precise definition of what constitutes a religion or religious belief or practice.

It is also hard to distinguish religious activity from forms of contemplation and transcendence that claim an association with spirituality if not faith or some type of theism. Claims to be a religion or a member of the clergy are more frequent in America than in most other societies, which demand stringent requirements for registration and require attendance and graduation from religious educational institutions or seminaries for official recognition. As a result the United States is the world's main greenhouse and seed bed for the production of new religious brands of all types including somethat are often defined as sects and cults. In the past two centuries the new religious groups grown in America have included Pentecostalism, Mormonism, Christian Science, Jehovah's Witnesses, Scientology, Eckankar, the Nation of Islam, and the Aryan Nations.

Claims to be a religion or a member of the clergy are more frequent in America than in most other societies.

This laissez-faire attitude by the state means that there is plenty of organized religion around for Americans to consume and numerous options and places to do so. In 2004 the National Council of Churches[7] reported there were 215 different denominations.

Local religious congregations number over 350,000 individual units and employ a paid staff of 1.3 million people. The vitality of the religious market is such that half these congregations have been founded since 1940.

At the congregational level too there is a multitude of forms and organizational variety. They cater to audiences ranging in size from a handful of devotees to tens of thousands in the new mega-churches. Some are local independent entrepreneurs or "boutiques" —for example the ubiquitous "store front church" of the inner city; others are vast cathedrals or large parishes that are local branches or franchises of large international corporations headquartered and directed from overseas.

Religion is recognized as of social and political importance but it is under-appreciated as a sector of the national economy so national data and studies of this topic are rare. However, the Independent Sector, the country's non-profit advocacy group, has produced two important national studies in recent years that have produced the following remarkable statistics relating to local religious congregations.

These 350,000 congregations are visited at least once a year by 76 percent of the American population.

Religious organizations received the largest single share of charitable contributions made by Americans in 2004, more than $88 billion, with education second at $34 billion, according to a report by the Indiana University Center on Philanthropy for the Giving USA foundation.

Moreover, individuals gave 94 percent of religious philanthropy.

Tangible as well as spiritual goods

Thus we can envisage the autonomous American consumer as being involved in two types of "religious shopping" or marketing: the search for the largely intangible products offered by the ideal brand and the purchase of specific items or tangible goods associated with participation in a specific ritual. Many congregations in all religious traditions have small shops where people can buy items such as candles, crosses, jewelry, icons, tracts, special foods, cook books, holy water, and wine. In addition gifts are almost obligatory for rites of passage such as baptisms, bar and bat mitzvahs, or weddings. Nor must we forget that since the 19th century the major retail sales seasons that have helped drive the national economy are associated with religious celebrations especially Christmas, Hanukkah, and Easter.

Beyond money, congregations also attract civic participation on a vast scale. Local congregations are the nexus of exchange at the heart of the nation's voluntary or independent sector. They are the main locus of the whole system of neighborliness—the informal giving and receiving of material assistance that is such a feature of American life. Over 45 million Americans volunteer their time to others through a religious congregation. This is because in addition to the core focus on worship and the religious education of members, congregations also engage in a variety of other activities particularly social services. Ninety-two percent of congregations offer human services such as homeless shelters, food pantries, soup kitchens, and 90 percent offer health programs. Nurseries and kindergartens and recreation and sports programs especially for youth also are typical congregational activities.[8] The immense humanitarian and philanthropic achievements of Catholic Charities, the Salvation Army, the Jewish Federations, and all the other denominations that often band together under the umbrella of the local United Ways are essential building blocks of civil society.

Ninety-two percent of congregations offer human services such as homeless shelters, food pantries, and soup kitchens.

Given this impressive level of activity it is not surprising to find that the total revenue of congregations in 1996 was estimated at $81.2 billion and the expenditures at over $79 billion which means that in many places religion is an important part of the local economy in terms of the purchase of goods and services. For example, 16 percent of local congregations reported that they bought paid advertising in commercial media for advocacy purposes in 1996.[9]

Most local congregations are connected organizationally in some way with others so that the religious landscape is dotted with state, regional, and national bodies and networks, the most typical of which is the national denomination. These religious organizations can be enormous operations involving millions of people in a variety of ways beyond the core activity of worship services. The most obvious example is the American Catholic Church, which is part of the oldest and largest bureaucratic organization in the world. The Church is a major employer nationally with 43,000 priests, 14,000 deacons, and 70,000 religious sisters. These clergy and ancillary professionals assist with 985,000 baptisms, 897,000 first communions, and 645,000 confirmations annually. They along with thousands of lay teachers educate 680,000 students in Catholic high school and 1,892,000 pupils in Catholic elementary schools.[10] These schools are major consumers of goods and services and so create another sort of real economic market in religion. Each of the life cycle events mentioned above and the celebrations they involve along with weddings and funerals entail the purchase or supply of numerous goods and services across a vast array of industries including catering, travel, entertainment, and clothing.

The numbers of students in Catholic education have fallen in recent years and most of the historic Mainline Protestant colleges adapted to the counterculture movement of the 1960s by cutting their denominational ties. Yet as Smith predicted the market for "religious education" just changed rather than disappeared. In recent decades, in a rejection of this same liberal cultural trend, "Christian" schools arose in the South and a new niche sector of the higher education scene has been the founding of over 100 Christian colleges now serving 250,000 students. The U.S. has allowed these new colleges, as they respect entrepreneurship and the dynamics of the market.

Religion is the most durable institution in human history. As a result organized religion can be envisaged as a well-established industry with a universal reputation and excellent goodwill among large sections of the public. Religion has tried and tested ways of imprinting lifetime loyalty that are second to none—baptism, circumcision, and naming ceremonies through marriage celebrations to funeral rites. The brand is relevant to every stage of lifecycle. It can also market itself through fear and promises—its claims to powerful intangible rewards and insurance.

American religion offers numerous brands with outlets in every community. Many of these outlets are located in prime city center sites. Many of the brands or religious traditions have visually well-defined and universally recognized logos such as the Cross, Star of David, or Crescent. As a result of their long presence in the marketplace many enjoy one hundred percent brand awareness and customer loyalty, little staff turnover, and global reach. The outlets and local branches are often open all day and are staffed by respected professionals wearing identifiable uniforms. To take the analogy further the after sales service is a key positioning feature for many of the brands in the eyes of their clients. Thus in current commercial terms religious traditions and faiths fall into the category of "über brands."

A Competitive Spiritual Marketplace

The market analogy applies in America because the social reality is that there is a competitive spiritual marketplace. It is not just a matter of the favorable economic and political situation referred to above. The nature of modern America as a residentially and socially mobile society makes it a necessity. Moreover for religious brands and religious entrepreneurs it pays good dividends if they get the package right. Using commercial marketing techniques has been best developed by Evangelical Christians who are at present the most successful firms operating in the religious market.

Expanding the flock through evangelism is a core principle of Christianity that is now linked to marketing through modern church growth movement. This is a major force in a competitive system built on proselytizing. It is a particularly important aspect of religious life for Evangelicals who hold to a theology that requires a personal commitment by individuals to Christ and a responsibility to bear witness and take the Word directly to the unchurched. The dynamic church growth movement began with Donald McGravan's 1955 book, *The Bridges of God*. It was written for overseas missionaries but its ideas were adapted by local pastors who were encouraged to engage their local communities by treating potential worshippers as consumers. Over the past few decades a whole industry of books and journals on religion, ministry, pastoral care, and associated themes of spiritual and psychological counseling for addictions and recovery, health, parenting, therapy, loss, and grief has emerged to assist pastors.

Expanding the flock through evangelism is a core principle of Christianity and a major force in a competitive system built on proselytizing.

Church growth and Evangelical religion is particularly associated with an important recent phenomenon on the religious scene—the mega-church. The modern master of church growth is Rick Warren of Saddleback in Orange County, California, who has established a so-called "seeker sensitive church" with a congregation of 15,000.

Through his 2002 book *The Purpose-Driven Life* and Saddleback's conferences, websites, and pre-packaged purpose-driven kits he has taught more than 100,000 pastors the techniques of informal marketing, and communication cards.

Warren is not unique. Another charismatic "salesmen type" pastor, Joel Osteen of Lakewood Church, Houston, Texas, has an even bigger mega-church in a former sports arena that seats 16,000 and is full most Sundays. Though the theology and social message is decidedly conservative the worship service style is up-to-date with far less emphasis on legalistic dos and don'ts. Another feature of such churches is the enthusiastic adoption of the latest technology—PowerPoint sermons and video screens—as well as many familiar aspects of consumer-oriented popular culture such as rock bands and coffee bars. Most have their own Christian retail store. Aside from an expected focus on books and Bibles they now have religious tee shirts that combine both a faith and a fashion statement. There are baseball caps with slogans plus "hoodies," jewelry, bumper stickers, skateboards, and even fortune cookies with Bible verses.

The sophisticated clergy and leadership of contemporary religious groups readily adopt the fruits of psychological and sociological research in their professional work. They realize that the market and the nature of a more mobile public means that reputation management and brand positioning are a major concern. Recruitment and retention of members across the generations has weakened much as Smith had predicted it would be. As a result religious groups and congregations are now major users of the services of experts in marketing and public relations on a *pro bono* basis as well as commercial terms. Consequently religious groups are big advertisers of their general message as well as specific activities and services. However most also depend on relationship marketing; for instance the Buddhists are big on weekend retreats on stress reduction.

Religion is a system of value but it is also a system with value. The mega-churches described above are not a new trend; there has been commercialization or commoditization of religion since ancient times. Ritual goods and services have long been obtained through cash payments. For most sophisticated religious systems the association is such that it can be claimed that to be religious is to be a consumer. This means the inevitable entanglement of personal professions of spirituality with institutional structures. Payment even enters realms such as self-help and healing.

One inevitable criticism of the competitive market system envisaged by Smith is that religion is created in the image of man. Religion becomes a product that can be marketed by entrepreneurs alert to the needs that religious affiliations can satisfy. Notions of what religion is and what can be offered under the rubric of faith will vary. Charlatans and fanatics will appear alongside saints and prophets. In a society as consumer oriented as the U.S. the market mechanism becomes a force of its own for keeping religion alive but also for making sacred many aspects of ordinary life and even some bizarre ones. For some critics this is as bad as when the sacred is made profane.

The places of worship

Places of worship are central to our cultural and national identity. They conjure up iconic images such as the small towns of New England with the white clapboard church on the green. The towers and spires of cathedrals, churches, and chapels still often dominate the skylines of the nation's cities. Many neighborhoods also now show the distinctive presence of synagogues, the Muslim mosque, the Hindu mandir, and Buddhist temple as testimony to the existence of those faith communities. The presence of different buildings representing different brands in a narrow space can be envisaged as rival symbols potentially aiding missionary activity. They are both a public statement and part of each group's public and self-image. Thus the religious architecture we observe on the streets is a tangible expression of religious observance and cultural diversity as well as historic continuity.

There is another more tangible aspect to religious architecture. Urban planners stress the need for us to appreciate the importance of places of worship in shaping the man-made environment of the past and how they will shape it for the future. The size and shape of religious buildings is not just a matter of the resources and wealth available to the congregation. Their architecture reflects different types of investment in buildings according to particular beliefs and rituals. Different ideas about the proper spatial organization of worship—whether the clergy lead or face the congregation—are reflected in the actual construction. Some religious groups downplay the importance of buildings. For some their buildings are sacred; for others they are not. Religious buildings do not just offer a place of contemplation, they are part of the built structure of American religion. Beyond its tens of thousands of churches and other places of worship, there are thousands of halls, cemeteries, and memorials. These are tax-exempt properties that supply commissions for architects, large contracts for the construction industry, and jobs for numerous occupations from ritual artists to janitors.

Impact on Many Industries

Religion creates products and economic opportunities but also has an impact on the consumption of specific products. An obvious area is the food and beverage industry, particularly alcohol consumption. The campaign for Prohibition was largely the work of abstinence-oriented groups in the Protestant tradition such as Methodists and Baptists. Still today Mormons, Adventists, and Nazarenes maintain this tradition so consumption of alcohol in markets where these groups are influential reflects this reality. Mainstream Protestants have no norms or sanctions against alcohol consumption yet many believe it is a sin associated with a negative moral character. As a result Americans who attend religious services frequently have been found to have lower rates of alcohol use and misuse.

However Jews and Catholics often have divergent values and beliefs and many regard alcohol or rather wine as a food and an important part of family life as well as religious ritual. This means that those wishing to market wine are likely to find the Northeast or California a stronger market than the Midwest or Utah. In fact kosher wines are a surprisingly large market with $27 million in sales in U.S. food and drug stores in 2004. That is the same dollar amount as imports from the French Burgundy region.[11]

Today most food manufacturers are cognizant of the food taboos and special preparation requirements associated with certain religious traditions such as Judaism, Islam, Mormonism, Adventism, Buddhism, and Hinduism. These involve both prohibitions on consuming certain food and beverages: pig products for Jews and Muslims, beef products for Hindus and alcohol, coffee and soft drinks by Mormons, as well as preferences for diets such as vegetarianism for Buddhists. These factors affect what is placed on the shelves of supermarkets in various areas and neighborhoods. The kosher food industry is the most developed and identifiable response to such demands and has its own labeling and certification system including special provision for the Passover season.

Since religions seek to explain life and death, health matters and biomedical issues are central concerns for clergy and their congregants. The nation's vast health industry has to be attentive to the varying demands and needs produced by different religious persuasions. In the past this was met in part by hospitals associated with particular religious groups and most major cities had Catholic, Jewish, Presbyterian, and other denominational hospitals that were responsive to the special needs of religious communities particularly concerning birth and death rituals and last rites. In their procedures and practices health professionals may need to be aware of their clients' religious identification due to the public's strong faith-based attitudinal differences and preferences on ethical issues of a medical nature such as contraception, abortion, resuscitation, organ transplants, and blood transfusions. Pharmaceutical companies, funeral parlors, and nursing homes also need to be responsive to the religious preferences of their clients.

Hallmark Cards is a business that is most attentive to religious markets, especially emerging ones. In 2003 it began to market Diwali cards to Hindus for the first time for a holiday that involves exchanges of cards and gifts, new clothes, and traditional sweets. This marketing decision was a direct result of the findings reported by the American Religious Identification Survey, which showed a tripling of the Hindu population between 1990 and 2001.[12] Hallmark Cards now produces an array of holiday and seasonal cards for Ramadan, Eid al-Fadr, saints' days, Three Kings' Day, Purim, Passover, Rosh Hashanah, Easter, Halloween, and Kwanzaa.

The commercial printing and publishing industry has been meeting religious needs ever since its inception five hundred years ago. CBA International, the trade association of the Christian bookstores and retailers reported sales by member suppliers at $4.2 billion in

2002. Today this market is not just the traditional fare of Bibles, prayer books, textbooks, religious tracts, newspapers, and magazines. It now consists of lucrative products in the self-help book segment of the market, best-selling novels, and an array of media. Over 25 million copies of *The Purpose Driven Life*, a 40-day religious course of self-improvement, have been sold. That is more copies than any other non-fiction title except the Bible.

Another recent publishing phenomenon has been Tim Le Haye and Jerry B. Jenkins, *The Left Behind* Series. Since 1995 their 12 books have sold over 62 million copies. Their fifth book *Apollyon*, reached the top of T*he New York Times* bestsellers list. Though the early volumes overwhelmingly relied on Christian bookshops for sales, mainstream distribution outlets, rather than religious bookshops have accounted for 75 percent sales of the later volumes. Wal-Mart has done particularly well with the series. Market research has revealed that 40 percent of readers reside in South. The core buyer is a married woman, aged 25 to 54 who is a college graduate and attends weekly worship services at an evangelical church.[13]

Publishers and booksellers have also benefited from the expression of secular opinions that challenge such beliefs but wrestle with the selfsame religious themes and issues. The most obvious case is *The Da Vinci Code*, which has also been a bestseller along with the non-fiction *Breaking the Da Vinci Code*. So in the present religious climate books that both affirm and deny people's deepest beliefs have engaged millions and provided a massive market for publishers.

Material culture helps the transportation of religious experience across time. In the past rosaries, prayer beads, and prayer wheels helped memory; today it is compact discs and the internet. Music has always been at the center of religion and given employment to composers, musicians, and singers. In the U.S., gospel music has had a long history but in recent years Christian lyrics and Christian bands such as Third Day, Switchfoot, and Mercy Me have enjoyed crossover success and climbed the popular music charts.

Evangelical Christianity has fueled this growth. This trend is somewhat unexpected but it is due to the changed attitude of Evangelicals towards popular culture. The change is also now evident in the movie industry. During the 1920s the Rev. Billy Sunday preached that movies were sinful. Now Evangelical and Fundamentalist Christians are seeing, producing, and acting in films. The Billy Graham Evangelical Association has its own production company, World Wide Pictures (WWP). This embrace of the new technologies shows the current desire of religious groups to have their viewpoint portrayed equally alongside "secular" offerings. The success of the recent Mel Gibson movie, *The Passion of the Christ* was an important development in this respect because it revealed the existence of a large niche market to which the main Hollywood studios now say they want to cater.

That other great new medium, the internet, has been enthusiastically embraced by religious groups (see Chapter 10). There are now millions of websites established by religious organizations and congregations or devoted to the teachings of numerous faiths and religious groups. The *Pew Survey* of April 2004 reported that two-thirds of the 82 million Americans who were then online used the net for faith-related activities.

Two-thirds of the 82 million Americans online used the internet for faith-related activities.

The ubiquitous home computer has created a market for Christian themed computer games that is supplied by new studios such as Virtue Games, a Christian multi-media game development studio. They offer content free of gratuitous violence, foul language, sexual immorality, and occultist themes. Their didactic products aim to instill positive values by focusing on epic story lines suitable for families rather than "shoot to kill" games. This development suggests a burgeoning Christian computer games market could be the next Christian media vehicle just as Christian music, movies and books have been in recent years.

Religious groups also operate as affinity groups. The Lutheran denominations in the Lutheran tradition are a good example of this. Thrivent Financial for Lutherans, a Minneapolis-based fraternal organization employs 3,000 field staff and has a base of nearly three million members. It sells financial products such as life insurance, annuities, and mutual funds to what it terms the "Lutheran marketplace." The Lutheran Services of America also operate the largest network of non-profit nursing homes in the nation.

Religious beliefs and religious groups are now recognized as central to understanding the electoral map of the country and this crucial issue will be dealt with in Chapter 13. However an appreciation of the importance of religion in the South and Bible Belt is important for accurate data collection and fieldwork in public opinion surveys in these markets. Wednesday night is "Church night" in these areas so for many voters it is a time unavailable for other activities. This directly affects opinion and election polling results because a key opinion type is not at home that evening. Ignorance of this fact has been a cause of the under-estimation of the "conservative" vote in several instances.

Given the size, importance, and variety of the diverse array of "religious markets" in the contemporary United States, access to reliable statistics on the religious preferences of the public should be of interest to a wide variety of social service, political, and commercial organizations. However, the constitutional separation of church and state means that this is one topic on which the U.S. Bureau of the Census is precluded from investigating or collecting data. The utility of this book and the data it contains is that it fills this gap in the nation's statistical map by providing counts of the main religious traditions and religious groups. It supplies reliable figures on the demography, geography, economics and politics of the American people according to their personal religious self-identification. The chapters that follow should enable interested parties to get an accurate feel for the size and shape of the potential market for their own specialized products, sales and activities within the larger, national free market of religion.

Notes

1. This Latin phrase was placed on the obverse of the Great Seal of the United States in 1782 and still appears alongside "In God We Trust" on the reverse of the one dollar bill.
2. Thomas Jefferson, *Letter to the Danbury Baptist Association,* January 1802.
3. Adam Smith, *An Inquiry into the Nature and Causes of the Wealth of Nations, Book Five, Chapter 1, Part 3, Article III,* The Modern Library, New York, 1965 [1776].
4. President George Washington from his *Letter to the Hebrew Congregation at Newport,* Rhode Island, August 1790.
5. Rodney Stark and Roger Finke, *Acts of Faith: Explaining the Human Side of Religion,* University of California Press, Berkeley, 2000.

6. For further reading on this theory see: Lawrence A. Young, ed. *Rational Choice Theory and Religion*, Routledge, New York & London, 1997. Laurance R. Iannaccone, "Introduction to the economics of religion," *Journal of Economic Literature*, XXXVI, 1465–1496 (1998).

7. Eileen W. Lindner, *Yearbook of American and Canadian Churches*, National Council of Churches in the USA, New York, 2005.

8. Virginia A. Hodgkinson & Murray S. Weitzman, *From Belief to Commitment: The Community Service Activities of Religious Congregations in the United States*, Independent Sector, Washington DC, 1993.

9. Susan J. Wiener et al., *Balancing the Scales: Measuring the Roles and Contributions of Nonprofit Organizations and Religious Congregations*, Independent Sector, Washington D.C., 2001.

10. *Official Catholic Directory*, P.J. Kennedy & Sons, New Providence, NJ, 2004.

11. Source: Manischewitz & ACNielson report.

12. Hallmark Press Room (August 2003).

13. *The Economist*, April 15, 2004.

TWO

The National Profile of Religious Identification in the United States

DESPITE the importance of religion in American life, the topic is a void as far as official information and governmental statistics are concerned. Nevertheless, religious people, especially clergy, often care passionately how many fellow believers are in their tent and how many in someone else's. "Church growth" is a major religious focus because numbers matter to most religionists for both practical operational purposes and for overall morale. Moreover, expanding the flock through evangelism is a core principle of missionary religions, especially Christianity and Islam.

However, the constitutional prohibition on religious establishment and the separation of church and state have been interpreted by the U.S. Bureau of the Census as precluding it from gathering religious statistics. As a result, the religious profile of the United States is normally provided by the various religious bodies themselves using their own specific criteria of membership. These criteria vary greatly among the various faiths and religious denominations; some religious groups are quite inclusive with regard to definitions of membership and adherence and others are exclusive and have high standards for recognition and membership. Some include children, others only adults. Levels of cooperation with investigations and surveys of membership by outsiders also vary greatly, with some groups being unwilling or even unable to fix their numbers.

The result is that most national religious statistics are a collection of "apples and oranges" and not directly comparable with each other nor even over time. In addition, data collections of membership are fraught with political problems and theological disputes, for all the main world religions are beset by arguments over authenticity, heresy, and non-recognition. This produces difficulties especially when analysts trying to make sense of vast amounts of rival and sometimes-contradictory statistics attempt amalgamations and aggregations. The alternative strategy of directly interviewing the populace is usually hampered by the fact that most national sample surveys of the general public have only one or two thousand respondents and so are just not large enough to do justice to the full range of religious groups that exist in American society. Such small sample sizes cannot provide robust numbers except for the very largest Christian churches and denominations.

The American Religious Identification Survey

The *American Religious Identification Survey* (ARIS) 2001 solves these problems. It is based on self-reporting of religious identification, so it evades the problems of data supplied by religious denominations. And its size allows it to provide useful information on a wide range of religious groups. Our innovation is to go directly to a large representative sample of the people of the United States on two occasions, in 1990 and again in 2001. We did this quite transparently through opinion polling. Polls are in principle both democratic and egalitarian because they attempt to find out the opinions of a sample of everyone, not just those who have an opportunity or a theological or political interest in being actively engaged in religion.

In practice there are problems in providing such equality of voice, but ARIS 2001 and the *National Survey of Religious Identification* (NSRI) 1990 strove toward that goal and succeeded in creating trend data that allow us to track changes over a decade. Just as we learn about population, demographic, and social change from the decennial U.S. Census, from NSRI/ARIS we learn about change and stability in American religious preferences. This initiative allows an assessment of the "common wisdom" about public opinion on religion as reported by the media in national social and political debates.

ARIS 2001 also provides data that allow an exploration of the overall balance of secular and religious outlooks among the population as well as "the three Bs" of religion—beliefs, belonging, and behavior.

Beliefs refers to belief in the existence of God, miracles, and the efficacy of divine intercession or help on the personal level.

Belonging refers to having membership in a religious congregation or institution.

Behavior refers to intriguing issues such as entering into interfaith marriage and the religious upbringing of children as well as changing one's religious identification by conversion or apostasy.

In the following chapters we dig deeper, examining how religious identification relates to demographics, geography, sociology, economics, politics, and racial and ethnic minority group membership.

Innovations between NSRI 1990 and ARIS 2001

The methodology[1] of the *American Religious Identification Survey* (ARIS) 2001 was based on a random-digit-dialed telephone survey of 50,281 American residential households in the contiguous 48 states. The methodology largely replicates the widely reported and pioneering *National Survey of Religious Identification* (NSRI) 1990, also carried out at the Graduate Center of the City University of New York and reported in the book *One Nation Under God: Religion in Contemporary American Society*.[2] ARIS 2001 thus forms part of a unique time series of information concerning the religious identification choices of American adults. The data were collected over a 17-week period, from February to June 2001. The primary question of the interview was open and unprompted: *What is your religion, if any?* The religion of the spouse/partner was also asked. If the initial answer was "Protestant" or "Christian" further questions were asked to probe which particular denomination.

The NSRI 1990 study was a large survey in which 113,723 persons were questioned about their religious preferences. However, it provided for no further detailed questioning of respondents regarding their religious beliefs or involvement or the religious composition of their households.

In the light of those gaps in the 1990 survey, ARIS 2001 took steps to enhance both the range and the depth of the topics covered. For example, new questions were introduced concerning the religious identification of spouses. Budget limitations necessitated a reduction in the number of respondents. Nevertheless, the 2001 survey still covers a national sample of over 50,000 respondents that provides a high level of confidence for the results and adequate coverage of most religious groups and key geographical units such as census divisions and the larger states.

For the sake of analytic depth, additional questions about religious beliefs and affiliation as well as religious change were introduced for a smaller representative sub-sample of 17,000 households. Even this sample is more than ten times greater than most typical opinion surveys of the U.S. population. This sub-sample as well as the larger sample was weighted by demographic factors to reflect the total U.S. adult population. These innovations have provided a much richer data set that goes far beyond the mere question of religious preference. The new data allow for a much more sophisticated analysis than NSRI 1990. They offer a more nuanced understanding of the complex dynamics of religion in contemporary American society and especially how religious adherence relates to countervailing secularizing trends. The information collected is also potentially more useful for the various national religious bodies.

Self-identification with religious groups

A distinguishing feature of this survey, as of its predecessor in 1990, is that respondents were asked with an open-ended question to describe themselves in terms of religion. Interviewers did not prompt or offer a list of potential answers. Moreover, the self-description of respondents was not based on whether established religious bodies, institutions, churches, mosques or synagogues considered them to be members. Quite the contrary, the survey sought to determine whether the respondents regarded themselves as adherents of a religion. Subjective rather than objective standards of religious identification were tapped by the survey. Significant numbers of responses were collected for over 100 categories of religious groups, faiths, denominations and orientations. The overall refusal rate for the question on religion (item non-response) was low, only 5.4 percent.

The Profile of Religious Self-Identification in 1990 and 2001

The first area of inquiry in ARIS 2001 concerns the response of American adults to the question: *What is your religion, if any?* This question generated more than a hundred categories of response, which we classified into the sixty-five categories shown in Figure 2.1. In 1990, 90 percent of the adult population identified with one or another religious group. In 2001, such identification dropped to 81 percent. Where possible, every effort was made to re-create the categories respondents offered to the nearly identical question in the NSRI 1990 survey.[3]

Figure 2.1 provides the most comprehensive and most widely recognized profile of religious identification among the U.S. adult population today. It compares the pattern of identification in 2001 with what the pattern was in 1990.[4] The major changes between the results of the 1990 survey and the current survey are:

- The proportion of the population that can be classified as Christian declined from 86 percent in 1990 to 77 percent in 2001.

- Catholics continued to be the largest religious group in the U.S. With a moderate increase in the number of adult adherents, they represented about one-fourth of the adult population in 2001.

- Although the number of adults who classified themselves in non-Christian religious groups increased from about 5.8 million to about 7.6 million, the proportion of non-Christians increased only by a small amount—from 3.3 percent to about 3.7 percent.

- The greatest increase in absolute numbers as well as in percentage terms was among those adults who do not subscribe to any religious identification; their number more than doubled from 14.3 million in 1990 to 29.4 million in 2001. Their proportion grew from just 8 percent of the total in 1990 to over 14 percent in 2001.[5]

- There was a major shift among Christian religious groups in the self-classification of adults who did not specify their denomination, with an increase in the "Christian" category and a decrease in the "Protestant" category. The generic Protestant classification decreased from 9.8 percent to only 2.2 percent. At the same time, the Generic Christian classification increased its share from 4.6 percent to 6.8 percent in 2001.

- There was a five-fold increase in the number of adults who self-identified as Evangelical and "Born Again" between 1990 and 2001. However, these adults represented less than 1 percent of the adult population in 2001. Another notable increase was in the non-denominational Christian category, to about 1 percent in 2001.

- Despite the overall population growth in the U.S. between 1990 and 2001, the absolute numbers of adult adherents remained almost the same between two major groups—Baptist and Methodist.

- Adults who self-identified as Jewish remained the largest non-Christian religious group. However, their overall number was declining.

- The number of adults who self-identified as Muslim doubled between 1990 and 2001. However, they still represented less than 1 percent of the adult population in 2001.

- The number of adults who self-identify as Hindu and those who self-identify as Buddhist increased two-fold between 1990 and 2001; together these groups represented about 1 percent of the adult population.

- Several religious groups that were too small to be cited in 1990 surfaced in 2001, including Druid, Santeria, Pagan and Spiritualist.

- There was a substantial increase in the number of adults who refused to reply to the question about their religious preference, from 2 percent in 1990 to over 5 percent in 2001. This is still a low percentage of non-response.

The dynamics of such changes reflect a number of factors including migration, natural growth as a result of age structure, as well as direct religious causes such as evangelism and apostasy. The churning and changing in the patterns of religious preferences demonstrates the atmosphere of religious liberty that prevails in the nation and the veritable "free market in religion" that prevails. This feature is a logical outcome of America's sanctification of individualism and personal autonomy and its positive indulgence of the human need to search for a spiritual home.

Figure 2.1

Self-Described Religious Identification of U.S. Adult Population, 1990 and 2001
(in thousands)

RELIGIOUS GROUP	1990	2001
Adult population, total*	**175,440**	**207,980**
Total Christian	*151,496*	*159,506*
Catholic	46,004	50,873
Baptist	33,964	33,830
Protestant—no denomination supplied	17,214	4,647
Methodist/Wesleyan	14,174	14,150
Lutheran	9,110	9,580
Christian—no denomination supplied	8,073	14,150
Presbyterian	4,985	5,596
Pentecostal/Charismatic	3,191	4,407
Episcopalian/Anglican	3,042	3,451
Mormon/Latter Day Saints	2,487	2,787
Churches of Christ	1,769	2,593
Jehovah's Witnesses	1,381	1,331
Seventh Day Adventist	668	724
Assemblies of God	660	1,106
Holiness/Holy	610	569
Congregational/United Church of Christ	599	1,378
Church of the Nazarene	549	544
Church of God	531	944
Orthodox (Eastern)	502	645
Evangelical	242	1,032
Mennonite	235	346
Christian Science	214	194
Church of the Brethren	206	358
Born Again**	204	56
Non-denominational	195	2,489
Disciples of Christ	144	492
Reformed/Dutch Reform	161	289
Apostolic/New Apostolic	117	254
Quaker	67	217
Full Gospel	51	168
Christian Reform	40	79
Foursquare Gospel	28	70
Fundamentalist	27	61
Salvation Army	27	25
Independent Christian Church	25	71

RELIGIOUS GROUP	1990	2001
Total other religions	*5,853*	*7,740*
Jewish	3,137	2,831
Muslim/Islamic	527	1,104
Buddhist	401	1,082
Unitarian/Universalist	502	629
Hindu	227	766
Native American	47	103
Scientologist	45	55
Baha'i	28	84
Taoist	23	40
New Age	20	68
Eckankar	18	26
Rastafarian	14	11
Sikh	13	57
Wiccan	8	134
Deity	6	49
Druid	(NA)	33
Santeria	(NA)	22
Pagan	(NA)	140
Spiritualist	(NA)	116
Ethical Culture	(NA)	4
Other unclassified	837	386
No religion specified, total	*14,331*	*29,481*
Atheist	(NA)	902
Agnostic	1,186	991
Humanist	29	49
Secular	(NA)	53
No religion	13,116	27,486
Refused to reply to question	4,031	11,246

*   Refers to the total number of adults in all 50 states. All other figures are based on projections from surveys conducted in the continental United States (48 states). NA means Not available.

** Because of the subjective nature of replies to open-ended questions, these categories are the most subject to fluctuation over time. They do not refer to clearly identifiable denominations as much as underlying feelings about religion. This is true of the categories "Evangelical" and "Nondenominational" as well.

Nearly every data collection concerning religion in America has had to face the enormous problem associated with defining its terms and categories. This is especially difficult because such a process inevitably touches upon theological issues for which there are sometimes no consensus solutions. In addition American patterns of religious identification have always been in flux. This is due to the dynamic nature of religion in America and particularly the constant schisms and unions within Protestant denominations. New religions arise and others fade away. Navigating the complex byways of the ever-changing religious scene is fraught with difficulties. For instance at the time of the Korean War in 1950, the Department of Defense listed 40 denominations under the general heading of Protestant chaplaincy, while today nearly 300 groups are authorized. In addition the number of non-Christian groups has grown. The Protestant tendency towards fragmentation has now spread and we can assert that at the general institutional level the free market that characterizes American religion tends to produce more and more "boutiques" as the "department stores" fragment while there appears little countervailing movement towards amalgamation.

Yet fragmentation seems to have its limits. In 2001, 89 percent of American adults who professed a religion identified themselves with a group or denomination that had one million or more adherents. This may be evidence that the forces of fragmentation are being at least partially offset by a counterforce of agglomeration. Americans may choose to adhere to the larger denominations and groupings for positive reasons (they are attracted to the denominations' beliefs and practices) or for negative reasons (many people just do not have the time or energy to seek out smaller denominations that might better suit their needs).

At first sight the possibilities of how individual people might consider themselves in terms of religion appear endless, particularly in a society where few seem to be embarrassed saying who they are religiously. Individuals are pulled by upbringing, education, longing, memory, family, and even guilt. Given this limitless potential coupled with an unprompted open-ended question, you might be surprised at the relatively limited number of categories of replies the NSRI and ARIS surveys actually elicited. Most Americans seem to know what they think they are or what the appropriate answer should be when a stranger inquires about their religious identification on the telephone. That process obviously has some effect on the outcome.

The cultural and political history of the nation undoubtedly influences the pattern of responses in Figure 2.1. The historic Mainline Christian denominations such as Presbyterian or Episcopalian seem to have greater resonance than more unfamiliar designations such as Armenian Apostolic Orthodox which seems to be dropped in favor of more familiar or generic responses such as "Christian" in this process.

Some other features of the responses set out in Figure 2.1 need explication while also providing an important message. Being asked to state their religion in a few words is a problem for many people since they may find it difficult to classify their local church according to recognized or official denominational labels. In what denomination should the respondent place the Christian Free-Will Baptist Church of Christ? Can we automatically expect someone who intermittently attends the First Congregational Church to know that he or she is really going to a constituent of the United Church of Christ (UCC)? The result is that most Methodists, Lutherans, and Baptist respondents provided no denominational specificity. Respondents who belonged to the Southern Baptists and American Baptists as well as the various Black Baptist conventions almost invariably replied "Baptist" or gave the full name of their local congregation and pastor. Hardly any of the Lutherans, for example, distinguished between the Missouri Synod, Wisconsin Evangelical Lutheran Synod, or the Evangelical Lutheran Church in America. This means we cannot easily distinguish between the "liberal" and "conservative" streams within the major denominational families.

One feature of the 2001 findings was the rise in the number of minority or previously suppressed religions and groups. For example, ARIS estimated 300,000 Neo-Pagans and other related earth-based religious groups in their family of religious and "magical paths" such as Wiccan. It is not our purpose here to delve into the complex issue of what the various religious groups believe or practice nor their origins and governance. The fairest approach to such questions is for us to advise our readers to search the vast literature available on the internet, which allows the groups to describe themselves in their own words.

The rise of the "Christian" and the decline of the "Protestant" generic labels

The finding in Figure 2.1 regarding the rise over the past decade in the preference for the Christian label and the decline in the prevalence of the Protestant label among American adults merits special attention for the insights it can offer on developments in contemporary American Christianity as well as on changes under way within U.S. religious preference. After all, the choice of label to describe one's faith is an important measure of beliefs and religious outlook. To reiterate, the estimated number of self-described "Christians" rose from 8.1 million in 1990 to 14.2 million in 2001 while the number of "Protestants" declined from 17.2 million to 4.7 million during this period.

We hypothesize that the dramatic shift is primarily caused by people re-labeling themselves, rather than by demographic changes. The shift appears too large to be explained by demographic growth in the size of the population groups that traditionally identify themselves as Christian versus decline in the demographic groups that traditionally identify themselves as "unspecified Protestants," i.e., without a specific denominational label.

The survey methodology of NSRI and ARIS provides unique opportunities for this analysis because of the two-stage nature of the screening process. Although the main question was: *What is your religion, if any?* when the given answer was either "Christian" or "Protestant" a further question was asked: *What denomination is that?* in order to try to obtain greater specificity. For example, in ARIS 2001 there were 5,838 first preference "Christian" respondents and 3,529 "Christian" respondents after the second screening question. There was more "switching" among Protestants. There were 4,239 "Protestant" first preferences but only 1,201 remained in this category after a second probing. This illustrates a greater willingness among the Protestant first preference group to offer an alternative denominational label.

Analysis of the re-categorization process is of inherent interest

and offers insights into patterns of self-identification and denominational loyalties. We have clear evidence that few Catholics use
the Christian label, since they comprised only 2.4 percent of first-
preference "Christians." In contrast Baptists, Methodists, and non-
denominational Christians were over-represented in this group.
Methodists, Presbyterians, and UCC adherents were over-represented among "Protestant" first preferences.

The popularity and rise in membership of the fundamentalist and
evangelical Christian movements, which favor the label *Christian* and
the numerical decline of membership (rather than identification *per
se*) in the historic mainline and liberal Protestant denominations,
may have contributed to the recent increase in people self-identifying themselves as "Christians." We can assume that the gains in identifiers for denominations such as the Assemblies of God, Disciples of
Christ, and Churches of Christ arose at the expense of the unspecified Protestant category. Certainly the fieldwork reported in Figure
2.1 reveals that the United Church of Christ, which was a new amalgamation in 1990, had better "brand recognition" in 2001. Of course
this may well be an artifact of better and more persistent questioning and data collection.

The appeal of new religious labels, such as "Evangelical/Born
Again" and the "Non-denominational," is both an important trend
in American Christianity as well as a probable cause of the changing pattern of identification. Blurring of theological differences, at
least in the eyes of the general public, may also explain the replacement of the generic label Protestant by the more ecumenical term
Christian. As will be discussed later, these patterns may also indicate
that social forces such as change in patterns of cultural geography
relating to migration and region of residence contribute to the religious "re-labeling" process that has recently occurred.

The national statistics produced by ARIS give rise to the following questions: How do we explain these significant changes in the
composition of religious identification? Do these changes in self-
identification reflect cultural or theological shifts? What types of people have changed in terms of age, sex, education, ethnic and racial
identity, educational attainment, socioeconomic status and geography? What are the characteristics of adults who self-identified as

Christians and those who self-identified as Protestants? And perhaps most importantly, do patterns of belief and outlook vary significantly between adults who identify themselves as Christian and those who identify themselves as Protestant? The rest of this chapter and those to come will focus on the answers to these types of crucial questions for contemporary American religion.

The profile of non-respondents to the religious identification question

As mentioned earlier, the rate of non-response to the religious identification question rose from 2.3 percent to 5.4 percent between 1990 and 2001. These non-respondents are composed of both the outright refusals and those who more politely replied "don't know." However, the number of Don't Knows is tiny, numbering only 12 persons out of 50,281 interviewees. The actual timing of ARIS in early 2001 meant that this trend towards reduced cooperation with a religious survey had nothing to do with the fear and anxiety over religious identification that began after 9/11/2001. To put this level of refusal into perspective it is interesting to note that this rate was only slightly higher than our sample's reaction to two other potentially controversial or personal issues, age and race or ethnicity. In these cases 3.6 percent and 3.7 percent of our total sample also refused to provide information. Moreover by international standards the willingness of our representative sample of Americans to reveal their religious preference in an unofficial poll is impressive since in the official 2001 U.K. Government Census 7.7 percent of the population of England refused to specify their religion.

In 1990 we interpreted this sub-population of people unwilling to participate in this survey as being composed of persons from rare and perhaps unpopular religious groups. This was because the numbers we uncovered for some groups such as the Orthodox churches, Mormons, Muslims, and Baha'is were far below the claims of their leaderships. However the 2001 experience suggested an improvement in the overall coverage of the smaller religious groups in society. More people came forward to identify with non-Christian religions and as mentioned earlier the number of Neo-Pagan respondents of various kinds rose considerably.

Nevertheless, the rise in the item refusal rate in 2001 leaves over

11 million adults without a designation. This is a gap in the national profile we can only partially fill. Fortunately the ARIS methodology allows us to look at some demographic, social and geographical characteristics of the non-respondents in order to see if there are certain patterns or if they are clustered in some way that could give us clues as to which religious groups these people might resemble.

Those who refused to answer the religious question also tended as we might expect to refuse other personal questions, for instance age (29 percent), race (38 percent), and education (27 percent). However we do know from their full replies to the question on sex that there was no gender bias and there were the expected proportions of men and women. The geographical distribution of the refusals shows that they were slightly more likely to be found in New England and the Pacific Census Divisions. The 73 percent who provided their level of education were more likely to be college graduates (42 percent) than our entire sample (33 percent). In terms of race/ethnicity those who refused were also more likely to be Asian than expected. This fits the pattern of a population skewed towards the well educated and California. The Asian over-representation does however reinforce our feeling that immigrants or New Americans are more reluctant to reveal their religion. This is not surprising because many come from societies and regions with deep religious hostilities or states where all or some forms of religion were persecuted or banned.

A Taxonomy of Religious Groups

The long list of religious classifications in Figure 2.1 calls for a shorter, more manageable list for most analytical purposes. Therefore, the 50,281 ARIS 2001 respondents have been collated into the following 13 religious groupings of varying sizes—the number of ARIS respondents is supplied:

Catholic   **10,741**
>   Roman, Greek and Eastern Rites

Mainline Christian   **9,339**
>   Methodist, Lutheran, Presbyterian, Episcopalian/Anglican, United Church of Christ/Congregational, Reformed/Dutch Reform, Disciples of Christ, Quaker, Orthodox (Greek, Russian, Eastern, Christian)

Baptist	**8,337**
Includes Southern Baptist, American Baptist and African-American denominations	
Christian Generic	**5,649**
Christian, Protestant, Evangelical/Born Again Christian, Born Again, Fundamentalist, Independent Christian, Non-denominational	
Pentecostal/Charismatic	**1,958**
Pentecostal, Assemblies of God, Full Gospel, Four Square Gospel, Church of God, Holiness, Nazarene, Salvation Army	
Protestant Denominations	**1,480**
Churches of Christ, Seventh Day Adventist, Mennonite, Brethren, Apostle, Covenant, Christian Reform, Jehovah's Witnesses, Christian Science, Messianic Jews	
Mormon/Latter Day Saints	**728**
Jewish/Judaism	**622**
Eastern Religion	**331**
Buddhist, Hindu, Taoist, Baha'i, Shintoist, Zoroastrian, Sikh	
Muslim/Islam	**219**
New Religious Movements and Other Religions	**474**
Scientology, New Age, Eckankar, Spiritualist, Unitarian, Deist, Wicca, Pagan, Druid, Indian Religion, Santeria, Rastafarian	
None	**7,551**
None, Humanistic, Ethical Culture, Agnostic, Atheist, Secular	
Don't Know/Refused	**2,852**

The 13 religious groupings in this taxonomy may appear rather arbitrary aggregations of denominations and traditions featured in Figure 2.1. However, we will show some flexibility in order to help our readers who require more specific categorization. For instance, the category of Mainline Christians contains large denominations such as Methodist, Lutheran, and Presbyterian that we analyze separately in several charts and tables. The taxonomy largely follows accepted practice among students of American religion. This system is adopted because we also needed to have a manageable number of religious groupings for presentational purposes and a sufficient number of cases in each grouping for statistical purposes. We have also deliberately not separated out the adherents of the historic black churches who are included in the logical theological position as Baptist, Methodist, or Pentecostal. The logic of this decision to give primacy to religion and values over race and sociology for most analytical purposes will be demonstrated in due course. However, in order to do full justice to the uniqueness of minority expressions of faith their religious profiles will be analyzed separately in a later chapter.

It is also necessary to say something about the Jewish population categorized here. These are people who identified themselves as Jews when asked their religion. Other questions in ARIS inquired into the ethnic or cultural background of the respondents, and these alternative or additional criteria elicited almost double the number and percentage of Jews in the U.S. population compared with Figure 2.2. However, for the purposes of this study these "secular" and "other religion" Jews have been placed in the relevant religious category, e.g., "Nones," New Religious Movements, Eastern religions, and Christian denominations (Messianic Jews).[6]

A Comparative Profile of Religious Traditions and Denominational Families, 1990 and 2001

When analyzing the statistics in Figure 2.2 it is important to remember the large increase in the U.S. population between 1990 and 2001 of over 32 million adults. Thus many of the 13 groupings that appear to have lost ground in terms of their proportion of the national population had real increases in actual numbers of identifiers. Only the Jewish and Christian generic categories (Number 4 in the taxonomy of groups) had real numerical losses, due in the latter case to the implosion of the Protestant identifiers previously discussed. Nevertheless, one of the most notable trends captured in Figure 2.2 is the fall in share between 1990 and 2001 of the various Christian groupings, with the exception of the "Pentecostal/Charismatic" and the "Protestant denominations" groupings.

Another clear trend is the increase in the size and proportion of the Eastern Religions category. Although the overall share is small, in 2001 they are estimated as more than two million adults. In real terms the actual numbers tripled during this decade mainly due to immigration. However, the lack of ARIS coverage of Hawaii, which is of little consequence for most groups, impacts Eastern religions nationally. It is estimated by Glenmary Research Center that around 100,000 Hawaiian adults belong to Eastern religions, particularly Buddhism.

Noteworthy is the substantial increase in the number and proportion of the so-called religious "Nones," those adults who profess no religion or self-identify as Atheist, Agnostic, Humanist or Secular.

Figure 2.2

Religious Identification of U.S. Adults According to the Taxonomy of the 13 Religious Traditions, 1990 and 2001
(weighted estimates)

RELIGIOUS TRADITION	NUMBER 1990	%	NUMBER 2001	%
Catholic	46,004,000	26.2	50,873,000	24.5
Mainline Christian	32,784,000	18.7	35,788,000	17.2
Baptist	33,964,000	19.3	33,830,000	16.3
Christian Generic	25,980,000	14.8	22,546,000	10.8
Pentecostal/Charismatic	5,647,000	3.2	7,831,000	3.8
Protestant Denominations	4,630,000	2.6	5,949,000	2.9
Mormon/LDS	2,487,000	1.4	2,697,000	1.3
Jewish	3,137,000	1.8	2,837,000	1.4
Eastern Religions	692,000	0.4	2,029,000	1.0
Muslim	527,000	0.3	1,104,000	0.5
NRM & Other Religions	1,296,000	0.7	1,770,000	0.9
Nones	14,331,000	8.2	29,481,000	14.1
Don't Know/Refused	4,031,000	2.3	11,246,000	5.4
Total	**175,440,000**	**100.0**	**207,983,000**	**100.0**

Notes

1. For a more detailed discussion of the survey methodology, please see Methodological Appendix.

2. Barry A. Kosmin & Seymour P. Lachman, *One Nation Under God: Religion in Contemporary America* (New York: Harmony Books, 1993).

3. In the 1990 survey, the question wording was: *What is your religion?* In the 2001 survey, the clause, *". . . if any"* was added to the question. A subsequent validity check based on cross-samples of 3,000 respondents carried out by International Communication Research (ICR) in 2002 found no statistical differences between the patterns of responses according to the two wordings.

4. The NSRI 1990 and ARIS 2001 survey findings provide religious identification data for the U.S. Bureau of the Census, *Statistical Abstract of the United States: 2003 (123rd Edition),* Washington D.C., 2003, (Table 79) p.67 (as well as the 2004 , 2005, and 2006 editions).

5. During the 1990s growth in the "no religion" population has also been noted widely in Western Europe, Canada and Australia.

6. See Egon Mayer, Barry Kosmin and Ariela Keysar, *American Jewish Identity Survey 2001,* The Graduate Center of the City University of New York, 2001.

THREE

Belief, Belonging, and Behavior

Religious or Secular Outlook

IN ORDER to enhance our understanding of the consequence and meaning of the data presented so far on the various religious groups as well as to comprehend where Americans stand on attitudes towards religion generally, we now need to use ARIS 2001 data that go beyond religious identification. The ARIS 2001 survey allows us to look at the religious identification of a representative sub-sample of 17,000 respondents who also provided answers to questions on beliefs, outlook, membership or affiliation with a religious institution, and religious switching (conversion and apostasy). Additionally they supplied information on spouses so we can extend it to an analysis of the religious mosaic among couples. This allows us in Chapters 3 and 4 to explore meaningfully "the three B's," of beliefs, belonging, and behavior.

We begin by examining a new concept in the study of American religion that is unique to ARIS—religious and secular outlook. The concept of "outlook" represents an attempt to apply in practical research the concept German phenomenologists have referred to as *weltanschauung* (sometimes translated as worldview or world-outlook).[1] Introduced into American sociology through the work of Alfred Schutz and his students, Peter Berger and Thomas Luckmann, the concept of *weltanschauung* was meant to resolve one of the fundamental paradoxes of social science: how to construct objective statements about what is essentially a subjective realm of experience. That paradox is all the more resistant to resolution when the subjective states social scientists are trying to describe include (as they nearly always do) ideological positions or value-laden behavior about which the social scientist him or herself can hardly claim neutrality. To address that paradox, those following in the intellectual footsteps of the phenomenologists have sought interpretive concepts that are clearly rooted in the language and worldview of the people whose ideas and behavior are to be interpreted.

The concept of "outlook" appears to us to be particularly well suited to describe the broad orientation of people to ideas they treat as plausible and to the criteria by which they judge plausibility. The value of this concept is that it is drawn directly from the ordinary experience of the everyday life of people and employs a method of measurement that emerges directly from the language of that experience.

Here we employ "outlook" both as a useful interpretive tool as well as a term that is readily understood by ordinary people in daily discourse about their own lives. The concept easily lends itself to binary distinctions because people often differentiate themselves that way, as for example: optimistic and pessimistic, liberal and conservative, or worldly and provincial.

Since the end of the 19th century, many students of religion have claimed that the process of secularization has transformed the theologies and institutions embodying religion and helped produce a secular "outlook." Max Weber described secularization as the "disenchantment of the world"—a characterization of the process of rationalization he adopted from the German poet Friedrich Schiller.[2] By this process Weber sought to capture the psychic and cultural transformation in which magical elements of thought and symbolism are progressively displaced by empiricism and rationality. On the wider societal level, Peter Berger defined secularization as "the process by which sectors of society are removed from the domination of religious institutions and symbols."[3]

People can be asked quite directly to describe whether they think their outlook is essentially religious or secular. Their replies to this question yield a distribution of answers that readily appear to be associated with a whole host of other indicators of opinion, belief, affiliation, association, and practice as well as demographic attributes. Thus great insights can be gleaned about the diverse mindscape of the American population as a whole.

Studying people's "outlook" as a means by which to differentiate various segments of the population allows us to view the objective facets of behavior associated with affiliation and identification as the consequence of meaningful intentionality. To say that people are "secular" or "religious" is at once both respectful of their own subjective perceptions about the universe and also makes no unwarranted inferences about the strength or weakness of their psychic attachments to their beliefs or their group loyalty. It thus allows us to characterize the subjective state of mind of the observed population without imposing a possibly invidious construct like identity.

To that end, ARIS 2001 asked a representative sub-sample of over 17,000 respondents the following:

"When it comes to your outlook, do you regard yourself as... (1) Secular, (2) Somewhat Secular, (3) Somewhat Religious or (4) Religious?"

Respondents were also permitted to indicate if they were unsure or a little of both. Ninety-one percent of survey respondents were able to provide an unequivocal reply to this question. In all, 16 percent described their outlook as secular or somewhat secular, while 75 percent described their outlook as religious or somewhat religious. Just 1 percent said they were "a little of both" and 2 percent said they were unsure. Five percent declined to answer the question. The distribution shown below in Figure 3.1 indicates that at least 10 percent of the population clearly and unambiguously considers itself "secular" rather than "religious." Another 6 percent regard themselves as "somewhat secular." The seculars were a smaller and more homogeneous group than the religious;

Figure 3.1

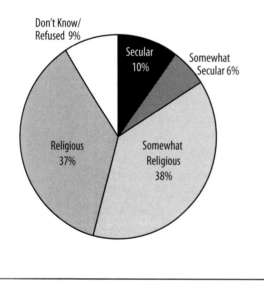

Outlook of U.S. Adult Population
When it comes to your outlook,
do you regard yourself as... ?

Don't Know/
Refused 9%

Secular
10%

Somewhat
Secular 6%

Religious
37%

Somewhat
Religious
38%

hence the larger proportion of them was to be found in the most definite category.

In contrast the religious option generated a fair amount of ambivalence, which was reflected in the equal proportions of respondents who fall into the category of "religious" and "somewhat religious."

This balance is obviously due to the great range of possibilities as to what "religious" could mean. It obviously means something very different in both belief and practice to a Catholic from what it means to a Seventh Day Adventist or to a Hindu. Many people are aware that though they are believers, their opinions and behavior are not completely in keeping with the precepts of their faith or religious group. Some in more liberal or less demanding groups are also aware that there are other religious groups in American society that are more exacting in their demands on believers and members and so they are more likely to say they are "somewhat religious." Even some of those who are to be found in the secular categories are not completely divorced from belief and religious membership but they are not willing to accept the external authority of scripture or clergy in their everyday lives or on political questions. They are examples of the secularization theory in practice.

Perhaps more interesting still are some of the demographic characteristics of the adult population, which seem to be associated with the disposition to be more or less secular, or more or less religious in one's outlook. Figures 3.2 and 3.3 provide a glimpse at some of those associations.

- Women were more likely than men to describe their outlook as "religious."

- Women were less likely than men to describe their outlook as "secular."

- Older Americans were more likely than younger to describe their outlook as "religious."

- Younger Americans tend to describe their outlook in more ambivalent terms, such as "somewhat religious."

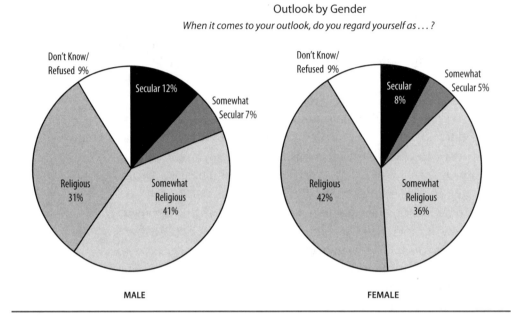

Figure 3.2

Outlook by Gender

When it comes to your outlook, do you regard yourself as . . . ?

MALE

Don't Know/Refused 9%
Secular 12%
Somewhat Secular 7%
Religious 31%
Somewhat Religious 41%

FEMALE

Don't Know/Refused 9%
Secular 8%
Somewhat Secular 5%
Religious 42%
Somewhat Religious 36%

Figure 3.3

Outlook by Age

When it comes to your outlook, do you regard yourself as . . . ?

	Religious	Somewhat Religious	Somewhat Secular	Secular	Don't Know/Refused
Aged 18 to 34	27%	43%	9%	14%	7%
Aged 35 to 49	38%	40%	6%	9%	7%
Aged 50 to 64	42%	36%	5%	10%	7%
Aged 65 and older	47%	34%	3	7%	9%

In order to offer detailed results for more groups, the following tables focus on the distribution of adults across the 22 largest religious faiths and denominations organized within the taxonomy of the 13 clusters or religious groupings.

Figure 3.4

Outlook by Religious Tradition

RELIGIOUS TRADITION/GROUP	Outlook Scale				ADULT POPULATION IN MILLIONS
	SECULAR	SOMEWHAT SECULAR	SOMEWHAT RELIGIOUS	RELIGIOUS	
Catholic	6%	6%	50%	33%	50.9
Mainline Christian	4	5	48	41	35.8
Methodist	3	5	48	42	14.2
Lutheran	3	6	48	41	9.6
Presbyterian	6	6	46	40	5.6
Episcopalian	7	7	52	32	3.5
United Church of Christ	4	4	55	34	1.4
Baptist	3	3	37	54	33.8
Christian Generic	6	6	37	45	22.5
Christian unspecified	4	6	37	47	14.2
Protestant unspecified	8	7	46	32	4.6
Evangelical/Born Again	7	1	19	70	1.0
Non-denominational	10	5	34	46	2.5
Pentecostal/Charismatic	2	2	26	63	7.8
Assemblies of God	0	2	18	72	1.1
Church of God	0	5	29	65	0.9
Pentecostal unspecified	3	2	27	61	4.4
Protestant Denominations	2	3	24	69	5.9
Churches of Christ	0	3	30	65	2.6
Jehovah's Witnesses	5	2	18	73	1.3
Seventh Day Adventist	3	4	19	73	0.7
Mormon	2	6	20	68	2.7
Jewish	26	16	41	11	2.8
Eastern Religions	15	11	42	27	2.0
Buddhist	7	15	46	24	1.1
Muslim	9	6	46	32	1.1
NRM & Other Religions	28	9	21	25	1.2
Nones/No religion	39	12	28	8	29.5
U.S. Total Adults	**10**	**6**	**40**	**38**	**208.0**

Note: Rows may not total to 100 pecent; Don't Know & Refused responses excluded from table.

Figure 3.4 highlights several important points about the religious outlook of America's adults. There is a clear contrast in outlook between those professing Christianity in any of its forms and the rest of society, with the possible exception of Muslims. Christians of all types were more likely to describe themselves as "religious." In contrast, those professing no religion, the New Religious Movements and Jews were the most likely to describe their outlook as "secular" or "somewhat secular." Respondents from the Pentecostal and Protestant Denominations groupings, particularly those identifying with Assemblies of God, Churches of Christ, and Church of God were the least likely to describe their outlook as "secular" or "somewhat secular."

Noteworthy was the wide range in the scores on the "religious" classification, from 73 percent of Seventh Day Adventists and Jehovah's Witnesses, to only 24 percent of Buddhists and 11 percent of Jews. As one might expect, self-defined Evangelicals had the most religious outlook closely followed by the Pentecostal and Protestant Denominations groupings along with Baptists and Mormons. Adults who chose the generic "Christian" label to describe their religious identification were more likely to describe their outlook as "religious" compared with those choosing the generic "Protestant" label—47 percent and 32 percent respectively.

The outlook scale creates a clustering of the religious groups from the most religious to the least religious along a theological spectrum. This clustering correlates with some critical social, economic and political attitudes and behaviors which will be discussed elsewhere in this volume.

Patterns of Belief

In addition to the question of outlook, survey respondents were asked about the nature of the Divine, i.e., their belief in the existence of God, belief in miracles, and the general benefit of a belief in God in terms of personal help. First, respondents were asked whether they agree (strongly or somewhat) or disagree (strongly or somewhat) with the proposition: *God exists.*

Figure 3.5

Belief that "God Exists" by Religious Tradition
(in percent)

RELIGIOUS TRADITION/GROUP	DISAGREE STRONGLY	DISAGREE SOMEWHAT	AGREE SOMEWHAT	AGREE STRONGLY	ADULT POPULATION IN MILLIONS
Catholic	0%	1%	12%	83%	50.9
Mainline Christian	1	1	11	84	35.8
Methodist	0	1	10	86	14.2
Lutheran	2	1	11	83	9.6
Presbyterian	0	1	14	82	5.6
Episcopalian	0	2	14	80	3.5
United Church of Christ	1	1	10	84	1.4
Baptist	0	0	4	93	33.8
Christian Generic	1	1	9	86	22.5
Christian unspecified	1	1	7	89	14.2
Protestant unspecified	1	2	14	77	4.6
Evangelical/Born Again	0	0	1	99	1.0
Non-denominational	1	2	8	84	2.5
Pentecostal/Charismatic	1	0	3	96	7.8
Assemblies of God	2	2	1	94	1.1
Church of God	0	0	11	88	0.9
Pentecostal unspecified	1	0	2	97	4.4
Protestant Denominations	0	0	4	94	6.0
Churches of Christ	0	0	6	92	2.6
Jehovah's Witnesses	0	0	2	97	1.3
Seventh Day Adventist	0	2	0	98	0.7
Mormon	0	1	6	92	2.7
Jewish	5	9	23	54	2.8
Eastern Religions	4	8	25	54	2.0
Buddhist	7	13	25	39	1.1
Muslim	1	1	8	85	1.1
NRM & Other Religions	6	3	18	60	1.2
Nones/No religion	12	9	22	45	29.5
U.S. Total Adults	**3**	**2**	**11**	**80**	**208.0**

Note: Rows may not total to 100 pecent; Don't Know & Refused responses excluded from table.

Belief in God's existence had a widespread consensus among American adults with over 80 percent of the populace strongly agreeing with this proposition. At the top of the belief scale were Pentecostals and the Protestant denominations such as Jehovah's Witnesses, with 97 percent agreeing strongly with the proposition "God exists." At the other extreme were the Eastern religions, Jews and "Nones" where 50 percent or less of adults agreed strongly that "God exists." However the results even among these more skeptical groups were surprising. Around 70 to 80 percent or more agreed (strongly or somewhat) about God's existence. That 39 percent of the non-theistic Buddhists and 45 percent of the "Nones" strongly agree was perhaps a surprising finding. As with the religious-secular outlook scale Catholics and Mainline Christians scored slightly below the other Christian groupings as regards the proportion of adults who were likely to strongly affirm God's existence.

Figures 3.4 and 3.5 suggest a notable, if not perfect, association between how people describe their outlook along the spectrum of "secular–religious" and what they affirm about belief in God. Among religious groups with the highest proportion of identifiers who describe their outlook as "religious" there was also a higher percentage which strongly agreed that *God exists*. The other indicators of God-beliefs (shown in Figures 3.6 and 3.7 below) similarly differentiate between those who describe their outlook as religious and as secular. This demonstrates that when people describe themselves as "secular" or "somewhat secular," they apparently do hold beliefs with respect to God that are quite different from those who describe themselves as "religious" or "somewhat religious." These designations are not simply *ad hoc* figures of speech. There was a tiny minority who said they had a religious outlook and yet rejected belief in God's existence. A more interesting finding was that 67 percent of adults who profess no religion ("Nones") nevertheless affirmed God's existence.

Inasmuch as the great majority of Americans profess a belief in the existence of God, it is interesting to probe further and to see whether there is any difference in the intensity or quality of that belief. All the respondents, regardless of how they replied to the question whether God exists, were asked their view of God's relationship to themselves as individuals, whether they agree (strongly or somewhat) or disagree (strongly or somewhat) with the proposition: *God helps me.*

Figure 3.6

Belief that "God Helps Me" by Religious Tradition

RELIGIOUS TRADITION/GROUP	Belief Scale				ADULT POPULATION IN MILLIONS
	DISAGREE STRONGLY	DISAGREE SOMEWHAT	AGREE SOMEWHAT	AGREE STRONGLY	
Catholic	2%	3%	17%	74%	50.9
Mainline Christian	2	3	19	72	35.8
Methodist	2	3	17	75	14.2
Lutheran	2	3	20	71	9.6
Presbyterian	2	3	20	71	5.6
Episcopalian	0	7	21	65	3.5
United Church of Christ	0	2	8	87	1.4
Baptist	1	1	6	90	33.8
Christian Generic	1	3	14	78	22.5
Christian unspecified	1	2	13	81	14.2
Protestant unspecified	2	5	23	64	4.6
Evangelical/Born Again	0	0	3	97	1.0
Non-denominational	1	2	12	77	2.5
Pentecostal/Charismatic	0	1	4	95	7.8
Assemblies of God	0	0	2	95	1.1
Church of God	0	0	9	90	0.9
Pentecostal unspecified	0	1	3	95	4.4
Protestant Denominations	0	0	7	89	6.0
Churches of Christ	0	0	8	87	2.6
Jehovah's Witnesses	0	0	10	88	1.3
Seventh Day Adventist	0	0	2	98	0.7
Mormon	2	1	8	89	2.7
Jewish	15	17	25	34	2.8
Eastern Religions	10	17	20	45	2.0
Buddhist	18	24	20	25	1.1
Muslim	1	1	15	73	1.1
NRM & Other Religions	18	5	16	50	1.2
Nones/No religion	20	11	22	34	29.5
U.S. Total Adults	**5**	**4**	**15**	**71**	**208.0**

Note: Rows may not tally to 100 percent; Don't Know & Refused responses excluded from table.

Note in Figure 3.6 that slightly fewer Americans believed in divine intercession—that God directly assists them—than agreed that God exists. In fact 9 percent fewer believed "very strongly" but 4 percent more "agree somewhat," so the net loss from agreement with the first proposition (Figure 3.4) was only 5 percent of the adult population. Thus most Americans firmly believe in a personal, active divinity. However, this question on intercession reveals quite a large gap among some religious groups. Almost all of Seventh Day Adventist and Evangelical/Born Again adherents strongly believed that God helps them (89 percent and 97 percent respectively). Conversely only 25 percent of Buddhists and only one-third of Jews and Nones and one-half those identifying with the New Religious Movements strongly believed that God helps them.

Most Americans firmly believe in a personal, active divinity.

Figure 3.7 deals with the ability of the Divinity to intervene in the world and perform miracles. Once again we have to factor in the minority that varies in size among the different groups that denies the existence of God from the outset. In addition different faiths conceive differently about what defines a miracle. For instance the Catholic Church defines it as a breach of Natural Law while Judaism has a lower threshold and includes serendipitous events. Those who agree strongly with the proposition *God performs miracles* total 70 percent of the national adult population while another 16 percent will entertain that possibility agreeing "somewhat."

The answers to the question in Figure 3.7 as to whether *God performs miracles* are especially instructive. They show once again a kind of triadic division among the religious groupings. The Pentecostals, Protestant Denominations, Mormons, and Baptists are the most agreeable to this belief, all scoring 80 percent or more. Practically all of Assemblies of God, Seventh Day Adventist, Evangelical/Born Again, and Pentecostal identifiers agree strongly that *God performs miracles*. The middle tier is made up of Catholics, Mainline Christians, and Muslims. The Non-Christian groups form the third tier, all scoring under 50 percent who strongly agree. This item underscores yet again that Jews, Buddhists, and adults who do not adhere to any religion are quite different in their religious worldview from the other religious groups. Large proportions of Jewish, New Religious

Figure 3.7

Belief that "God Performs Miracles" by Religious Tradition

RELIGIOUS TRADITION/GROUP	Belief Scale				ADULT POPULATION IN MILLIONS
	DISAGREE STRONGLY	DISAGREE SOMEWHAT	AGREE SOMEWHAT	AGREE STRONGLY	
Catholic	1%	5%	22%	70%	50.9
Mainline Christians	3	6	21	68	35.8
Methodist	2	5	18	73	14.2
Lutheran	4	6	21	68	9.6
Presbyterian	4	4	24	66	5.6
Episcopalian	3	8	28	58	3.5
United Church of Christ	1	14	30	53	1.4
Baptist	1	1	8	90	33.8
Christian Generic	2	5	15	78	22.5
Christian unspecified	2	4	13	80	14.2
Protestant unspecified	3	8	23	64	4.6
Evangelical/Born Again	0	0	4	96	1.0
Non-denominational	1	2	14	82	2.5
Pentecostal/Charismatic	2	1	4	93	7.8
Assemblies of God	0	1	1	98	1.1
Church of God	2	0	9	89	0.9
Pentecostal unspecified	2	1	3	94	4.4
Protestant Denominations	3	2	12	81	5.9
Churches of Christ	5	2	15	77	2.6
Jehovah's Witnesses	5	4	13	74	1.3
Seventh Day Adventist	0	3	1	96	0.7
Mormon	1	4	7	87	2.7
Jewish	16	26	23	32	2.8
Eastern Religions	16	16	22	43	2.0
Buddhist	16	24	23	34	1.1
Muslim	4	7	13	70	1.1
NRM & Other religions	21	14	15	45	1.2
Nones/No religion	19	19	22	35	29.5
U.S. Total Adults	**4**	**7**	**16**	**70**	**208.0**

Note: Rows may not total to 100 pecent; Don't Know & Refused responses excluded from table.

Movement identifiers, Eastern religions, and Nones disagree (somewhat or strongly) that *God performs miracles.*

The scores in Figure 3.7 were hardly different from those in Figure 3.6. This means that overall, adult Americans were just as likely to believe in the general power of God to perform miracles as in intercession or God's helping them personally. The pattern of beliefs shown in Figures 3.5 through 3.7 seems to suggest that the "secular–religious outlook" scale works well as a representation of religious reality as regards levels of belief among the various religious groups and groupings. These patterns also tend to validate the ARIS methodology with regard to the self-identification process and the accuracy of the data collection, i.e., our Pentecostals, Mormons, and Buddhists seemed to respond as they should in theory.

The data show extraordinarily high degrees of consensus in the expected directions among some groups such as respondents identifying with the Assemblies of God, which treat the Bible as fact and believe in miracles, faith healing, and speaking in tongues. The responses of our Evangelical respondents too, are what we would expect from religious "conservatives"—people using this self-description who "stress the constancy of the Bible." The aggregation of religious groupings in our taxonomy, such as "Mainline Christians" and "Protestant Denominations," also seems to be validated as the taxonomy brings together like-minded denominations and groups.

The overall levels of consensus and dissensus within the religious groups provide insights into the terminology often used in analysis of religion. Figures 3.4 through 3.7 allow us to distinguish which are "broad churches" or communities composed of people adhering more to a cultural heritage with a range of beliefs such as Catholics and Jews and those which are "sects" that put more emphasis on beliefs and are as a result more consensual and homogeneous. The former are designated "communitarian" in outlook and the latter "associational." The findings on the more "liberal" groups show that for some people identifying with a religion does not preclude thinking of that identification in secular terms. Identification with a religion can grow out of outlook and beliefs but it can also grow in a more "secular" way out of a stock of knowledge and customs and a wellspring of affinities that link individuals to larger societal entities, from a family to a community to an ethnicity or a racial group.

One set of statistics that might appear at first glance anomalous relates to the None/No Religion group. Over one-third claim a religious outlook though half are, as might be expected, secular in some way. More surprising might be that 45 percent believe in the existence of God while only 21 percent are atheists. This is a somewhat disparate group only united by their agreement that they apparently do not identify with any of the multitude of offerings available in the religious marketplace. Some obviously have their own private forms of religiosity and find God at home or outdoors and not in an institution or building alongside others. Some may simply be searching for the right religious home. This ambivalence and shading of responses is not a new phenomenon in American society. Abraham Lincoln was never baptized and was a religious "None" all his life. Yet he had a good knowledge of the Bible and quoted from it extensively in his speeches and he also accepted the existence of a Divine Creator.

Membership in Religious Congregations and Institutions

Closely akin to religious group identification in the minds of most people is membership in or affiliation with a place of worship. Indeed, in his classic definition of religion, the 19th-century sociologist Emile Durkheim characterized religions as systems of belief. These systems unite a group of adherents into common modes of worship, which in turn are shared activities that organize adherents into churches (or synagogues, temples, mosques or whatever else a group may chose to call the place in which kindred spirits come together to celebrate, worship and recognize the commonality of their beliefs).[4]

More than half (54 percent) of the adult population in America resided in a household where either they themselves or someone else belonged to a religious congregation or place of worship. To be sure, the significance of membership (its importance, its criteria, and even its definition) varies greatly from one denomination or faith to another. This study is not in a position to evaluate the meaning or importance of religious institutional membership for particular individuals or groups but only to report on claimed patterns of affiliation.

Yet even this one single statistic provides important information, for given that about 80 percent of adults identify with some religious group, there appears to be a considerable gap between "identification" with a religion and reported "membership" or "belonging" to an institutional embodiment of that faith. About 30 percent of American adults or over 60 million people who identify with a religious group are "unchurched" in that they live in households without any current membership ties to a congregation. That difference between religious identification and belonging could well contain the seeds of a potent cultural shift in which religion means something quite different from those who adhere to one, to those who see themselves as the institutional custodians of a faith group. One can probably assume that the "unchurched" are those who seek only episodic, life-cycle events such as baptism, weddings, and funerals from their religious institutions. Many may be antipathetic to "organized religion," anticlerical, or just averse to joining anything.

More than thirty years ago, the sociologist Thomas Luckmann anticipated the emergence of an increasingly de-institutionalized form of religious identification in an incisive analysis of modern religious life, *The Invisible Religion*. In that work he concluded: "The modern sacred cosmos legitimates the retreat of the individual into the 'private sphere' and sanctifies his (or her) subjective autonomy."[5] Luckmann's analysis may have been ahead of its time. Aggregated survey data from the *General Social Survey* 1972–1994 showed a persistence of church membership. Among a nationally representative sample of 1,481 American adults surveyed by GSS between the early 1970s and the early 1990s, 61 percent indicated membership in a church.

However, the decade of the 1990s appears to have been a period in which religious institutional membership slid, underscoring what Luckmann described as the rise of "invisible religion." Figure 3.8 describes the varied pattern of religious institutional membership among the 22 largest religious groups that encompass nearly 190 million adults, or nearly 92 percent of the adult population

About 30 percent of American adults or over 60 million people who identify with a religious group are "unchurched."

(including "no religion," the choice made by an increasingly growing number).

Figure 3.8

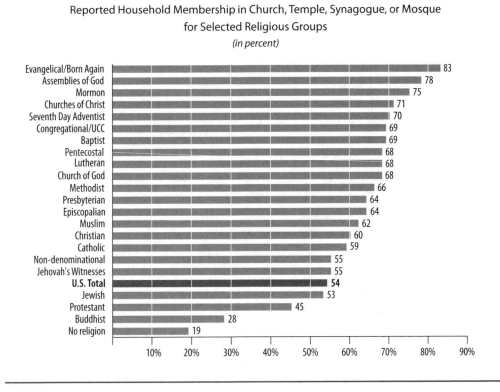

Reported Household Membership in Church, Temple, Synagogue, or Mosque
for Selected Religious Groups
(in percent)

As Figure 3.8 illustrates, there are notable differences between
various religious groups with respect to the relationship between
identification and *affiliation*. For example, 68 percent of those identifying themselves as Lutheran also report church membership, while
only 45 percent of those who describe themselves as Protestant
(without a specific denominational identification) report church
membership. Nearly 80 percent of those identifying with the Assemblies of God report church membership. Church membership is
reported by 59 percent of Catholic adults. About 53 percent of adults
who identify their religion as Jewish or Judaism report temple or
synagogue membership. Among those calling themselves Muslim or

Islamic, 62 percent report somebody in the household holds membership in a mosque. It is noticeable that the theologically conservative and most demanding denominations are the most "churched" groups. The exception is the Jehovah's Witnesses, who as we have seen, normally score similarly to other "sects." They stand out on this particular variable because their affiliation criteria are "exclusive" or exacting and there are barriers to full membership.

It is possible that as with reports of attendance at worship services, respondents who self-identified with a religious group in the survey might then have felt pressure to "belong," resulting in an overall a tendency to exaggerate affiliation ties. However, that does not seem to have happened in the two cases where we can test for this tendency. In fact there is good correspondence between the actual reported number of Presbyterian and Episcopalian church members for 2000 and the extrapolated ARIS numbers. Both these churches keep reliable membership statistics and if one applies the ARIS membership rates of 64 percent to the estimated number of Presbyterians and Episcopalians in Figure 2.1 then the figures show a remarkable level of precision. They are within a hundred thousand or so of each the actual current national rolls for those churches (2,208,000 for the Episcopal Church and 3,584,000 for the Presbyterian Church).

Perhaps, it will come as no surprise to religious leaders, but nearly 20 percent of adults who described themselves as Nones, including even some "atheist" and "agnostics," also reported that either they themselves or someone else in their household was a member of a church, temple, synagogue, mosque, or some other religious institution. Affiliated "Nones" are usually linked to congregations through spouses or parents but some may well feel the need for community or the impulse to "search together" with others. They are an anomaly and yet the other side of the phenomenon or paradox of the 37 percent of all adults who identify with a religion but indicate that neither they themselves nor anyone else in their household belongs to a church or some other similar institution. It is this latter group in particular that best exemplifies the notion of "invisible religion" first proposed by Luckmann.

The obvious difference between the percentage of the total adult population that identifies with one or another religion and the percentage that report living in a household where either they themselves or someone else is a member of an organized religious body draws attention to the difference between *identification* as a state of heart and mind and *affiliation* as a social condition.

This difference in the proportions between *identification* and *affiliation* in each group suggests the possible differences in the value and meaning attached to affiliation within various religious movements. For example, note that among adults identifying themselves as Buddhists, just 28 percent reported affiliation with a temple.

Differences between the percentages of *identification* and *affiliation* may also indicate differences in meaning associated with religion itself. For some, religious identification may well be a social marker as much as a marker designating a specific set of beliefs. For others, it may be an anchor to one's sense of self through family or community. For others still, it may simply be the "gut response" evoked by the question: *What is your religion, if any?* without any wider emotional, social or philosophical ramifications. In Chapter 11 we will compare the socioeconomic and demographic profiles of adults who report household membership in religious institutions to adherents living in households where nobody belongs to a religious body.

Notes

1. Peter L. Berger and Thomas Luckmann, *The Social Construction of Reality* (New York: Doubleday Anchor Book, 1966, 1967). P. 15 "The sociology of knowledge must first of all concern itself with what people 'know' as 'reality' in their everyday non- or pre-theoretical lives."

2. Hans Gerth & C. Wright Mills, *From Max Weber: Essays in Sociology*, (New York: Oxford University Press, 1958), p. 51.

3. Peter L. Berger, *The Sacred Canopy: Elements of A Sociological Theory of Religion*, (New York: Doubleday, 1967), p.107.

4. Emile Durkheim, *The Elementary Forms of The Religious Life* (New York: Free Press, 1955).

5. Thomas Luckmann, *The Invisible Religion* (New York: The Macmillan Co., 1967).

FOUR

Religious Switching

Lifetime Change in Adults' Religious Identification

ONE facet of the market analogy in the religious sphere is that Americans can and do pick and choose between the products on offer in the religious marketplace. Hence the rise of new religious offerings and the cycle of "religious awakenings" that have marked the nation's religious history. In the U.S. the sovereign consumer or religious shopper has the freedom to join and leave religious groups and individual congregations. Though most Americans still tend to remain in the religious group into which they were born, the trend shows that Americans are increasingly partial to exercising these consumer rights and do not feel obligated to give lifetime loyalty to one particular "religious brand."

One fascinating and unique finding from ARIS is that we can track this trend in some detail. ARIS 2001 asked if respondents had ever changed their religious identification. If they replied in the affirmative they were then asked: *What was your religious preference, if any, before you changed?* More than 33 million American adults, about 16 percent of the total U.S. adult population, reported that at some point in their lives they had changed their religious preference or identification. Perhaps this phenomenon of "religion switching" is a reflection of a deeper cultural phenomenon in contemporary America. In the early 1990s, the sociologist Wade Clark Roof described the increasingly middle-aged baby boomers as a "generation of seekers."[1] However, the 1990s were also a period of great immigration and an economic boom. Therefore, the religious life of the nation has been influenced by social forces that are wider and more varied than simply the aging of the baby boomers.

About 16 percent of the total U.S. adult population reported that at some point in their lives they had changed their religious preference or identification.

Figure 4.1

Lifetime Change in Adults' Religious Identification for Selected Religious Groups

RELIGIOUS GROUP	NUMBER	SWITCHED IN	%	SWITCHED OUT	%	# IF NO SWITCHING
Catholic	50,873,000	4,282,909	8	9,493,912	19	56,084,003
Baptist	33,830,000	4,401,587	13	4,619,653	14	34,048,066
No religion	29,481,000	6,622,494	23	1,118,081	4	23,976,587
Christian	14,190,000	2,873,155	20	1,486,614	10	12,803,459
Methodist	14,140,000	2,631,703	19	3,776,077	27	15,284,374
Lutheran	9,580,000	1,755,644	18	1,857,875	19	9,682,231
Presbyterian	5,596,000	1,316,068	24	1,432,118	26	5,712,050
Protestant	4,647,000	316,587	7	1,088,409	23	5,418,822
Pentecostal	4,407,000	1,340,583	30	730,540	17	3,796,957
Episcopalian/Anglican	3,451,000	899,908	26	745,376	22	3,296,468
Jewish	2,831,000	171,447	6	291,390	10	2,950,943
Mormon	2,697,000	427,068	16	431,692	16	2,701,624
Churches of Christ	2,593,000	302,633	12	358,183	14	2,648,550
Non-denominational	2,489,000	721,683	29	43,548	2	1,810,865
Congregational/UCC	1,378,000	183,916	13	269,776	20	1,463,860
Jehovah's Witnesses	1,331,000	517,540	39	380,983	29	1,194,443
Assemblies of God	1,105,000	221,398	20	144,514	13	1,028,116
Muslim/Islamic	1,104,000	182,859	17	98,333	9	1,019,474
Buddhist	1,082,000	340,523	33	221,035	20	962,512
Evangelical/Born Again	1,032,000	384,339	37	78,049	8	725,710
Church of God	944,000	241,296	26	195,733	21	898,437
Seventh Day Adventist	724,000	247,780	34	177,635	25	653,855

As seen in Figure 4.1, switching involves not only the shift of people's spiritual loyalties from one religion to another, which could reflect some kind of spiritual seeking, but also, and perhaps more importantly, a dropping out of religion altogether. The second column in the table shows that the largest net gainer in terms of numbers was more than six-and-a half million new preferences for the "no religion" option. To be sure, there is no indication in the current data when the "religious switching" actually occurred—in the 1990s or earlier. Surely, for our older respondents the switching very likely had occurred earlier.

The methodology used in Figure 4.1 requires some explanation. The numbers in the table are the current number of adherents of each denomination; the number who switched in, and the number who switched out. The last column to the right, "number if no switching," is an artificial, "what-if" construct consisting of the current number of adherents, minus those who switched in, plus those who switched out. Also, the percentages switching in and switching out are calculated as shares of the current number of adherents. It is impossible from the data available to construct a past number of adherents to use as the denominator, given that the numbers are affected by many other factors, including births, deaths, and migration.

The findings in Figure 4.1 go some way to explaining some of the recent changes in the national religious profile recorded in Figure 2.1. They describe the patterns of religion switching only among the 22 largest aggregates that taken together constitute over 90 percent of the entire adult population currently residing in the United States. The top three gainers in America's vast religious market place appear to be Evangelical Christians, those describing themselves as Non-Denominational Christians, and—at the other extreme— those who profess no religion. Figure 4.1 shows powerful cross-currents; many Americans are drawn to religious groups that demand strong commitment, while others are abandoning religion altogether. Among the nation's largest religious group, Catholics, there were 50.9 million self-identified adherents in 2001. About 4.3 million were newcomers, who "switched in." Yet 9.5 million adults who had at one time in the past identified as Catholics had "switched out" to other religious groups or to no religion as of 2001. That implies a net loss of about 5 million adults, or around 9 percent, due to the process of religious switching.

Some pro-active, missionary groups such as Adventists and Jehovah's Witnesses have a large turnover since they appear to attract a relatively large number of converts ("in-switchers") but also have nearly as large a number of apostates ("out-switchers"). It is also interesting to note that Buddhists fall into this category of what one might call high-turnover religious groups. Probably more unexpected is the high rate of "churning" of identifiers exhibited by some of the mainline denominations, such as Episco-palians and Presbyterians, though it made little dif-ference to their overall positions.

Figure 4.2 summarizes the analysis shown in Figure 4.1 and focuses on the net gain or loss of each religious group due to religious switching. Evidently, the trend appears to be towards polarization with groups at opposite theological poles growing— the Nones and the Evangelical/Born Again and non-denominational Christians. Interestingly the latter two groups are most associated with the mega-church phenomenon of church growth. If we go further down the list it seems again that the most liberal offerings, such as Buddhism, and most con-servative religious groups—Pentecostals, "Chris-tians" and the Protestant sects—were gaining followers. By contrast, though the losses were not spectacular aside from the anomalous "Protestant" category, the net losers from switching were groups in the theological middle ground, mostly the main-line Protestant denominations, Judaism, and Catholicism. These societal transformations have immense consequences for "cultural wars" and the political dynamics in U.S. society.

This ARIS data is unique because it offers the opportunity for some compelling insights into change in contemporary American religion. The rel-atively large sample size yields reliable data on the top losers and gainers. The Catholics and Methodists clearly lost out as millions of their adherents "switched out" of these churches and we are able to show where they went. At the other end of the spectrum we can also look at the gainers, the Evangelical/ Born Again, non-denominational and the no-religion groups, to find out whom they attract—that is the former religious identification of those who "switched in" to these groups.

Figure 4.2

Gain and Loss of Religious Groups*

RELIGIOUS GROUP	CHANGE
Evangelical/Born Again	42%
Non-denominational	37
No Religion	23
Pentecostal	16
Buddhist	12
Christian	11
Jehovah's Witnesses	11
Seventh Day Adventist	11
Muslim/Islamic	8
Assemblies of God	7
Episcopalian/Anglican	5
Church of God	5
Mormon	0
Baptist	-1
Lutheran	-1
Presbyterian	-2
Churches of Christ	-2
Jewish	-4
Congregational/UCC	-6
Methodist	-7
Catholic	-9
Protestant	-14

* Difference between actual number of adherents and the number there would have been if there had been no religious switching, from Figure 4.1.

Former Catholics

Figure 4.3 answers the crucial question: where did more than nine million former Catholics go? Clearly a plurality of former Catholics distanced themselves from any organized form of religion, opting for the "no religion" group. This is the largest destination and represents more than one-quarter of former Catholics, so that over 2.5 million former Catholics professed no religion in 2001. The other religious identifications, each attracting more than one million former Catholics, were the generic Christian and Baptist groups.

Figure 4.3

Current Religious Identification of Former Catholics

CURRENT RELIGION	NUMBER OF ADULTS	%
No Religion	2,599,000	28
Christian	1,566,000	17
Baptist	1,056,000	11
Lutheran	597,000	6
Methodist	482,000	5
Pentecostal	443,000	5
Presbyterian	293,000	3
Non-denominational	294,000	3
Episcopalian/Anglican	256,000	3
Evangelical/Born Again	158,000	2
Mormon	138,000	2
Other Religions	1,329,000	14
Don't Know/Refused	134,000	1
Total	**9,494,000**	**100**

Some former Catholics became Lutheran, Methodist or Pentecostal. About half a million adults switched to each of these groups. Other smaller groups are listed in Figure 4.3. "Other religions," amalgamates several groups, each one too small to represent, but summing to 14 percent of former Catholics.

Since Catholics are the largest religious group in the nation, it is not surprising that they lost the largest number of adherents. However, more significantly, despite attracting over four million newcomers they still lost over five million souls to other types of religious identification.

Figure 4.4

Current Religious Identification of Former Methodists

CURRENT RELIGION	NUMBER OF ADULTS	%
Baptist	863,000	23
Catholic	682,000	18
No Religion	394,000	11
Lutheran	367,000	10
Presbyterian	324,000	9
Christian	231,000	6
Episcopalian/Anglican	188,000	5
Other Religions	642,000	17
Don't Know/Refused	35,000	1
Total	**3,776,000**	**100**

Former Methodists

The other major movement out of a particular religious identification recorded by ARIS was among the denominations and churches making up the Methodist tradition. Figure 4.4 answers the question: Where did almost four million former Methodists go? Unlike former Catholics, few dropped out of organized religion entirely. As shown in Figure 4.4, the "none" option attracted a much smaller proportion of former Methodists, only 11 percent. This is similar to the proportion of switchers who became Lutheran and Presbyterian. In fact, the most popular choice for former Methodists, over 800,000 adults or 23 percent of switchers, were to the various Baptist groups. A substantial number of Methodist switchers, 18 percent, also became Catholics. The comparative numbers in Figures 4.3 and 4.4 show the complicated nature of the switching phenomenon and the religious crosscurrents it highlights. While 682,000 Methodists turned to Catholicism only 482,000 Catholics or 5 percent of its switchers went to Methodism thus giving a net gain of 200,000 converts to the Catholic Church.

The "New Nones"

The growth in the proportion and number of religious "Nones" is the most significant change in the national religious profile from both a statistical and social perspective. The data on switching can help us understand a little more of this dynamic. Thus we can learn, for example, the point of origin in religious and theological terms of the new "Nones," namely the six million adults who in 2001 chose to profess no religion, yet previously professed a religion. These new Nones, are predominantly former Catholics. In fact former Catholics are much more likely to be found in this category (43 percent) than they are as a proportion of the nation's total population (25 percent).

Figure 4.5

Previous Religious Identification of "New Nones"

PREVIOUS RELIGION	NUMBER OF ADULTS	%
Catholic	2,599,000	43
Baptist	815,000	14
Christian	420,000	7
Methodist	394,000	7
Lutheran	264,000	4
Presbyterian	138,000	2
Protestant	134,000	2
Pentecostal	115,000	2
Mormon	114,000	2
Jehovah's Witnesses	80,000	1
Episcopalian/Anglican	56,000	1
Jewish	53,000	1
Other Religions	61,000	11
Refused	163,000	3
Total	**6,045,000**	**100**

Figure 4.6

Previous Religious Identification of "New Pentecostals"

PREVIOUS RELIGION	NUMBER OF ADULTS	%
Baptist*	513,000	38
Catholic	443,000	33
Methodist	56,000	4
Charismatic	47,000	4
Episcopalian/Anglican	45,000	3
Lutheran	37,000	3
Presbyterian	33,000	2
Christian	32,000	2
Churches of Christ & Christian Churches	27,000	2
Other Religions	80,000	6
Refused	39,000	3
Total	**1,341,000**	**100**

* Includes Southern Baptist

As shown in Figure 4.5, more than 2.5 million adults who self-identified as Catholics at one point in their lives switched to the no-religion option.

Looking at Figure 4.5, we realize that adults who switched from a religion to no religion came from many religious backgrounds. However, the overall Catholic predominance means that all the other religious groups, aside from Mormons, are under-represented among the "new Nones" in comparison with their share of the population as reported in Figure 4.1 and Figure 4.3. Other major sources of these "new Nones" are Baptists (of all types including the American, black and Southern Baptist denominations), the generic Christian group, and Methodists.

The New Pentecostals

One of the religious trends most noticed by commentators over the past few decades has been the growth of Pentecostalism. Figure 4.6 shows the religious origins of those newcomers who gave this designation in 2001. It excludes those who provided a particular Pentecostal denomination such as Assemblies of God or the more problematic answer "Church of God" (the title of more than one denomination).

These "new Pentecostals"—adults who switched their religious identification and became Pentecostal—were most likely to be previously Baptist or previously Catholic. Together these two groups encompass more than 70 percent of new Pentecostals. Both groups, but particularly Baptists, are over-represented among the switchers to Pentecostalism. This dominance means that once again most other religious groups are under-represented in Figure 4.6. Interestingly, only a tiny fraction (about 1 percent) were previously of "no religion." Likewise Figure 4.5 shows only two percent of "new Nones" are former Pentecostals.

The new Evangelical/Born Again and non-denominational Christians

There are not enough cases even in ARIS to provide reliable numbers on the previous religious identification of persons who specifically identified themselves as new Evangelical/Born-again and non-denominational Christians. However, it is possible to summarize the main trends. The biggest source of new Evangelical/Born Again Christians is former Catholics, since more than 40 percent of adult switchers who in 2001 self-identified as Evangelical/Born Again Christian were ex-Catholics. The new non-denominational Christian adults appear to have two major religious sources; once again America's largest religious groups are over-represented, for about 40 percent of them were formerly Catholics and about 30 percent previously identified as Baptists.

Theological and Social Trends in Religious Switching

The ARIS findings shed statistical light on the well-known phenomenon of "religious switching." They show us the main trends in contemporary American religion, and provide details particularly on the origins of the growing religious groups as well as the trend towards "no religion." Two important findings on this topic—that Catholics tend to reject other religious options when they reject Catholicism and that there are no major flows of switchers between the no-religion group and Pentecostals—seem to confirm earlier research findings and sociological theory. It has long been observed that switching most often occurs between religious groups similar in social class composition. It seems that people cognitively map similarities and differences between denominations—in other words they place various religious groups in some kind of order of compatibility. They then use their mapping system when switching groups (and, as we shall discover, choosing spouses). This is because religious distance is very closely associated with social distance.

Sociologist Milton Rokeach suggested in his 1960 work *The Open and Closed Mind* that switchers moving between Christian denominations usually change to a denomination only one or two steps away from their own in terms of liturgy or theology. His "R-order" formula is Catholic, Episcopalian, Lutheran, Presbyterian, Methodist and Baptist—to which we might add "Christian," Pentecostal and the Protestant sects. The first three share the liturgical tradition, with communion the focal point of the service; the latter three share the sermon-centered liturgies of the Reformation. We can see indications of this pattern of staggered movement in Figures 4.3 to 4.6. In this model Catholic "losses" can be explained because this church is

Switchers moving between Christian denominations usually change to a denomination only one or two steps away from their own in terms of liturgy or theology.

disadvantaged by lying at one extreme on the theological scale. Probably more important than theological factors in contributing to the decline is the increasing number of Catholics living in a more open social environment since World War II. The suburbanization process and migration to the sunbelt has entailed the movement of white Catholics out of small, homogeneous communities and greater mixing with people from different religious backgrounds. This has simultaneously coincided with a decline in Catholic school enrollment. Paradoxically a sense of loyalty to Catholic culture and to the echoes of ancestral ethnic ties may have reinforced the secularization trend and the movement into the no religion column. Many former Catholics (and Jews) may see it as less disloyal to be a "None" than to identify with another faith, hence the contrast between these "out-switchers" and the ex-Methodists who are probably typical of most people raised in the Protestant tradition.

Religious switching, which involves the dynamics of conversion and apostasy, is however only one factor, and not the prime force, in reshaping the national religious profile. Another important factor is immigration and the entry of newcomers bringing either new faiths or differentially reinforcing various existing religious groups on the American scene. Unfortunately ARIS does not have migration data except for the Hispanic population (see Chapter 14). Instead in that chapter we will use ethnic minority status as a surrogate to supply some insights into the effect these new Americans are having on the national profile. The other major influence in changing the national profile is demography. We will now turn to this crucial topic to see how the natural replacement of older Americans by a new generation of young adults pans out. We will also examine how the patterns of family formation and fertility—traditionally key issues of interest to religion—vary among religious groups to strengthen or weaken their numbers.

Notes

1. Wade Clark Roof, *A Generation of Seekers: The Spiritual Journeys of the Baby Boom Generation* (San Francisco: HarperSanFrancisco, 1993).

FIVE

Who Are the Religious and Non-Religious?

The Demographics

L IFECYCLE events in the human drama such as marriage, procreation, birth, and death have always been at the core of
organized religion and religious rituals. Most religious traditions
set out in detail the duties and responsibilities of individuals to one
another, particularly their parents, children, and spouses. Religious
literature, particularly the Bible, is full of stories, parables, and teachings about family relationships. However, the religious thinkers of
the past lived in relatively stable and closed societies with clear and
fixed relationships between young and old and between men and
women. They could not have envisaged the unprecedented social
upheaval of the past few decades, particularly as regards the status
of the family.

A biomedical revolution has also had an enormous influence in
improving health standards and extending life expectancy. The
resulting advances in the area of sexual reproduction, fertility and
contraception have posed new ethical and moral challenges to religious teachings. One result of these changes is that formal marriage
is entered into at later ages and less frequently. The women's and
gay liberation movements have made dramatic progress. Since the
1960s divorce laws have been liberalized, abortion legalized, and the
Pill introduced. Out-of-wedlock births now account for more than
one in four of the national total. Women's lives especially have
undergone striking changes as they have increased their independence from men and marriage.

These developments pose challenges for most religious groups
because they have religious implications in terms of what constitutes
acceptable human behavior. Most of these changes have run counter

to the religious prescriptions and traditional norms of Judaism, Christianity, and Islam. The rapidity of these changes and the increasing break with past patterns of behavior and morality disconcert many clergy and believers, who have tried to re-direct society back onto its previous course. This battle for the hearts and minds of the American public has produced a polarized debate between modernizers and traditionalists, or liberals and conservatives, across all religions. The ARIS data allow us to study the scorecard as American religion attempts to respond to the newly emerging social structures of the 21st century. We will discover which religious groups are most successful in attracting the loyalties of particular segments of an increasingly socially diverse American population.

In this chapter we explore the interplay of demography and religion in the overall American population as well as within various religious groups. Different generations see the world differently, both because they are at different stages of life and because their experiences growing up have differed. One's outlook and approach to the world are influenced by the era in which one is raised, educated, and socialized into society. Living through the Great Depression and World II had a different impact from being raised during the 1960s or the age of the internet. In addition, being a boy or a girl in various eras was also very different in its impact.

We can thus expect the forces of history and differing generational patterns of socialization to influence people's personal beliefs and outlooks. We discover these in the aggregate by examining the interplay between religious identification and the key demographic characteristics of age and gender. These are important because the future of a religious group is also often shaped by the relative distribution of the old and the young and the proportion of males and females. One caveat is necessary here; confounding variables such as race play a significant role in the American population's demographic characteristics and processes and they will be dealt with in a later chapter. However, in this chapter religious identification *per se* will be the focus.

Gender

The lay and professional literature on modern American religion has consistently shown what clergy and parishioners have observed:

women are more likely than men to join religious organizations and participate in worship services. In a previous chapter we demonstrated that women are more likely to say they have a religious outlook. One explanation is the different standing in society of women, reflecting a division of labor by sex. Historically the religious and family spheres in the West were feminized and separated from the mainstream workplace activities which were male-dominated. Another explanation has it that men are less religious than women because of what psychologists refer to as sex-type personalities. In this view, being religious is consistent with feminine orientation, which includes a religious experience of "otherness," a personal experience of "connectedness," and a sharing of the "we-ness" of religious community. In the jargon of the men's movement, being religious is not conducive to masculinity since it demands submission and is more left-brain-oriented i.e., feminine.

It appears that Christianity is especially associated with female spirituality. Church participation has always been lower for men in all the Christian traditions in America. Historically, European Christianity, with its experience of feudal society and monarchy, has shown antipathy to maleness, the hero, the achiever, activism, and assertiveness. Its preferred definition of maleness has focused on fathering: either on the male role as priest leading the flock in the ways of God or the father as the representative of Christ in the family and as head of the home. In America, as early as 1692, Cotton Mather wrote, "So still there are far more Godly women in the world than there are men; and our Church Communions give us a little demonstration of it." In Victorian times, women's organizations were forces for benevolence, and for the establishment of schools and churches. By contrast, on the frontier where single men and their interests dominated, the saloon took precedence.

One social change stressed by most commentators on contemporary America is the emergence of a gender-neutral society among today's young. Society increasingly provides similar educational opportunities for young boys and girls and in most areas of the country gender gaps have diminished in both secular and religious educational attainment. Traditional differentiated gender roles were the standard way of life in the older generations, primarily those now over 60 years old. In contrast, adults who at the turn of the 21st century were in their 20s, 30s, and even 40s experienced different and more egalitarian upbringings and patterns of socialization. Younger men and women have had access to similar life opportunities and benefited from more similar career opportunities.

Given the increasing gender neutrality of civil society, we might have expected gender differences in religion to have narrowed. In fact, ARIS 2001 discovered that the national "gender gap" in religion persists. Females were more likely than males to profess a religion in 2001. As shown in Figures 5.1 and 5.2, 17 percent of adult males compared with only 12 percent of adult females did not identify with any religion. This phenomenon corroborates the previously mentioned finding that males have a more secular outlook than females, and that conversely women were more likely than men to describe their outlook as "religious"—42 percent and 31 percent respectively.

The social consequences of gender differences in religious expressions are potentially vast. On a societal level, in Chapter 13 we will show different political patterns among men and women, partly attributed to their religiosity. On the family level, mothers are generally ascribed more authority over child socialization ("the hand that rocks the cradle") particularly with regard to the psycho-emotional development of their children. This gives women considerable leverage in determining their children's religious upbringing. In interfaith families the religious upbringing of children is a critical issue. This matter will be further discussed in this chapter.

Once we allow for the greater male preference for no religion, the rest of the distributions are relatively balanced. In 2001, about one-fourth each of males and females self-identified as Catholic and about one-half of adult males and females were non-Catholic Christians. Altogether 74 percent of males and 80 percent of females self-identified as Christians of some kind. There were only small differences among the distributions of the various Christian denominations. Baptist was the next largest group, self-identified by 16 percent of males and 18 percent of females. Similarly, equal proportions of adults, regardless of gender, did not provide a specific answer to the question about their religious preference.

Figure 5.1

The Profile of Religious Identification of Adult Males, 2001

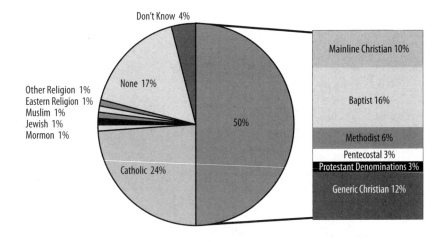

Figure 5.2

The Profile of Religious Identification of Adult Females, 2001

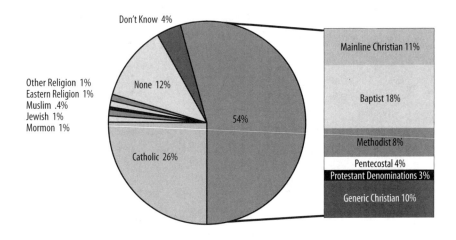

Figure 5.3

The Gender Balance among Religious Traditions/Groups

RELIGIOUS GROUP	PERCENT MALE	PERCENT FEMALE	ADULT POPULATION IN MILLIONS
Catholic	47	53	50.9
Mainline Christians	45	55	35.8
Methodist	42	58	14.2
Lutheran	48	52	9.6
Presbyterian	45	55	5.6
Episcopalian	41	59	3.5
United Church of Christ	43	57	1.4
Baptist	46	54	33.8
Christian Generic	51	49	22.5
Christian unspecified	52	48	14.2
Protestant unspecified	50	50	4.6
Evangelical/Born Again	51	49	1.0
Non-denominational	46	54	2.5
Pentecostal/Charismatic	41	59	7.8
Assemblies of God	50	50	1.1
Church of God	42	58	0.9
Pentecostal unspecified	41	59	4.4
Protestant Denominations	43	57	5.9
Churches of Christ	45	55	2.6
Jehovah's Witnesses	31	69	1.3
Seventh Day Adventist	55	45	0.7
Mormon	45	55	2.7
Jewish	49	51	2.8
Eastern Religions	59	41	2.0
Buddhist	59	41	1.1
Muslim	60	40	1.1
NRM & Other Religions	50	50	1.2
Nones/No religion	59	41	29.5
U.S. Total Adults	**48**	**52**	**208.0**

In 1990, the *National Survey of Religious Identification* (NSRI) discovered that 87 percent of American males identified with a religion, 83 percent as Christians. Again, these figures were higher for women. Overall in 1990, 92 percent of women identified with a religion, 89 percent as Christians.[1] So despite our earlier expectation of social change impacting gender patterns, the statistics remained stable during the 1990s. On identification with any type of religious group (i.e., excluding Nones and refusals) the gender gap remained five points: 87 percent vs. 92 percent in 1990 and 79 percent vs. 84 percent in 2001. As far as identification with any of the Christian churches and denominations is concerned, the gap was six points in both surveys: 83 percent vs. 89 percent in 1990 and 74 percent vs. 80 percent in 2001. The overall national pattern does, however, hide some very interesting differences among the various religious groups and faiths, as Figure 5.3 illustrates.

Since women have greater life expectancy than men, there are more adult American women than men. Women are 52 percent of the total national population. We might expect, given this demographic statistic and the above religious data, that nearly every Christian religious group contains more female than male identifiers.[2] However, a pattern does emerge. The more conservative groups such as the Mormons, Pentecostal grouping, and the Protestant denominations seem to be the most feminized. The more communitarian or ethnic-based religious groups (Catholics, Lutherans, Jews) tend to have a gender balance closer to the national norm. The non-Christian groups, with the exception of Jews and those identifying with the diverse grouping labeled New Religious Movements and Other Religions, are the exception to this pattern of feminization. The Nones, Muslims and Eastern religions have unbalanced sex ratios and are all around 60 percent male. This suggests that these religious options are more appealing to men than women but age of course is a confounding variable with regard to gender since some groups attract more widows than others. For Muslims and Eastern religions, such trends are reinforced by immigrant status since men are more likely to be immigrants.

Age

Age and age structure also make a difference in the religious realm. The youngest respondents to ARIS were aged 18 years (born in 1983 during the Reagan Presidency). The oldest respondents were in their late nineties (born around 1910 during the Presidency of William H. Taft). The world has undergone amazing changes in the eight decades that separate our oldest and youngest respondents. In 1910 more Americans worked on the land than in any other occupation; by the 1980s there were more computer programmers than farmers. Technological change has affected society in fundamental ways. It has changed people's relationship to natural and social environments: how they live, what they eat, how they move from place to place, how they spend their working and leisure hours, and how they relate to one another. Given the astonishing speed of technological change, we should expect dramatic change in how people see the world and their place in the universe, and thus in religious outlook and identification.

In Figure 3.3 in Chapter 3 with regard to secular–religious outlook we saw clear evidence of the process of secularization among the younger elements of the American population. The self-identified secular and somewhat secular were 23 percent of the under 35s but only 10 percent of those over age 65. This trend justifies taking a detailed look at the situation in terms of actual religious identifi-

Figure 5.4

Age Cohort Profiles of Males by Religious Tradition

RELIGIOUS TRADITION	AGE 18-34	AGE 35-49	AGE 50-64	AGE 65+
Catholic	25.0%	25.5%	23.8%	20.7%
Mainline Christians	9.9	15.3	19.5	27.3
Baptist	14.4	15.9	17.3	15.0
Christian Generic	13.5	11.6	9.5	10.0
Pentecostal/Charismatic	2.9	4.0	3.5	2.2
Protestant Denominations	2.2	2.4	2.8	3.1
Mormon/LDS	1.4	1.0	1.4	1.4
Total Christian	**68.7**	**75.7**	**77.8**	**79.7**
Jewish	1.0	1.1	1.9	2.2
Eastern Religions	2.2	0.9	0.7	0.3
Muslim	1.3	0.5	0.2	0.1
NRM & Other Religions	0.9	0.9	0.9	1.1
Nones	23.1	16.5	13.6	10.5
Refused	2.8	4.3	4.9	6.2
Total	**100.0**	**100.0**	**100.0**	**100.0**

cation by age and sex since these demographic variables have many consequences for religious groups. Although a young age structure bodes well for the future, on the assumption that such loyalties are permanent, having significant numbers of older people can be valuable for leadership and resource purposes.

The columns in Figure 5.4 present the religious profiles of males in four age groups from the young to the old: 18–34; 35–49; 50–64; and 65 years and over. Older males are more likely to identify with a Christian group of some kind. Almost 80 percent of the males aged 65 and over, compared with only 69 percent of adults under age 35, identified with some form of Christianity. Figure 5.5 shows that the inter-cohort age differences have an almost identical linear relationship for women. The male-female differential for Christianity is 6 to 7 percentage points across all the cohorts. Women over 65 years of age are far more likely to self-identify as Christians (87 percent) compared to adult women less than age 35 (75 percent).

When we examine the proportionate distribution among the religious groupings or traditions within the overall Christian category in Figures 5.4 and 5.5 we can see that the Catholic component of the American population is now flat across the generations and gender.

Figure 5.5

Age Cohort Profiles of Females by Religious Tradition

RELIGIOUS TRADITION	AGE 18-34	AGE 35-49	AGE 50-64	AGE 65+
Catholic	25.8%	27.0%	25.5%	22.2%
Mainline Christians	11.6	17.5	21.5	30.2
Baptist	16.3	17.2	19.6	17.4
Christian Generic	12.3	11.3	8.7	8.1
Pentecostal/Charismatic	4.1	4.8	4.6	3.6
Protestant Denominations	3.1	2.8	3.5	4.1
Mormon/LDS	1.7	1.4	1.4	1.1
Total Christian	**74.9**	**82.0**	**84.8**	**86.7**
Jewish	0.8	1.1	1.5	2.5
Eastern Religions	1.4	0.8	0.6	0.2
Muslim	1.1	0.2	0.1	0.0
NRM & Other Religions	0.8	0.8	0.7	1.1
Nones	18.0	11.5	8.0	5.1
Refused	3.0	3.8	4.5	4.4
Total	**100.0**	**100.0**	**100.0**	**100.0**

In fact most of the Christian groupings are flat in terms of age structure. One exception is the Generic Christians, who are on the rise.
However, by far the most noticeable change between the younger
and older age groups is the precipitous decline of the Mainline Christian grouping, which has the loyalty of only about one-third of the
proportion of younger adults compared with older people. In fact the
Mainline losses appear to account for all the intergenerational losses
of Christianity as a whole.

After the combined Christian groups the next largest religious
category in society is the "Nones." Once again, the ARIS data emphasize that the most striking trend of recent decades has been the major
increase in the number and the proportion of adults who profess no
religion. Figures 5.4 and 5.5 illustrate the changing patterns among
the various age groups separately for males and females. Still, some
trends are universal. For instance, young adults both male and
female are by far the most likely to profess no religion. In all, 23 percent of males and 18 percent of females under age 35 did not identify with any religion in 2001.[3] Even more significantly, among men
under 35 years the Nones are now challenging the Catholics to be
the largest identification category. Once again the inter-cohort
gender gap is consistent, at five percentage points. However, the
proportion of males who profess no religion is double that of females
among the oldest age group, those age 65 and over: 10 percent of
males and 5 percent of females profess no religion. Thus the share
of Nones is more than twice as high among the young than the old
and more than three times as high among young women as old
women. The data suggest that the move away from identification
with religion that began with males is now spreading to young
females.

As far as the remaining religious groupings are concerned, adults
who self-identify as Jews by religion are older. Although a small
minority, their proportion is double among the oldest age group
compared with the youngest. In fact among women the Jewish proportionate decline seems to mimic the Mainline Christian losses. In
contrast the Eastern Religions and Muslims are much more "popu-

*In all,
23 percent of
males and
18 percent of
females under
age 35 did not
identify with any
religion in 2001.*

lar" among the younger cohort, both among males and females. We can assume these patterns largely reflect the new waves of Asian immigrants, who tend to be young. In contrast the New Religious Movements and Other Religions are perhaps surprisingly not any more popular among young people than they are among older persons.

The comparison of the various age groups offers us a glance at the situation among cohorts that grew up in different eras. If these are indeed generational changes, as we pointed out earlier—the oldest generation grew up in the 1920s and 1930s, while the youngest generation grew up in the 1970s and the 1980s—then the data suggest that we can expect further changes in the American religious profile as young non-Christians replace aging Christians. On the other hand it could be that they are merely age dependent patterns. In that case as the younger cohort gets older, perhaps marries and has children, it will "Christianize" and the balance among the groupings may not change as drastically.

Figures 5.6 and 5.7 show the internal situation regarding age for men and women separately in some selected religious groups,. This allows us to look a little more closely at the age structure of denominations or "brands." Clearly, identifiers with some religious groups are dominated by young people while others by more aging adherents. Religious groups with the younger age structures in 2001 were Muslims, Buddhists, Jehovah's Witnesses, Nones and Catholics. Adults who self-identified as "Christians" without further specification were also remarkably young with well over 40 percent of the adult adherents under age 35. At the other end of the spectrum, the religious groups most attractive to older persons were the United Church of Christ, Presbyterian, the generic Protestants, and Episcopalian, all of which had at least 30 percent of the adherents aged 65 and older. Similar old age patterns were found among female Jews, Methodists, and Churches of Christ. Well-balanced age structures, which suggest an appeal across the generations or irrespective of age, are a feature of the Assemblies of God, the Church of God, and the Lutherans.

Figure 5.6

Male Age Cohort Composition of Selected Religious Groups

RELIGIOUS GROUP	AGE 18-34	AGE 35-49	AGE 50-64	AGE 65+	TOTAL
Assemblies of God	28%	31%	23%	18%	100%
Baptist	31	31	24	13	100
Buddhist	63	24	11	2	100
Catholic	35	32	21	12	100
Christian, unspecified	49	31	14	6	100
Churches of Christ	25	28	29	18	100
Church of God	26	31	22	21	100
Episcopalian	15	27	31	27	100
Evangelical/Born Again	24	40	18	18	100
Jehovah's Witnesses	33	33	27	7	100
Jewish	25	24	30	21	100
Lutheran	24	30	26	20	100
Methodist	19	32	26	23	100
Mormon	37	24	24	15	100
Muslim	66	24	7	3	100
Non-denominational	29	39	20	12	100
No religion	45	29	17	8	100
Pentecostal/Charismatic	34	36	23	7	100
Presbyterian	18	25	28	29	100
Protestant, unspecified	19	24	28	29	100
Seventh Day Adventist	35	34	17	14	100
UCC/Congregationalist	15	29	22	33	100
U.S. Total Male Adults	**34**	**31**	**21**	**14**	**100**

Marital status

Given most faiths' attention to and rulings regarding sexuality and marriage we should expect to find that marital status is strongly correlated with religious identification. Generally speaking, married and widowed people should be the most likely to belong to conservative religious denominations. Singles should be the most likely to belong to liberal religious denominations or to profess no religion. Once-married persons who are divorced or separated should be closer to married people than to singles in their religious identification.

The ARIS data on marital status is only a "snapshot" and relates solely to the current marital situation of the respondents. This

Figure 5.7

Female Age Cohort Composition of Selected Religious Groups

RELIGIOUS GROUP	AGE 18-34	AGE 35-49	AGE 50-64	AGE 65+	TOTAL
Assemblies of God	21%	34%	21%	24%	100%
Baptist	28	30	24	18	100
Buddhist	46	29	17	8	100
Catholic	30	32	22	16	100
Christian, unspecified	43	35	13	8	100
Churches of Christ	18	23	29	30	100
Church of God	28	20	24	28	100
Episcopalian	14	35	23	29	100
Evangelical/Born Again	22	40	24	14	100
Jehovah's Witnesses	42	30	16	12	100
Jewish	18	24	24	34	100
Lutheran	22	30	23	25	100
Methodist	18	26	25	30	100
Mormon	35	30	21	15	100
Muslim	80	14	6	1	100
Non-denominational	33	37	16	14	100
No religion	46	31	15	8	100
Pentecostal/Charismatic	31	37	22	11	100
Presbyterian	17	26	26	31	100
Protestant, unspecified	15	24	30	31	100
Seventh Day Adventist	22	24	26	28	100
UCC/Congregationalist	11	24	24	41	100
U.S. Total Female Adults	**30**	**31**	**21**	**18**	**100**

discrepancy between individual experience and the statistics is most obvious in the case of divorce. In recent times nearly half of all marriages have ended in divorce, but the number of currently divorced persons is much smaller. Unmarried persons living with a partner is another marital status category that is often in transition and requires consideration. Some of these partnerships are indeed permanent, some are temporary, and some are a prelude to marriage. In fact the average American young couple now lives together for about three years before they get formally married. Just over half of these marriages are ceremonies under the auspices of a religious group.

Surprisingly, the patterns revealed for men in Figure 5.8 reflect only slightly the norms advocated by the various religions. For instance, Mormons and Catholics strongly disapprove of divorce but it is unproblematic for Muslims and Jews. However, the findings do not reflect this. One reason is that marital status patterns are also affected by the patterns of the age profile of the religions. Religious groupings whose adherents are mainly young, such as Islam, have many people who are single and never married, while religions with older adherents such as the Mainline Christians have many widowed people. Figures 5.8 and 5.9 on religious identification by marital status tend to resemble Figures 5.4 and 5.5, which show religious identification by age.

Christians of all types are less likely to be in the single living-with-a-partner category, or "living in sin" as many believers would term it. In contrast the Nones have the highest share of the marital status groups in this "common law" marriage category. Catholics stand out as being neither very over- nor very under-represented in any marital status category. Baptist men and women are over-represented among the separated as are those identifying as Pentecostal. One interesting and intriguing finding is that separated men are the least likely to refuse to reveal their religious identification while married men are the most likely to refuse this question.

Figure 5.9 shows that female patterns parallel those for men. Those most likely to adhere to a Christian group and least likely to profess no religion were the widows and widowers. Second, single adults living with a partner were the most likely to profess no religion and least likely to adhere to a Christian group, again among men and more so among women. To illustrate, only 4.8 percent of widows professed no religion compared with 23.8 percent of single women living with a partner.

Single adults who live with a partner (cohabiting) were the most likely to profess no religion. Nones represent 29 percent of cohabitating men, thus surpassing the total of Catholics in that marital status category. They represent about 24 percent of cohabiting women, similar to Catholics. This is a sizable demographic group, given that among all American adults 6 percent of males and 5 percent of females were unmarried singles living with a partner in 2001.

Figure 5.8

National Profile of Marital Status by Religious Tradition for Adult Males

RELIGION	SINGLE NEVER MARRIED	SINGLE LIVING W/ PARTNER	MARRIED	SEPARATED	DIVORCED	WIDOWED
Catholic	25.4%	24.4%	24.0%	22.8%	24.4%	19.5%
Mainline Christians	9.9	10.4	18.2	10.0	15.8	27.0
Baptist	13.0	15.3	16.1	20.3	17.1	16.6
Christian Generic	13.1	9.7	11.3	9.4	11.5	9.1
Pentecostal/Charismatic	2.4	1.9	3.6	6.3	3.4	3.6
Protestant Denominations	2.0	1.4	2.7	3.6	3.3	2.9
Mormon/LDS	1.1	0.4	1.4	0.2	1.0	1.8
Total Christian	**66.9**	**63.6**	**77.2**	**72.6**	**76.5**	**80.5**
Jewish	1.5	1.5	1.4	0.8	1.1	1.9
Eastern Religions	2.1	1.0	1.0	0.7	0.6	1.0
Muslim	1.2	0.9	0.5	1.4	0.5	0.0
NRM & Other Religions	1.1	1.4	0.7	1.3	1.1	0.9
Nones	24.1	28.9	13.8	22.3	16.8	10.4
Refused	3.2	2.9	5.4	1.0	3.3	5.2
Total	**100.0**	**100.0**	**100.0**	**100.0**	**100.0**	**100.0**

Figure 5.9

National Profile of Marital Status by Religious Tradition for Adult Females

RELIGION	SINGLE NEVER MARRIED	SINGLE LIVING W/ PARTNER	MARRIED	SEPARATED	DIVORCED	WIDOWED
Catholic	25.7%	23.9%	26.4%	26.0%	22.0%	21.0%
Mainline Christians	12.1	12.3	19.9	9.1	18.6	28.7
Baptist	16.6	17.0	16.2	26.0	21.3	20.0
Christian Generic	11.3	10.0	10.7	8.4	10.4	7.9
Pentecostal/Charismatic	3.6	2.7	4.1	8.8	6.4	4.8
Protestant Denominations	3.0	2.4	3.3	2.7	1.9	4.4
Mormon/LDS	1.1	0.5	1.6	0.9	1.4	1.1
Total Christian	**73.4**	**68.8**	**82.2**	**81.9**	**82.1**	**87.8**
Jewish	1.2	1.0	1.3	1.5	1.0	2.2
Eastern Religions	1.6	1.1	0.7	0.0	0.6	0.2
Muslim	0.7	0.4	0.4	0.5	0.1	0.1
NRM & Other Religions	0.7	2.1	0.6	1.5	1.7	0.8
Nones	18.3	23.8	9.7	11.4	10.6	4.8
Refused	4.2	2.9	5.0	3.2	3.9	3.9
Total	**100.0**	**100.0**	**100.0**	**100.0**	**100.0**	**100.0**

ARIS 2001 provides detailed data that allows the distinction to be made between single adults who never married and single adults who live with a partner. This helps us better understand some of the attitudes of religious institutions toward unwed couples living together. It is clear that new social attitudes have begun to affect the religious patterns. NSRI 1990 found that married people were the most likely to be Christians. Eleven years later, ARIS 2001 found that divorced and separated people were just as likely as married people to be Christians of some kind. However, single people who have never married were far less likely than widowed, married, or divorced people to identify with a Christian tradition.

Male Marital Status Patterns within Religious Traditions

Now we have analyzed the overall national picture as regards the market share of different types of marital status according to religious traditions we can switch the mode of analysis to patterns within the religious traditions to see what types of people they attract and the overall composition of their 'clientele'. Thus statistics are provided for the various religious groupings or traditions according to whether their male or female adherents are single, married, divorced or separated.

Single men

As was noted earlier, the marital status composition of the various religious groups is shaped both by their demography and by their religions' norms. Naturally, religious groups with many young people will have many singles that were never married. As illustrated in Figure 5.10, the best example is Muslims, who attract many young males. While over 40 percent of Muslim males were single and never married in 2001, only 14 percent of Mainline Christians were single, never married.

Overall in 2001, 22 percent of American males were single, never married. The largest group, Catholics, is close to the average—24 percent were single, never married.

The marital status profile of adherents in strict religions is influenced by norms and beliefs confining sexual activity and procreation to matrimony. In contrast the more liberal groups are more likely to

Figure 5.10

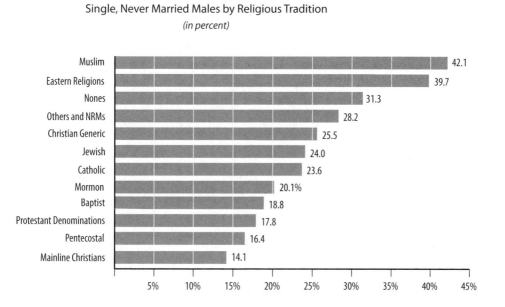

Single, Never Married Males by Religious Tradition
(in percent)

Muslim — 42.1
Eastern Religions — 39.7
Nones — 31.3
Others and NRMs — 28.2
Christian Generic — 25.5
Jewish — 24.0
Catholic — 23.6
Mormon — 20.1%
Baptist — 18.8
Protestant Denominations — 17.8
Pentecostal — 16.4
Mainline Christians — 14.1

Figure 5.11

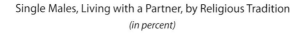

Single Males, Living with a Partner, by Religious Tradition
(in percent)

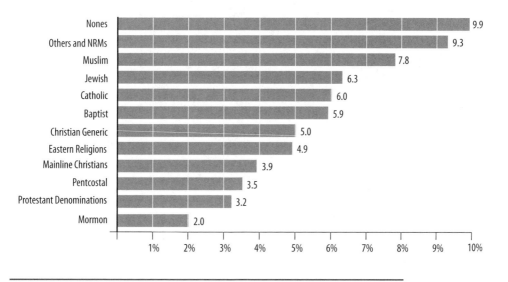

Nones — 9.9
Others and NRMs — 9.3
Muslim — 7.8
Jewish — 6.3
Catholic — 6.0
Baptist — 5.9
Christian Generic — 5.0
Eastern Religions — 4.9
Mainline Christians — 3.9
Pentcostal — 3.5
Protestant Denominations — 3.2
Mormon — 2.0

accept cohabitation of unmarried couples and the inevitable result of "unwed parents." Therefore, we find the Nones at the top of Figure 5.11 with almost 10 percent of adult men living with a partner. In contrast, placed at the bottom of the chart were the Mormons with only 2 percent of single adult men living with a partner. This reflects the Mormon's successful transmission of their message on marriage and family values to their adherents. Overall, 6 percent of American adult males were single, living with a partner in 2001.

Separation and divorce

As regards the propensity of being separated among American men, at one time the separated status was largely composed of people from religious groups, among which the most prominent was the Catholic Church, where marriages had broken down but faith disallowed divorce. This no longer appears to be the case. Overall, only 1.6 percent of American males were separated in 2001. Again, the largest group, the Catholics, is at about that level. Proportionately this index varied quite widely between the various religious groups. It ranged from 3.4 percent of Muslim males to less than 0.5 percent of Mormon males.

Statistics on the proportion of currently divorced people in the population are not very informative because they do not cover the population that has ever been divorced but only that which is currently divorced. Whereas some churches deny divorce others will not remarry divorcees. So the divorced population comprises some for whom this is a permanent status as well as many for whom this is a transition stage before a second or subsequent marriage. Overall, 6.6 percent of American men were currently divorced in 2001. In all, the variation in the proportion of divorced males among the religious groupings was quite small. At the highest end of divorced males we found the Protestant Denominations while at the lowest end were Eastern Religion males. Interestingly the Catholic and Mainline Protestant Churches (Lutheran, Episcopalian) who traditionally have had some sanctions against divorce or remarriage are now very much in the middle range on this variable.

However, divorce rates are clearly correlated with marriage rates since one cannot be divorced unless one was once married. This correlation produces some statistical quirks. For example, because relatively few males professing no religion have ever been married, the proportion that is divorced is no higher than that of the general population.

Married men

Religious values held by most traditions place major importance on marriage and family life, so it is natural to look at marriage rates among the different religious groups as a measure of their "success." Figure 5.12 shows that overall, 60 percent of males were married in 2001, but the rate varied widely by religious group. The Catholic rate was very close to the national average. The highest marriage rates, at around 70 percent of all men, were for Mainline Christians and Mormons, and the lowest was among Muslim with only 41 percent. Both demography and religious norms play a role in shaping these marriage rates. Three other groups form a cluster with relatively low rates of marriage, whereby less than half of the males were married in 2001, Eastern Religions, New Religion Movements, and No Religion.

Figure 5.12

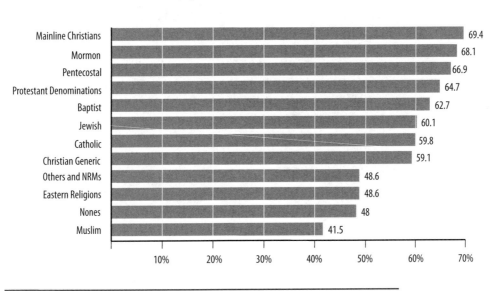

Married Males by Religious Tradition
(in percent)

Female Marital Status Patterns within Religious Traditions

Single women

Overall, 16 percent of American adult females were single, never married in 2001. Similar to the marital status profiles of males, although at lower rates, Figure 5.13 shows Eastern Religion and Muslim females lead other groups in their odds of being singles who never married. Females who profess no religion were in the third place, with more than one-quarter never married in 2001. The figures highlight the gap between the top three groups and average American women in their marital status. The most likely explanation is that these three groups attract young people who have not had a chance to get married. As with men, Mainline Christian women were less likely to be single and never married, reflecting the older age structure of their female and male adherents.

Figure 5.13

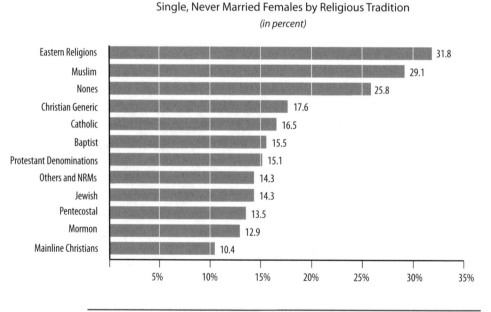

Single, Never Married Females by Religious Tradition
(in percent)

Figure 5.14

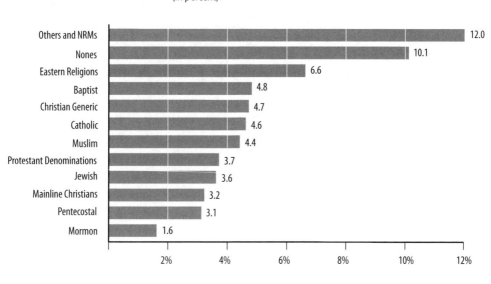

Single Females, Living with a Partner, by Religious Tradition
(in percent)

Overall, 5 percent of American females were single, living with a partner in 2001. This is slightly lower than the figure for American males. Figure 5.14 shows the proportions of single females living with a partner were quite similar to that of males in almost every religious group, with the exception of Jews and Muslims (see Figure 5.11), where female rates are considerably lower. Females that self-identified with New Religion Movements (including Unitarian-Universalists, Neo-Pagans, Scientology, and New Age) and those professing no religion were the most likely to be single living with a partner. These two groupings were more than five times as likely to be single living with a partner as the Mormons with only 2 percent.

Divorce and separation

Overall, only 1.1 percent of American females were separated in 2001, quite similar to the fraction of American males. Pentecostal females were leading the way in their tendency to be separated. They were three times more likely to be separated than Mormons. However the rank order for most groups was different for men and women in this marital status category. Yet once again the expected tendency for Catholic women to be more likely to be separated than others does not occur. This is another indicator of the current situation among Catholic identifiers that seems to challenge the traditional Catholic doctrine on the sacrament of marriage.

Overall 8.5 percent of American females were currently divorced in 2001. It might be thought that the pattern would be best explained by religious laws on marriage and divorce but this is untrue. Muslim women are in theory most vulnerable to divorce under *Sharia* law but they are at the bottom of the scale. This suggests the pattern is related more to gender roles assigned to women by the various religions. Pentecostal women were more likely to be divorced than women on average. Females self-identifying as Jewish and as of Protestant Denominations were below the average.

The New Religion Movements were more than nine times as likely to be divorced as Muslim women but for the former group this could be the result of "religious switching" after the break-up of a marriage. Certainly some religious groups such as some Unitarian-Universalist congregations and some evangelical churches regard divorcees as a niche market for recruitment. Another factor affecting the scores on separation and divorce is differential rates of re-marriage among adherents of the various religious groups since some are particularly concerned with "match-making" and assisting people to re-marry.

Some religious groups such as some Unitarian-Universalist congregations and some evangelical churches regard divorcees as a niche market for recruitment.

Married women

The expectations of females to be married are quite universal across cultures and are especially strong in most religious traditions. This is illustrated in Figure 5.15. The variation in the proportion of females married by religious group is not as wide as the variation among males (see Figure 5.12). Overall, 57 percent of American women were married in 2001. Most religious groups fall within the range of 52 percent to 61 percent of females being married. There are only a few exceptions. As was the case among men, Mormon women were the most likely to be married. On the other end of the scale, women identifying with the New Religious Movements and those professing no religion were the least likely to be married.

Figure 5.15

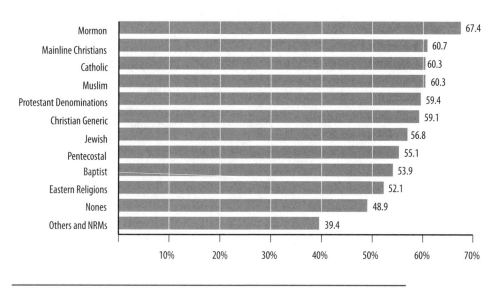

Married Females by Religious Tradition
(in percent)

Marketing Challenges

The answer to the question of who the religious and non-religious Americans are has been revealed in this chapter. In terms of a typology based on gender, age and marital status, the Americans most likely to identify with a religious tradition tend to be female, middle aged or older, and married or widowed. In contrast the irreligious American adults, those not identifying with a religious tradition of any kind, tend to be male, younger, and unmarried.

Yet the demographic statistics on individuals presented in this chapter show just how complicated it is to assess the current market position and prospects of each specific religious tradition or group if one tries to factor in the gender, age and marital status characteristics of their current identifiers. Obviously all religious groups are affected and concerned by the societal tendency towards lower rates of marriage as well as marrying at older ages. It appears that just as religion tends to endorse marriage so married people tend to endorse religion. This poses a recruitment problem for most religious groups.

Can they attract the increasing numbers of single cohabiting young people without validating their lifestyle? Most groups worry about their ability to attract the young but the aging of the population due to greater longevity offers an alternative strategy for recruitment and retention. An ability to attract and hold the loyalty of the ever increasing numbers of older people from the baby boom generation is also an asset in today's and tomorrow's religious marketplace.

Notes

1. Kosmin, Barry A., and Seymour P. Lachman, *One Nation Under God*. New York: Harmony Books, 1993.
2 . The relatively small sample sizes for the Seventh Day Adventist (300 cases) and Evangelical groups mean that there are large confidence intervals in their sex ratios so we cannot confirm their outlier status on this variable.
3. It is possible that among the oldest age group (65+), the relatively large "Refused" category includes adults who did not feel comfortable self-identifying as "no religion."

SIX

Household and Family Characteristics

Household Size

A VERAGE household size is a useful composite indicator or surrogate index used by demographers and sociologists to provide insights into the nature of populations. Many religions' emphasis on the family, the home, and the importance of relationships and duties across the generations encourage people to dwell together until they form their own families. This ethos can be contrasted with more secular values such as personal autonomy and individualistic lifestyles that encourages people, especially unmarried young adults, to seek "freedom" by living on their own. Large household sizes suggest the group has more families with children or more multi-generational families. The reason for this can be economic circumstances as well as cultural values. Average household size is related to the standard of living of its members and other socioeconomic indicators that will be further discussed in a later chapter. Smaller household sizes are usually associated with higher income groups having more persons living alone and an older age profile because of fewer children in the home.

The average household size in the U.S. in 2001 was 2.74 persons. As illustrated in Figure 6.1, Muslims are most likely to live in larger households, followed by Evangelicals and Mormons, with over three people on average. Jews, Mainline Christians such as Episcopalians and Presbyterians, and UCC identifiers lived in the smallest households, with fewer than 2.3 persons on average.

Figure 6.1

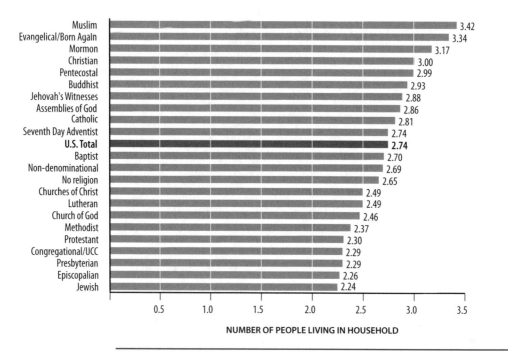

Average Household Size for Selected Religious Groups

NUMBER OF PEOPLE LIVING IN HOUSEHOLD

Single-person households

Figure 6.2 compares religious groups on the prevalence of single-person households. Single-person households are not homogeneous. Some are young people who have not yet formed families, while others are old people, many of whom have lost their spouses. A religious group with a higher share of single-person households usually reflects not only a small family size but also an aging community with a larger share of older people who live alone. It also means that the group has many people with sufficient income to enable them to rent or buy their own home. As illustrated in Figure 6.2, Jews had the highest share of single-person households. At the other extreme we find the Evangelical/Born Again with only 11 percent of the households occupied by a single adult. This is less than one-third the rate of the Jewish households.

Figure 6.2

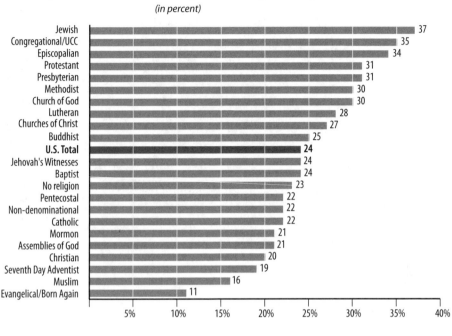

Single-Person Households among Selected Religious Groups
(in percent)

The national age composition of adults who live alone tilts heavily toward older people. Among 25 million adults who lived alone about 40 percent were 65 years or older compared with only 17 percent who were under age 35.

Figure 6.3 illustrates the age composition of single-person households for 11 major religious groups. Clearly there are groups, such as Presbyterians, Methodists, Jews, and Episcopalians, with a high concentration of older people living alone. In these populations more than half of the adults living alone were over 65 years old. Young adults (under age 35) living alone were found in particular among the no religion group and the unspecified Christians.

Figure 6.3

Age of Respondent in Single-Person Households for Selected Religious Groups

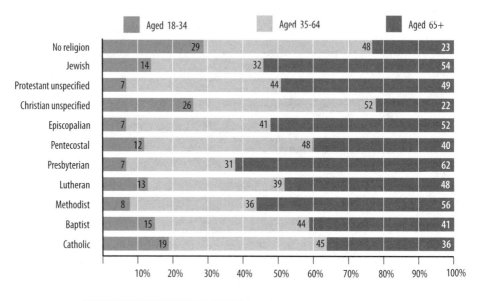

Households with children

In the Book of Genesis the Bible enjoins believers to "be fruitful and multiply." Most religions and faiths have traditionally adopted a pro-natalist policy as well as pro-marriage and family orientation. In fact large family size is usually an indicator of religious traditionalism in modern societies. Thus the number of children living in a household is an important religious as well as social indicator.

Figure 6.4 provides an assessment of the number of children present in households of the various religious groups. It looks at the distribution of households with 0 children, 1–2 children, and 3 or more children. We chose to restrict the analysis to respondents aged 18–60 years and exclude single-person households. This is done as a surrogate measurement of fertility, since ARIS 2001 did not have a specific question on number of births for each woman.

Households with no children suggest either young families or the opposite, older "empty nesters" in which the children have already left their parents' home. Figure 6.4 indicates that multiple-person households where the respondents aged 18 to 60 were Jewish, unspecified Protestant, Buddhist or Mainline Christian were those most likely to have no children present. Half of these homes had no children present. The most child-friendly households were found among the Evangelicals, "Christians," the various Pentecostal denominations, Mormons, and Jehovah's Witnesses, in other words the more conservative Christian groups.

Figure 6.4

Numbr of Children in the Household by Religious Tradition

(only respondents ages 18 to 60 in multiple-person households)

RELIGIOUS TRADITION/GROUP OF RESPONDENT	0 CHILDREN	1-2 CHILDREN	3+ CHILDREN	NUMBER OF HOUSEHOLDS IN MILLIONS
Catholic	43%	44%	13%	15.6
Mainline Christian	47	43	10	9.2
Lutheran	44	44	12	2.6
Presbyterian	51	42	8	1.4
Episcopalian	49	42	9	.9
United Church of Christ*	50	46	4	.3
Baptist	40	46	14	10.6
Christian Generic	42	45	13	7.2
Christian unspecified	38	48	14	5.0
Protestant unspecified	58	34	8	1.1
Evangelical/Born Again*	35	39	25	.3
Non-denominational	47	42	11	.8
Pentecostal/Charismatic	35	48	17	2.6
Assemblies of God*	36	46	18	.3
Church of God	33	57	9	.3
Pentecostal unspecified	35	47	18	1.5
Protestant Denominations	45	39	16	1.7
Churches of Christ	49	38	13	.7
Jehovah's Witnesses*	39	41	20	.4
Seventh Day Adventist*	43	46	11	.2
Mormon	39	36	25	.9
Jewish	52	40	8	.7
Eastern Religions	49	40	11	.7
Buddhist*	50	34	16	.4
Muslim*	46	35	20	.4
NRM & Other Religions*	44	44	12	.5
Nones/No religion	48	43	9	10.1
Refused	53	37	10	2.3
U.S. Total Households	**44**	**44**	**12**	**62.4**

*Based on only 100–200 cases

Although ARIS 2001 data do not allow us to estimate fertility rates for each religious group, we can identify the religious groups with a high number of children. Figure 6.5 provides the ranking from high to low on the percentage in each category having 3 or more children in the household. This again focuses on respondents aged 18 to 60 living in multi-person households. This is a graphic illustration of the data presented in Figure 6.4.

Figure 6.5

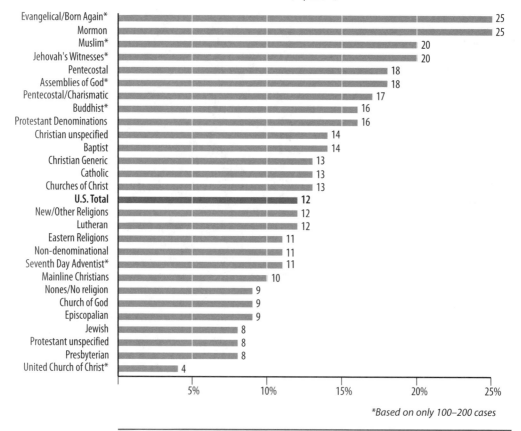

Households with 3 or More Children among Respondents Aged 18 to 60 in Multiple-Person Households for Selected Religious Groups
(in percent)

Group	Percent
Evangelical/Born Again*	25
Mormon	25
Muslim*	20
Jehovah's Witnesses*	20
Pentecostal	18
Assemblies of God*	18
Pentecostal/Charismatic	17
Buddhist*	16
Protestant Denominations	16
Christian unspecified	14
Baptist	14
Christian Generic	13
Catholic	13
Churches of Christ	13
U.S. Total	**12**
New/Other Religions	12
Lutheran	12
Eastern Religions	11
Non-denominational	11
Seventh Day Adventist*	11
Mainline Christians	10
Nones/No religion	9
Church of God	9
Episcopalian	9
Jewish	8
Protestant unspecified	8
Presbyterian	8
United Church of Christ*	4

Based on only 100–200 cases

As indicated in Figure 6.4, overall, 12 percent of the multi-person households nationally had 3 or more children. A cluster of religious groups emerges as child-oriented. At the higher end were Evangelicals and Mormons, with one-fourth (25 percent) of the households having 3 or more children. They were followed by Muslims and Jehovah's Witnesses with one-fifth of the households having 3 or more children. At the low end were Presbyterians, unspecified Protestants, Jews, and finally the United Churches of Christ households, with only 4 percent having 3 or more children.

These findings confirm that there are big gaps across the religious groups as regards the propensity to have children. The high Mormon and Evangelical numbers reflect the pro-family and pro-natalist ethos of these groups. For example, the Mormons' temple-centered culture interprets all activities in the context of the ultimate Mormon goal: preserving the family into eternity. The result is that the heavily Mormon state of Utah has a fertility rate almost double that of the U.S. average.

The heavily Mormon state of Utah has a fertility rate almost double that of the U.S. average.

Lone parents

One of the most noticeable sociological changes that took place during the 20th century was in the structure of the family and the household. First, the extended multi-generational family, often associated with rural life, was replaced by the "nuclear" two-generation family, a married man and woman living with their offspring. Second, as a result of out-of-wedlock births and family break-ups there are growing numbers of families headed by "lone" parents today. This trend poses challenges for many religious groups socially and economically as well as theologically and morally.

Of course there are joint custody and other complex arrangements to be factored into this picture but overall women are more likely to be the custodial parent. Pentecostal, Baptist, and Catholic women are far more likely to be in this situation than Nones or women from the smaller groupings where lone fathers are more common.

Married and single mothers

Figure 6.6 shows that 65 percent of mothers—women with children under 18 years in the household—are currently married. The Mormons and Jews had the highest proportion of nuclear families

at 80 percent. The lowest proportions of mothers currently married
were found among the Other Religions grouping and the Nones. Single motherhood has a complex meaning since it describes women in
different marital situations. The ARIS data allow us to look at three
specific types of single mothers: First, single mothers who never married; second, single mothers who are living with a partner out of
wedlock; and third, single mothers who are divorced, separated or
widowed. Children under age 18 are living in all three types of single-mother households. One of the major causes of poverty in contemporary society and reduced life chances for children is single
motherhood. Generally children of lone or single mothers do not
benefit from the same standard of living as children raised in two-
parent families.[1]

Figure 6.6

Marital Status of Mothers by Religious Tradition

MOTHER'S RELIGION	NEVER MARRIED	LIVING WITH A PARTNER	DIVORCED, SEPARATED, WIDOWED	MARRIED	TOTAL
Catholic	13%	6%	12%	69%	100%
Mainline Christian	9	4	12	75	100
Baptist	18	6	17	59	100
Christian, unspecified	15	4	11	69	100
Pentecostal/Charismatic	13	3	21	62	100
Protestant denominations	17	4	12	67	100
Mormon*	10	1	9	80	100
Jewish*	10	1	9	80	100
Eastern Religions	17	2	9	73	100
Muslim*	25	6	3	66	100
NRM & Other Religions*	9	10	26	48	100
No religion	21	10	11	58	100
U.S. Total Mothers	**15**	**5**	**13**	**65**	**100**

* Based on small sub-samples

As demonstrated earlier, marital status correlates with religious
identification for both males and females. Subsequently we ask ourselves, does single motherhood also correlate in any way with religion? Figure 6.6 shows the variations in the three types of single
motherhood by the religious identification of the mother. Since the
phenomenon of single motherhood is relatively infrequent, even

with such a vast sample as ARIS 2001, we are limited to showing the results for only the largest religious groupings.

Since out-of-wedlock births are anathema to most religious groups it is to be expected that single mothers (unmarried without a partner) and out-of-wedlock mothers living with a partner are most common among those of no religion. Unmarried mothers are rare among Mormons and Pentecostals. Clearly there is no uniformity by religious group. Although Baptists scored high on all three types of single mothers,[2] there are other groups in which particular types of single motherhood was more prevalent. For instance, divorced, separated, or widowed mothers were found most often among Pentecostals.

These complicated relationships raise some religious and social issues regarding the welfare of the children living in single-mother households. While some psychologists may be concerned about families where the mother never married and the children are raised with no male role model, the concern of many clergy would be that when the partners live out of wedlock, important religious teachings regarding morality and values are being rejected.

Mixed-religion couples

Much as normative marriage patterns serve as a sociological buttress to traditional religious identification and belonging, they can also be associated with social change. Therefore in this section we look at the incidence of marriage across religious lines. We should add that ARIS 2001 is the first national survey that has looked at the religious composition of marriage and domestic partners in large enough numbers to be able to make generalizations among different groups. Because of the size of our sample and the nature of our questions, this survey has generated a wealth of unique data that will require much further mining with regard to issues pertaining to interfaith households.

ARIS 2001 discovered that 11 percent of our nationally representative sample of households contained either a married or domestic-partner couple who reported a difference in religious identification between the partners. That amounts to 28 million adults (Figure 6.7). This of course is *an ex post facto* situation in that those 14

Figure 6.7

Adults in Mixed Religious Identification
Households for Selected
Religious Groups

RESPONDENT'S RELIGIOUS GROUP	MIXED HOUSEHOLDS
Episcopalian	42%
Buddhist	39
Protestant	33
Non-denominational	32
Jehovah's Witnesses	30
No Religion	28
Lutheran	28
Presbyterian	27
Jewish*	27
Pentecostal	24
Methodist	24
Congregational/UCC	24
Seventh Day Adventist	24
Catholic	23
Muslim	21
Christian	21
Evangelical/Born Again	18
Churches of Christ	18
Church of God	18
Baptist	18
Assemblies of God	18
Mormon	12
U.S. Total**	**22**

Total U.S. Adults in Mixed Religion Couples   28,400,000

* Category refers only to Jews by religion.

** Note: Base includes adults married or living with a partner, where the religious self-identification reported by respondent did not match that reported for spouse/partner.

million couples do not include those partners who "switched" in order to please or accommodate their spouse or where the couple reached a compromise and both switched to a more comfortable religious environment. In effect ARIS counted mainly couples who decided not to join the other's group. The sheer number of mixed relationships means that religious differences are no longer seen as an obstacle to marriage by many Americans. Undoubtedly our contemporary mobile society has snipped at the ties to parents and community, so that to such people faith is just another lifestyle choice. The incidence of mixed-religion couples can be put in perspective by comparing it with mixed race rates (using Hispanic as a race). In 2001 there were 7.4 million Americans in such unions and in 2000 about 1 in 15 marriages involved persons of differing racial backgrounds.

However, religious groups vary considerably on this statistic. Very conservative faiths with high requirements for members, such as Mormons, are less likely to be involved in interfaith marriages. Only 12 percent of Mormon "coupled" adults had spouses or partners of other religious groups. Also low, at around 18 percent, were Baptists, those adhering to the Churches of Christ, Assemblies of God, the Evangelicals, and those adhering to the Church of God. The low rate of intermarriage among Mormons is particularly impressive because they constitute such a small share of the population. If Mormons chose marriage partners from among the general population without regard to religion, nearly all of them would end up by chance in intermarriages. There were also religions with "soft" boundaries that have become non-exclusive groups. So at the high end of intermarriage we find the Episcopalians at 42 percent and Buddhists at 39

percent living in mixed-religion families. The public tends to understand these basic distinctions and sorts itself out accordingly. The rate
for Episcopalians was much higher than that for the overall Mainline Grouping, which was 28 percent.

Buddhists were well above the overall rate for the Eastern Religions, which was 23 percent. This suggests that other groups in this
tradition had much lower rates. The most mixed marriages were
among groups where couples do not have to agree with each other
on theology or that welcome non-adherents to participate in their
worship. The rate for the Other Religions and New Religious Movements Grouping (not shown in table) was 50 percent.

Some intermarriages are much more "distant" or culturally distinct than others. A Methodist marrying a Baptist or even a None
marrying a Buddhist is not as rare or "religiously complicated" as a
Catholic–Jehovah's Witness marriage or a Pentecostal-Hindu one.
Obviously inter-denominational Protestant marriages are not the
equivalent of inter-faith marriages. Mixing is more common among
groups within similar religious traditions and groupings such as
within the Mainline Christian churches or among generic Christian
categories such as "Protestant" and "Non-denominational." Nones
are also likely to be living with people who identify with a religion
of some kind. In fact a substantial portion of Catholics in mixed
marriages are living with Nones, many of whom are former or
lapsed Catholics. To some extent the pattern of choice of "mixed marriages" tends to follow the pattern of religious switching analyzed in
Chapter 4.

However, crucial demographic variables also affect the rates in
Figure 6.7. The size of the group and the availability of suitable mates
is a key factor. Propinquity is also important since geographical concentration will help to maintain homogenous marriages. Mormons
and some other small religious groups are assisted to marry in-group
by their tendency to cluster geographically (see Chapter 7 for more
on geographic patterns in religion).

At the high end of intermarriage we find the Episcopalians at 42 percent and Buddhists at 39 percent living in mixed-religion families.

The Religious Upbringing of Children in Mixed Families

One of the most challenging objectives of a religious community,
regardless of size, is retaining its adherents and especially the next

generation, the children. Interfaith relationships and marriages challenge these objectives. Overall, in the study of the religious or secular upbringing of children we can identify two tiers of authorities which play an important role. On one tier are the religious institutions themselves, mainly the local congregations. On the other tier are the individual families and kin, especially parents and grandparents. We will consider them one at a time.

On the institutional level, there are requirements regarding religious practices and beliefs. Some churches set strict obligations for membership and participation and others are more flexible. The growing phenomenon of interfaith marriages and the large number of mixed-faith families compel many religious denominations to accommodate their needs. For example, the Roman Catholic Directory on Mixed Marriages from 1983 realizes the joint responsibility of both parents in the religious upbringing of children. It even states that each parent should be able to share something of his or her own tradition with their children. Although leaders of religious groups seek uniformity, they realize that they must compromise on the religious upbringing of interfaith families or lose some adherents entirely.

On the individual level, interfaith parents must bridge their differences with each other. They may choose to attend different churches themselves. But where will the children go? What about the children's religious education? Parents face difficult decisions when their religious denominations require—or at least urge—conflicting choices. Some couples may attempt to raise children in two faiths. Others may pick a single religion. Still others may raise children without religion. Each of the choices is bound to leave someone unsatisfied.

Thus, interfaith marriages and relationships result in losers and gainers. Finding out which religions lose adherents and which religions gain adherents as a result of intermarriages, and what factors may explain these patterns, is important for assessing trends in American religion. However it is important to consider the arithmetic of this phenomenon. If groups like Episcopalians or Buddhists have around 40 of every 100 of their identifiers in mixed couples, that means 60 are married to each other—producing only 30 Episcopalian couples. So the mixed households outnumber the homogeneous or all-Episcopalian families. Even among Mormons where only 12 of every 100 "out-marry," the result is 44 all-Mormon couples for every 12 mixed ones involving a Mormon partner.

The ARIS 2001 enables us to look at the religious diversity of American children.[3] Parents in mixed relationships were asked: *In what religion, if any, were/are your children being/going to be raised?*[4] We operationally chose to define interfaith families as families where the responding parents classified themselves and their spouses or partners in different religious groups, where "no religion" is counted as one of the groups. The questions on religious identification were open-ended. Some sociologists of religion might argue that many of these couples are in closely related religious groups and are thus better described as interdenominational families. Perhaps so, but the respondents clearly felt that the differences were important enough to identify themselves differently from their spouses or partners. The challenges of deciding how to raise their children are real and the numbers suggest that mixed couples are less likely to produce offspring than other couples.

Mixed couples are less likely to produce offspring than other couples.

One aspect of the religious freedom enjoyed by Americans is that parents have the right to choose the religious upbringing of their children. When parents choose a religious identification for their children they exercise their religious autonomy and power. Sometimes they choose to adhere to their religious institutional requirements regarding religious upbringing. For instance, Catholic partners in a mixed marriage may fulfill their "promise" to bring up their children in the Catholic faith.

Still, in choosing a religion for their children, parents have to renegotiate their own preferences and choices. Given the differences in their religious identification these decisions are hard to make. As the children grow they may choose to adhere to a different faith but the religious or secular environment set at home by their parents is important. These childhood experiences are critical in shaping children's beliefs and outlooks as they grow up and develop their own identity. Some parents defer making decisions until the children are of school age. Some parents are forced to make immediate choices early on for religious rituals. For instance, Jewish parents have to decide whether to have a circumcision for their newborn sons, and Catholics must decide whether to baptize their newborn offspring. Many parents are influenced by their extended family members, who might pull them in different directions. Often, confusing messages create more tension between the couple and with their families.

Figure 6.8

Religious Identification of Children in Mixed Religious Identification Families[5]

RELIGIOUS TRADITION CHILDREN RAISED IN	NUMBER OF CHILDREN IN MILLIONS	PERCENT
Catholic	2.0	23
Mainline Christians	1.5	17
Baptist	1.4	16
Christian Generic	1.2	14
Pentecostal/Charismatic	0.4	5
Protestant Denominations	0.3	3
All other religious traditions	0.3	3.5
Nones	1.2	14
Don't Know/Refused, and "whatever they choose"	0.4	5
U.S. Total Number of Children in Mixed Religion Families	**8.7**	**100**

In 2001, almost 9 million children lived in intact mixed religious families with parents who were either married or cohabitating. Figure 6.8 shows a detailed profile of the religious identification groupings of these children. It is important to state that the data are a "snapshot" relating to the consequences of millions of decisions at a certain point in time but they are not the "movie." Almost one-quarter of children in intact interfaith families were raised as Catholics, 17 percent as Mainline Christians, 16 percent as Baptists, and about 14 percent were raised with no religion. Thus two million Catholic children had a parent who was not Catholic. In some aspects the child population in interfaith families closely resembles the national pattern of religious identification of the adult population. Yet, parents have a tendency to choose the generic Christian labels for their children more than for themselves: 14 percent of children compared with less than 7 percent of the adult population.

These statistics are affected by the rates of mixed marriage reported in the previous table. Rates were low for Mormons and Baptists. Mixed marriage was also relatively rare among the Pentecostal grouping (Assemblies of God, Church of God, and Pentecostals in Figure 6.7) yet when they inter-marry the children are likely to be raised as Pentecostals. Interestingly, only a small fraction of interfaith parents, about 5 percent refused to reveal the religious identification they were raised in or did not make choices regarding the religious upbringing of their children and preferred for them to choose their own religious identification when they grow older.

The finding on the small proportion of children that are raised in no religion at 14 percent is perhaps surprising. One might have expected more children in interfaith families to be raised with no religion, as a compromise or default option, since decision-making on the religious upbringing of children in interfaith families can be quite complicated. Each parent probably tilts toward his or her own religious upbringing but they probably negotiate and compromise. Who takes the lead? Traditionally, the mother, as the caregiver, is responsible for the religious upbringing of the children. She is the one to pass on her faith, home practices and beliefs, to take the children to religious school and socialize them with other children of the same faith. True, the whole family often attends religious services together, yet mothers are usually perceived as the driving force.[6] So the gender patterns discussed earlier that show women are more likely to identify with a religious group than men can be assumed to play out in the realm of how children are raised, to the detriment of the no religion option.

The above example of social processes at work demonstrates how the various demographic indices of gender, age, marital status and family type all interact to affect the current and future national patterns of religious identification. We have observed that religious groups and traditions not only vary in actual size but also have different demographic profiles and therefore consist of distinct subpopulations and can be envisaged as segmented markets. Because the demography of American religion focuses on the individual

Parents have a tendency to choose the generic Christian labels for their children more than for themselves.

and the family or household, it cannot provide the whole picture; people do not live in isolation but in neighborhoods and communities of all types. In order to understand more fully the contemporary social reality, we need next to examine the geography of religion— literally the situation on the ground in the nation's states and regions.

Notes

1. In 2001, median household income of married couples was more than double the household income of a female householder, husband absent. (*Statistical Abstract of the United States 2003*, Table No. 685).

2. As mentioned at the outset of this chapter factors such as race may play a role here. We will look at the ethnic and racial composition of religious groups in other parts of this book.

3. The previous large national study on religious identification, 1990 *National Survey of Religious Identification,* did not have any information on religious identification of children. See: Barry A. Kosmin and Seymour P. Lachman *One Nation Under God: Religion in Contemporary American Society*, 1993.

4. Only parents of children under age 18 whose children live with them are included. For the sake of simplicity, we assume that all children in a family are raised in the same religion.

5. The analysis includes married or cohabiting couples who do not share the same religious identification.

6. Roger L. Dudley and Margaret G. Dudley, "Transmission of Religious Values from Parents to Adolescents," *Review of Religious Research* 28, no. 1 (1986).

SEVEN

Geographic Distribution of Religions

THE GEOGRAPHY of American religion is about social rather than physical scenery. Location, particularly region and state of residence, is important in American culture and especially in religious matters. Since colonial times the adherents of the various religious traditions and groups in America have not been randomly distributed across the country. Strong regional and state religious cultures persisted in the United States even though for more than two centuries, wherever they resided, Americans practiced and acted on their religions under the same legal framework and regime of the First Amendment.

However, the decade prior to 2001 saw massive and unprecedented population changes: an increase in the total adult population by over 27 million people, the entry of record numbers of immigrants, and interstate migration resulting in residential relocation of nearly 20 million people. This churning of the population begs the question of how it has impacted the country. Do the religious traditions and groups Americans identify with and the way and extent to which they practice religion differ substantially from place to place?

Casual observation might suggest that spatial differences will persist over time because certain locations and habitats attract certain types of people, and religion is an activity practiced in groups. Alternatively one might suggest that this same outcome will occur for structural reasons because there is not perfect competition in the religious marketplace.

In effect, a series of local religious markets exists. The process by which these markets occur is complicated to explain beyond the congregational level (see Chapter 11). Elements of fashion and camaraderie are present in the practice of religion in a specific time and place, and this reinforces a cultural status quo. Migration itself is selective, and a cultural milieu attracts and repels different sorts of people even in a dynamic and migratory society like the contemporary United States. The peer group perpetuates religion and reinforces the tendencies of the majority, which in turn produce the regional religious cultures we will describe. In any given community, churches and religious organizations may exist for some faiths and not others. Because it requires less effort to choose within the existing infrastructure than to establish new forms of religious organization, the institutional inheritance factor serves to bolster established religions.

The most obvious symbol of a religion is its house of worship. The mere physical presence of a chapel, church, or synagogue on the landscape is a form of advertising for potential members. Houses of worship are testimonies to faith, not merely symbols of belief, and they are statements about the place of their congregants in the local environment.

In this chapter we will examine differences in degree of identification with regard to specific religious faiths, traditions, and groups according to census regions and divisions, the states, and the rural-suburban-urban classification. This chapter will attempt analysis on the basis of social and community geography, viewing religion as a group phenomenon that reflects a population's social environment. There are obviously gaps between religious affiliation and daily conduct, yet a certain linkage between religious preference and some aspects of personal conduct is demonstrable.

Religious preference does not operate very accurately as a predictor of behavior on the individual level, but it becomes important when it influences norms of group behavior. Religious preference has a noticeable effect on social beliefs and logically should have an effect on delinquency and drug or alcohol abuse for individuals who are part of a circle of people acting according to a defined value system. We should look for its impact on social outcomes such as out-of-wedlock births, abortion rates, birth rates, and even crime. It has been increasingly recognized in recent years that religious differences, which inevitably involve differing world views and approaches to moral and ethical issues, shape public cultures in different parts of the country and in turn are shaped by them. So the politics and public policies that emerge via the politicians elected at the state level or sent to Washington likewise reflect the regional religious realities on the ground.

The Faith Profiles of the States

One of the questions most often asked is how Christian is the United States, this region, state or city? Unfortunately even the ARIS data cannot provide a large enough number of respondents in order to supply reliable counts on all the religious traditions or religious groups down to the level of the smaller states and certainly not for counties or individual cities. However, if we confine ourselves to three large categories of faith we can see with some precision how the various states differ in the general religious make-up of their populations.

Figure 7.1 represents the results of aggregating the 13 religious traditions previously used in many tables into three "faith groups." The "Christian Faith" group is composed of the seven traditions that claim a Christian heritage. The "Other Faiths" group consists of an amalgamation of four alternative traditions: Jewish, Muslim, Eastern religions, and the Other religions & New Religious Movements. The third group is "No Faith" which is composed of the "Nones" combined with the "Don't Know" and "Refusal" category. This group is probably more accurately termed "No faith or religious identification currently claimed." The high correlation between the proportions of "Other faiths" and "No Faith" by state does suggest that religious diversity or alternatively "Christian Faith" homogeneity affects how people respond to surveys on this topic in different communities and environments.

All this may seem complicated but the first column in Figure 7.1 showing the actual position on the ground should make the situation clearer. The national U.S. average shown earlier in Chapter 2—

Figure 7.1

Faith Identification by State[1]

STATE	PERCENT CHRISTIANS	PERCENT OTHER FAITHS	PERCENT NO FAITH	STATE	PERCENT CHRISTIANS	PERCENT OTHER FAITHS	PERCENT NO FAITH
Alabama	86.0%	1.7%	12.3%	New Hampshire	73.3%	2.2%	24.5%
Arkansas	82.4	0.6	17.0	New Jersey	72.7	7.0	20.3
Arizona	74.8	3.5	21.7	New Mexico	77.5	1.6	20.4
California	68.9	6.1	25.0	New York	71.5	9.6	18.9
Colorado	69.7	3.7	26.6	Nebraska	83.8	0.6	15.6
Connecticut	77.0	4.7	18.3	Nevada	74.8	2.8	22.4
Delaware	67.3	6.2	26.5	North Carolina	82.6	2.0	15.4
D.C.	74.3	9.7	16.0	North Dakota	87.8	2.4	9.3
Florida	76.5	5.0	18.5	Ohio	77.2	2.0	20.8
Georgia	81.3	2.8	15.9	Oklahoma	80.0	1.4	18.6
Idaho	73.3	1.3	25.4	Oregon	65.9	3.1	31.0
Illinois	76.8	4.4	18.8	Pennsylvania	80.1	2.4	17.5
Iowa	80.7	1.5	17.9	Rhode Island	77.9	2.6	19.5
Indiana	79.3	2.1	18.6	South Carolina	88.4	0.7	10.9
Kansas	78.0	1.6	20.4	South Dakota	87.4	2.4	10.2
Kentucky	79.8	1.3	18.9	Tennessee	85.0	1.5	13.5
Louisiana	83.5	1.0	15.5	Texas	82.2	2.4	15.4
Maine	79.4	1.1	14.5	Utah	76.6	3.2	20.2
Maryland	76.1	4.7	19.2	Vermont	67.9	2.1	30.0
Massachusetts	71.4	5.6	23.0	Virginia	79.5	3.0	17.5
Michigan	76.3	2.6	21.1	Washington	66.0	3.7	30.3
Minnesota	78.2	2.3	19.5	West Virginia	79.8	1.3	18.9
Mississippi	87.6	0.9	11.5	Wisconsin	79.0	1.2	19.8
Missouri	77.8	1.2	21.0	Wyoming	73.6	2.2	24.2
Montana	74.2	2.1	23.7	**U.S. Total**	**76.8**	**3.7**	**19.5**

76.8 percent Christian Faith, 3.7 percent Other Faiths and 19.5 percent No Faith—is provided as a general comparison. Though every state in Figure 7.1 had a clear majority self-identifying with one form or other of the Christian faith in 2001, some states varied considerably from the national norm in the proportion of the population that does so.

At one extreme is a number of "Bible Belt" states centered on the Great Plains or in the South with over 80 percent of the population self-identifying as Christians. The two "most Christian" states are North Dakota and South Carolina each with 88 percent of adults pos-

Figure 7.2

Percentage of Christians in Each State

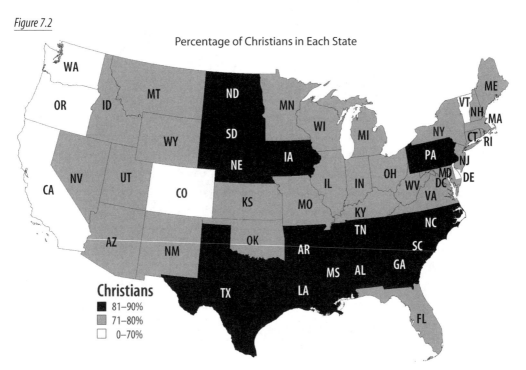

Christians
- ■ 81–90%
- ▨ 71–80%
- □ 0–70%

Figure 7.3

Percentage of Other Faiths in Each State

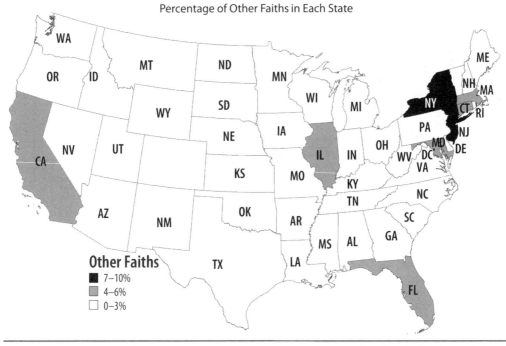

Other Faiths
- ■ 7–10%
- ▨ 4–6%
- □ 0–3%

itively identifying as Christians. Interestingly among the big, urban states only Pennsylvania and Texas reach above the 80 percent level.

At the other end of the scale are some states where religious diversity or "irreligion" is much stronger and Christianity relatively weaker. Most of these states with less than 70 percent of the population identifying as Christians of some type lie in the West. The most diverse or alternatively least Christian state is Washington where 34 percent do not identify as Christians. It is part of an obvious cultural unit that consists of the three Pacific coastal states of California, Oregon and Washington. Two other states with similar faith profiles are Colorado and Vermont each of which is known for its mountains and recreational open air lifestyles. The final one in this category is tiny Delaware, one of the original 13 colonies on the eastern seaboard.

Interestingly the range of the state scores for those with No Faith is 22 percentage points, from North Dakota (9.3 percent) and Mississippi (11.5 percent) to Oregon (31 percent), Washington (30 percent) and Vermont (30 percent). This is the same figure as the range

Figure 7.4

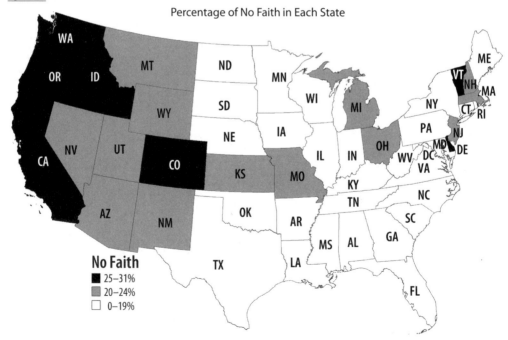

Percentage of No Faith in Each State

of scores for Christianity (66 percent to 88 percent). Given that the No Faith category is a smaller group nationally, this suggests that irreligion is a much more localized and varied cultural phenomenon.

The Regional Geography of the Religious Traditions

In order to provide more accurate detail on religion *per se* it is necessary to use larger geographic units and to rely on data at the level of the four census regions and nine census divisions which comprise the official classification system of the U.S. Bureau of the Census.[2] Figure 7.5 shows how each religious tradition was distributed geographically. Some religious traditions are clearly regional in nature and others are much more national or more evenly spread across the country.[3] The one that stands out most at the regional level as the most geographically concentrated religious tradition is the Mormons, more than 70 percent of whom live in the West; more than half resided in the Mountain area and another one-fifth resided in the Pacific division. Conversely Mormons have very low concentrations

Figure 7.5

Distribution of Religious Traditions by Census Division*
(percent)

CENSUS REGION	NORTH EAST		MID WEST		SOUTH			WEST	
CENSUS DIVISION	NEW ENGLAND	MID-ATLANTIC	EAST NORTH CENTRAL	WEST NORTH CENTRAL	SOUTH ATLANTIC	EAST SOUTH CENTRAL	WEST SOUTH CENTRAL	MOUNTAIN	PACIFIC
Catholic	8.0	20.4	15.7	6.3	12.6	2.5	10.6	6.2	17.7
Mainline Christian	4.0	14.9	21.0	10.5	20.6	5.9	9.4	5.0	8.9
Baptist	2.2	7.2	12.1	4.8	32.7	15.0	16.9	3.2	6.0
Pentecostal/Holiness	2.5	10.6	16.0	6.1	24.2	9.7	16.9	4.2	9.9
Protestant Denominations	2.6	10.2	16.4	7.7	15.7	9.7	15.4	6.8	15.4
Mormon	3.1	3.5	4.1	2.4	8.4	2.7	3.4	51.4	20.9
Christian Generic	4.8	11.6	17.9	6.9	16.1	4.6	9.6	7.1	21.6
Jewish	3.6	38.9	9.5	1.8	21.2	1.5	3.3	4.2	16.0
Muslim	5.1	30.3	22.3	2.2	17.4	1.8	9.0	2.1	9.8
Eastern Religions	4.8	19.9	8.3	3.0	11.8	2.0	5.7	4.4	39.9
NRM & Other	10.7	11.4	12.2	5.3	18.8	4.4	7.3	9.1	20.8
None	5.5	13.5	17.0	6.4	15.6	3.8	8.6	8.3	21.3
Don't Know/Refused	6.1	14.6	14.8	7.0	18.4	6.0	9.6	5.6	17.8
U.S.	**5.1**	**14.4**	**16.2**	**6.8**	**18.9**	**6.1**	**10.9**	**6.4**	**15.2**

* All rows total 100%

in New England, the Midwest, or Deep South. The Baptists, the
nation's second largest religious tradition, remain an overwhelmingly Southern phenomenon. Nearly two-thirds are found in the
South and 33 percent in the South Atlantic division alone. Only very
small proportions of Baptists are found in New England or the Mountain states. Other geographically concentrated groups at the regional
or census division level are Eastern Religions, with 40 percent in the
Pacific and 20 percent in the Mid-Atlantic; Jews, with 40 percent in
the Mid-Atlantic and 20 percent in the South Atlantic; Muslims, with
30 percent in the Mid-Atlantic and 22 percent in the East North Central divisions.

Some religious traditions have a more even national spread:
Catholics, Mainline Christians, Protestant denominations, and, interestingly, the Nones. In general the traditions with the largest numbers are the most geographically diffuse, with the exception of the
large but regionally concentrated Baptists.

Catholics, while not highly concentrated skew to the Northeast
with over-representation in both New England and in the Mid-
Atlantic Divisions and also in the Pacific Division. If there is a
"Catholic market" for some purposes then given the large population of Catholics in the U.S., one-fifth of 50 million residing in the
Mid-Atlantic means 10 million adults. People who professed no religion are more likely to reside in the Pacific Division (21 percent).
Once again, this represents a large population, with over 6 million
adults who profess no religion living in this region.

Religious compostion of census regions and divisions

Figure 7.6 reverses the previous analysis and looks at the religious composition of the various geographical units. At the regional
level it is quite clear that the Northeast was heavily Catholic in 2001.
In New England almost 40 percent of adults self-identified as
Catholic. The Mid-Atlantic division was also a stronghold of Catholics
and had the highest percentage of Jews, almost 2.5 times the
national average.

The Midwest is notable for having above the national average of
Mainline Christians. This is particularly evident in the West North
Central Division where 28 percent of the adults self-identified with

the denominations comprising the Mainline Christian tradition. On the other hand Mainline Christians are considerably under-represented in Pacific Division.

The South is the bastion of Baptist tradition. Notably, Baptists are almost 40 percent of all the adults in the East South Central. This is almost 2.5 times the national average of 16 percent adults self-identifying as Baptist. Pentecostals are also much more of a factor in the Deep South than elsewhere in the country.

The West had well above the national average of adults who profess no religion. In the Pacific Division the percentage of Nones reaches 20 percent of the adults and the Pacific states also seem particularly popular with those in the Generic Christian tradition. Mormons are over 10 percent of the Mountain Division, around 2 percent in the Pacific but have almost a negligible presence elsewhere. The Eastern religions are similarly skewed and are a significant presence only in the Pacific Division.

Figure 7.6

Religious Traditions as a Percentage of Census Division

(percent)

CENSUS REGION	NORTH EAST		MID WEST		SOUTH			WEST		U.S.
CENSUS DIVISION	NEW ENGLAND	MID-ATLANTIC	EAST NORTH CENTRAL	WEST NORTH CENTRAL	SOUTH ATLANTIC	EAST SOUTH CENTRAL	WEST SOUTH CENTRAL	MOUNTAIN	PACIFIC	
Catholic	38.5	34.6	23.7	22.6	16.3	10.0	23.6	23.8	28.6	24.5
Mainline Christian	14.2	17.9	22.6	27.7	18.0	15.4	13.8	13.9	10.7	17.3
Baptist	6.9	8.2	12.2	11.4	28.2	39.7	25.1	8.2	6.4	16.3
Pentecostal/Holiness denominations	1.9	2.8	3.7	3.4	4.8	6.0	5.8	2.4	2.5	3.8
Protestant	1.5	2.0	2.9	3.2	2.4	4.5	4.0	3.1	2.9	2.9
Mormon	0.8	0.3	0.3	0.5	0.6	0.6	0.4	10.4	1.8	1.3
Christian Generic	10.2	8.7	12.0	10.9	9.2	8.2	9.5	12.0	15.4	10.8
Lutheran	1.8	4.1	8.3	14.0	2.6	1.9	2.5	4.3	3.1	4.6
Jewish	1.0	3.7	0.8	0.4	1.5	0.3	0.4	0.9	1.4	1.4
Muslim	0.5	1.1	0.7	0.2	0.5	0.2	0.4	0.2	0.3	0.5
Eastern Religions	0.9	1.3	0.5	0.4	0.6	0.3	0.5	0.7	2.6	1.0
NRM & Other	1.8	0.7	0.6	0.7	0.8	0.6	0.6	1.2	1.2	0.9
Nones	15.2	13.2	14.9	13.2	11.7	8.8	11.2	18.4	19.8	14.1
Don't Know/Refused	6.5	5.5	5.0	5.6	5.3	5.3	4.8	4.7	6.4	5.4
Total	100.0	100.0	100.0	100.0	100.0	100.0	100.0	100.0	100.0	100.0

Interestingly, the range in the percentage of adults who refused to respond to the religious identification question is quite narrow across the geographical units, as shown in Figure 7.6. This uniformity suggests that non-cooperation with the ARIS survey owed more to individual traits than cultural or social factors.

Religious Composition of the Larger States

ARIS provides a representative sample of sufficient size so that for the various traditions we can present state level data for twenty large states. It offers a finer grain of detail which is important and useful for the media or those interested in electoral politics.

The religious traditions are shown as a percentage of the population of the 20 selected states in Figure 7.7. Some of the patterns that were highlighted for the census regions and divisions reappear, sometimes more vividly. The most evident is that Massachusetts was the most Catholic state in 2001 with Catholics comprising over 44 percent of its adult population. Other heavily Catholic states are New York, New Jersey and California. Wisconsin and Minnesota have almost one-third of the adult population who say they are Mainline Christians and one quarter of adults in Pennsylvania identify themselves that way as well. Among the large states Tennessee, North Carolina and Georgia are the most Baptist all having more than a third Baptist adherents while in Tennessee almost 40 percent of adults self-identified as Baptists.

Particular strongholds of the Pentecostal tradition are Missouri, Georgia, North Carolina and Tennessee. Tennessee also has well above average proportions in the Protestant Denominations. The Mormons are only a significant presence in Washington State in this list. Washington along with Indiana and California are particularly popular for adherents of the Christian Generic tradition. Jews have their most significant presence in New York, New Jersey, Florida, and Maryland whereas for Muslims it is New York and Illinois. The Eastern religions are significant only in California while the Other Religions and NRM tradition surface in a significant way only in Massachusetts. The "Nones" are the largest tradition in Washington accounting one-quarter of the adult population but perhaps more importantly from a national, political, and cultural perspective they

Figure 7.7

Religious Traditions as a Percentage of the Population of the Larger States*

	CATHOLIC	MAINLINE CHRISTIAN	BAPTIST	PENTECOSTAL /HOLINESS	PROTESTANT DENOMS.	MORMON	CHRISTIAN GENERIC	JEWISH	MUSLIM	EASTERN RELIGIONS	OTHER /NEW RELIGIONS	NONES	DON'T KNOW REFUSED
California	31.7%	9.3%	6.6%	1.9%	2.9%	1.4%	15.2%	1.6%	0.4%	3.0%	1.1%	18.5%	6.5%
Florida	26.4	16.2	18.4	4.2	2.3	0.5	8.5	2.9	0.2	0.7	1.2	12.6	5.9
Georgia	7.9	18.2	36.7	5.5	2.2	0.7	10.1	0.3	0.7	1.1	0.6	11.5	4.4
Illinois	28.9	19.3	11.1	2.7	2.0	0.2	12.6	1.4	1.2	0.8	0.8	14.6	4.2
Indiana	20.0	20.5	13.9	5.0	3.5	0.3	16.2	1.4	0.2	0.2	0.3	15.5	3.1
Massachusetts	44.3	11.5	4.3	2.3	1.4	0.2	7.4	1.7	0.4	1.5	2.1	15.6	7.4
Maryland	22.2	21.3	16.5	3.6	3.1	0.9	8.4	2.6	1.1	0.4	0.7	13.5	5.6
Michigan	22.7	22.0	13.8	3.6	3.5	0.1	10.7	0.5	0.9	0.4	0.8	14.9	6.1
Minnesota	25.0	32.8	5.1	1.3	2.8	0.0	11.1	0.3	0.3	0.6	1.1	13.9	5.6
Missouri	19.4	14.9	22.4	6.0	2.6	0.6	11.9	0.5	0.0	0.4	0.3	15.3	5.7
N. Carolina	9.6	16.9	38.3	5.4	2.0	0.7	9.7	0.7	0.2	0.2	0.9	9.8	5.6
New Jersey	37.3	15.5	8.4	2.1	1.7	0.5	7.4	4.4	0.8	1.6	0.3	14.8	5.5
New York	38.4	13.4	7.4	2.8	1.6	0.2	7.7	5.0	1.9	1.7	1.0	13.4	5.5
Ohio	18.9	21.8	14.0	5.4	3.6	0.8	12.7	0.3	0.5	0.5	0.6	15.4	5.4
Pennsylvania	26.9	26.5	9.1	3.2	2.9	0.4	11.1	1.2	0.2	0.6	0.4	11.9	5.6
Tennessee	6.5	17.5	39.2	5.3	7.1	0.3	9.2	0.4	0.3	0.2	0.6	8.7	4.8
Texas	27.8	14.6	20.6	4.8	3.9	0.5	10.0	0.5	0.7	0.7	0.5	11.0	4.4
Virginia	13.8	17.3	30.3	4.1	2.9	0.5	10.6	1.3	0.7	0.5	0.5	12.3	5.2
Washington	19.6	16.0	6.1	3.5	2.9	3.0	14.8	1.3	0.0	1.1	1.3	24.5	5.9
Wisconsin	27.8	34.4	6.2	1.3	1.9	0.1	7.4	0.2	0.4	0.3	0.3	14.0	5.8
U.S. Total	26.0	17.1	15.0	3.5	2.8	0.6	11.0	1.6	0.6	1.1	0.8	14.3	5.5

* Rows total to 100%

are the number two tradition by size in California, the largest state in the Union.

The Mainline Christian denomiations in the larger states

Because of the political and social prominence of its adherents, the Mainline Christian tradition, continues to have a cultural influence on the nation that is more significant than its numbers would suggest even in the 21st century. Figure 7.8 disaggregates the three largest denominational families in the Mainline Christian tradition to reveal important differences among them in their geographies. The oldest denomination, the Presbyterians, who were most influential during the American Revolution and the early days of the Republic, are the smallest today accounting for less than three percent of Americans. In numerical terms they are significant only in Pennsylvania.

Methodism which was a powerful force nationally in terms of influence and numbers in the 19th century, also tends to be well distributed across most of the states and exceeds ten percent of the state populations in a geographic variety of states: Georgia, Maryland, Ohio, and Tennessee. The indices of dissimilarity with the national population are low for all the "WASP-dominated" denominations in the Mainline tradition.

Figure 7.8

Large Mainline Christian Denominations
(percentage of selected state populations)

	METHODIST	LUTHERAN	PRESBYTERIAN		METHODIST	LUTHERAN	PRESBYTERIAN
California	2.2%	2.4%	2.5%	North Carolina	8.8%	2.6%	3.2%
Florida	6.1	2.7	3.9	New Jersey	5.5	2.6	3.5
Georgia	10.8	2.3	2.9	New York	5.5	2.2	2.0
Illinois	6.0	7.5	3.2	Ohio	10.4	4.9	3.5
Indiana	9.4	5.7	1.9	Pennsylvania	9.3	7.8	5.1
Massachusetts	2.2	1.1	0.8	Tennessee	10.4	1.6	3.0
Maryland	10.4	4.6	2.5	Texas	7.5	3.1	1.9
Michigan	8.8	7.2	3.0	Virginia	7.4	2.3	2.9
Minnesota	4.3	23.8	2.4	Washington	6.2	6.2	3.2
Missouri	6.6	4.2	2.0	Wisconsin	7.1	22.0	1.9
				U.S. Total	**6.8**	**4.6**	**2.7**

The exceptions to this rule are the Lutherans, who will be por-trayed in more detail later in this chapter. Lutherans are much more skewed in their geographical location and as a result are particularly prominent in the Upper Midwest, represented in Figure 7.8 by Wis-consin and Minnesota, but had a negligible presence in many states, notably Massachusetts and Tennessee.

The emerging New America: Florida, California and Texas

ARIS offers valuable insights into the contemporary religious character of the emerging America of the large sunbelt states which increasingly dominate the nation politically and culturally. A new economic and social environment of shopping malls, condominium developments, and freeways has emerged in recent decades in the Sunbelt states. As people, and with them political and economic power, have migrated south and west, American religion has fol-lowed. This is imperative for religious organizations because the Sun-belt states contain disproportionately large numbers of children, who are the future of all religious groups in America.

Close observation of Figure 7.7 reveals that the one large state with a religious profile that most closely approximates that of the total United States is Florida. We might have expected this. Florida has achieved its national resemblance through the migration of peo-ple from many areas of the country. It has been the fastest-growing state in recent decades and epitomizes the realignment of the U.S. population toward the Sunbelt. As Florida's population increased from less than 2.8 million in 1950 to 16 million in 2000, it became the fourth most-populous state in the Union. A magnet for retirees from the Northeast and the Midwest, it also attracted other people, including immigrants from overseas. The relocation of the elderly and the new trend of seasonal migration have had an impact on both sending and receiving states, transforming Florida in particular from a typical southern agricultural state to a more suburban one with a national character.

If we wish to understand what is happening and will happen cul-turally in the United States in the 21st century, we cannot ignore developments in California. California also has undue cultural influ-ence over the nation and large sections of the world by means of the

economic domination of Hollywood over the entertainment industry, particularly television and motion pictures. It is also pre-eminent
demographically. The 2000 Census revealed that the state had a population of nearly 34 million, or 12 percent of the country's inhabitants. No one state has ever before had such a large share of the total
population of the nation. This demographic fact has been translated
into political power by the congressional redistricting that followed the
2000 census. The other demographic trend evident in California is
immigration from Asia and Latin America. Hence the above-average
numbers of adherents of Eastern religions and of Catholics.

How California developed its religious profile is interesting and
relevant. Like the inhabitants of all western states except Utah, 19th-
century Californians demonstrated a low level of religious interest
compared with other Americans of the period. They also tended to
reject the Mainline tradition and to favor alternative religious traditions such as Unitarianism, Spiritualism, Adventism, Christian Science, and Theosophy. These radical religions had in common
spirituality that could be practiced on an individual basis. This
appealed to independent-minded Californians separated from family
and traditional communities by hundreds of miles of wilderness and
thousands of miles of sea. Though such groups accounted for only 5
percent of the population, according to the 1906 Census of Religious
Bodies, their presence tended to challenge and undermine the traditional Protestant denominations. This prevented the creation of a religious establishment in any cultural or political sense and so laid the
basis for a more secular local society. In 1872, California officially
became a secular society when the state legislature overthrew the
restrictions on Sunday business, the so-called Sabbath laws.

Understanding the state's history, we can now analyze the contemporary religious scene in California. As we have already noted
from Figure 7.1, California is the one really big state with the smallest Christian majority. The 1960s revealed the Golden State as America's center of unconventional religious movements and unorthodox
religions. Though the ARIS found relatively few explicit devotees of
the New Religious Movements such as Scientology, Eckankar, and
Neo-paganism those we did find tended to be over-concentrated in
California. The numbers are not as important as their very existence,

which demonstrates the acceptance of mysticism, occultism, and other spiritual alternatives by the general population. Surveys conducted by the sociologist Phillip E. Hammond and reported in 1987 found that nearly one third of Californians believed in reincarnation and that over 20 percent practiced meditation. Californians were also more likely to adopt the "new morality," and were less likely to belong to a church or a synagogue, or to pray, or to read the Bible.[4] Other surveys have also established a particular Californian preference for autonomy, spiritualism, and the practice of personal piety over involvement in religious institutions.

When we consider contemporary religious culture or national politics, we cannot ignore that other powerhouse of the Sunbelt, the Lone Star State, with over 20 million inhabitants in 2001. Texas is no longer the rural society made familiar by history and Hollywood westerns. It is not simply the cotton fields of East Texas, with its black and white Baptist farmers, nor the stereotypical irreligious Anglo cowboys and Mexican Catholic peons out on the plains and in the Rio Grande Valley. Though many Texans still wear ten-gallon hats and cowboy boots to the office and even to church on Sunday, Texas is largely a modern urban society dominated by two great metropolitan centers. Houston is now the fourth largest city by population in the United States, and Dallas stands seventh.

Texas can be described as both a southern and a western state, and this is reflected in its religious profile. Over 82 percent of Texans were Christians in 2001. The state has a bedrock of fundamentalist Protestant churches like the Churches of Christ and conservative Evangelicals from numerous denominations. Hence the Pentecostal and Protestant denominations traditions are over-represented along with the Baptists. Yet like many western states it has a Mexican heritage and growing contemporary presence that means it is nearly 28 percent Catholic.

Urban, Suburban and Rural Residency Patterns of the Religious Traditions

The types of neighborhoods or communities people reside in often reflect the type of occupations available to them and greatly affect their lifestyles and recreational habits. Figures 7.9 and 7.10 use a tripartite classification system that identifies similar types of residential

areas and built environments across the nation according to whether
they are located in a) central cities of metropolitan areas or typical
urban areas with high population densities, b) the suburbs of metropolitan areas and metropolitan areas without a central city or c)
rural areas, the Non-Metro counties comprising farmland and other
places with low population densities as well as small towns of under
30,000 people.

Figure 7.9 shows the distribution of each religious tradition
according to the three types of residential location of its adherents.
For historical and socioeconomic reasons some traditions have much
greater proportions of city residents; others have a bias towards suburbanites; and still others seem to be more popular among rural
dwellers. Today less than a third of all Americans are "true urbanites," inhabitants of cities. Figure 7.9 indicates that in 2001 Muslims
were the most likely to be city dwellers. Half of them resided in an
urban area, double the rate of Mainline Christians and Mormons. The
identifiers with Eastern Religions were also more urban with 48 percent residing in cities.

Figure 7.9

Proportion of Religious Tradition Residing in Urban/Suburban/Rural Areas

	URBAN	SUBURBAN	RURAL	TOTAL
Catholic	32.9%	54.6%	12.5%	100%
Mainline Christian	24.3	51.7	24.0	100
Baptist	30.1	41.9	27.9	100
Pentecostal/Holiness	29.1	43.4	27.6	100
Protestant denominations	27.5	43.8	28.7	100
Mormon	25.2	49.9	24.8	100
Christian Generic	30.8	49.6	19.6	100
Jewish	36.1	59.7	4.2	100
Muslim	50.6	45.8	3.6	100
Eastern religions	47.8	46.4	5.8	100
Other/New religions	36.1	46.1	17.7	100
Nones	33.2	48.4	18.4	100
Don't Know/Refused	28.4	55.2	16.4	100
U.S. Total	**30.5**	**49.8**	**19.7**	**100**

Rural folk comprise one in five of all Americans but several traditions were biased towards rural residents. These were Protestant Denominations, Baptists, and Pentecostals, with about 28 percent each. Mainline Christians and Mormons had proportions above the national average.

Half of all Americans now live in the suburbs so it was not surprising to find that most traditions are well represented in such neighborhoods. Figure 7.9 shows that Jews stand out with the highest national average of adherents in suburban areas. Almost 60 percent of Jews and 55 percent of Catholics reside in the suburbs. Yet even the traditions with lower suburban scores are not far off this figure. The suburbs contain 42 percent of Baptists, 43 percent of Pentecostals and 44 percent of those in the Protestant Denominations. This finding suggests that the real residential divide between the constituencies of the various religious traditions is whether they are urban-suburban or suburban-rural in nature.

The Religious Composition of Urban, Suburban, and Rural Areas

The religious composition of rural areas in the contemporary U.S. shown in Figure 7.10 is quite different from that of urban and suburban areas. Rural communities are more culturally homogeneous than urban America and tend to have distinctive cultural values, folkways, customs, and traditions. County fairs, agricultural shows, and rodeos dot the rural landscape. Today, a single tradition or denomination still dominates most rural counties. Historically, church participation was higher in rural areas, particularly where there otherwise was social deprivation combined with religious and ethnic homogeneity. Going to church on Sunday remains the highlight of the hardworking farm family's week, especially the poor family that cannot afford other social outlets. Rural religion reflects America's historical settlement patterns of the previous century, and because most of agriculture has shed labor, rural counties have been shielded from the recent influx of immigrants from non-Western societies. Calculations based on Figure 7.10 reveal that more than 80 percent of rural Americans are Christians and two-thirds of rural people identify with Christian traditions aside from Catholicism.

There is no doubt that rural residents are more religious in their belief and behavior than urban dwellers.

In modern Western societies there is no doubt that rural residents are more religious in their belief and behavior than urban dwellers. Aside from differences in education and class, the explanation often given is that rural people are simply more in touch with nature, or "real life." In contrast, life in industrial cities, with its accompanying fixation on material goals, tends to deprive people of the capacity for contemplation of world and self that leads to wonder and amazement. Modern technology, more prevalent in cities, gives the impression, or at least fosters the illusion, that people are not fundamentally dependent on powers outside or above themselves.

Several key differences between the various traditions emerged in 2001. First, rural areas had more Baptists. They made up 23 percent of the rural population as compared with 14 percent of the suburban population. Rural areas also had more Mainline Christians: 20 percent of the rural population versus 14 percent of the urban population. Third, rural areas had far fewer Catholics: 16 percent of the rural population versus 26 to 27 percent of urban and suburban areas. Fourth, the Protestant Denominations and the Pentecostal-Holiness traditions were more strongly represented in rural areas. In contrast rural communities had only a fraction of some of the religious minorities, such as Jews, Muslims, and Eastern Religions.

The rural and agricultural nature of religious enthusiasm in America goes back to the first half of the 19th century. Older religious traditions seem to survive better in the countryside. For instance, the urbanization of both whites and blacks in the 20th century weakened Methodism. Other groups in the Pentecostal and Protestant Denominations traditions that are overrepresented in the rural areas are the Church of the Nazarene, the Churches of Christ, the Churches of God, the Brethren, the Assemblies of God, and the Holiness churches. These religious preferences reflect a conservative temperament that inevitably has social outcomes in terms of the political atmosphere and lifestyles of many rural communities, which are typically resistant to changing fads and fashions.

The profiles of central cities, the urban classification in Figures 7.9 and 7.10, were remarkably consistent with those of suburban and smaller metropolitan areas. Nationally, the real contrast is between these two types of residential settings and rural America.

Undoubtedly, much 'of the nation believes that the crisis of urban America as shown in crime rates and declining educational and family standards is due to an observable deterioration in moral conduct in its great cities. However, this trend cannot be associated with major changes in the religious loyalties of city dwellers. Change in urban religion today is more notable for its declining practice rather than ideological or theological innovation. The data for the urban areas also dispute some commonly held views of big-city dwellers for it can be seen in Figure 7.10 that they were less likely to refuse to answer the religious identification question than suburbanites. Furthermore, urban America had only slightly above average proportions of religious "Nones."

Change in urban religion today is more notable for its declining practice rather than ideological or theological innovation.

Figure 7.10

Composition of Urban / Suburban / Rural Areas by Religious Tradition

	URBAN	SUBURBAN	RURAL	U.S.
Catholic	26.4%	26.8%	15.5%	24.5%
Mainline Christians	13.8	18.0	20.3	17.3
Baptist	16.1	13.7	23.1	16.3
Pentecostal/Holiness	3.6	3.3	5.5	3.8
Protestant Denominations	2.6	2.5	4.2	2.9
Mormon	1.1	1.3	1.6	1.3
Christian Generic	11.0	10.8	10.8	10.8
Jewish	1.6	1.6	0.3	1.4
Muslim	0.9	0.5	0.1	0.5
Eastern Religions	1.5	0.9	0.3	1.0
NRM & Other Religions	1.0	0.8	0.8	0.9
Nones	15.4	13.7	13.2	14.1
Don't Know/Refused	5.1	6.0	4.5	5.4
Total	**100.0**	**100.0**	**100.0**	**100.0**

Religion and Regional Cultures

The geographical data presented in Figures 7.1 to 7.10 provide important insights into the influence different religious communities have on specific areas of the country. ARIS is particularly valuable because it conclusively confirms the continuing existence of some geographically specific religious subcultures within the nation. Obviously the religious geography of Colonial times could not be maintained as evangelists persuaded, colonies united, immigrants arrived, frontiers expanded, and pioneers migrated. However, distinctive heartlands still persist, especially for five religious traditions: Baptists in the South, Lutherans in the Upper Midwest farm belt, Roman Catholics in the Northeast, Mormons in Utah and the other Rocky Mountain states, and Nones in the Pacific Northwest. To some extent this finding belies the conventional wisdom about contemporary society, which suggests that America has become more socially uniform and culturally homogeneous and thereby religiously integrated under the influence of a pervasive mass culture and high residential mobility.

The Baptists and the South

The concentrated strength of the Baptists, the nation's largest Protestant denominational family, in the American South contrasts with their relative lack of significance in other areas. That Baptists dominate the South is of enormous cultural significance to the nation. As we have mentioned before, Baptists come in many varieties and are split by race into black and white groups; nevertheless, they form a formidable cultural force in shaping the outlook of the populace and social institutions of the region. The most influential organization is the 17-million-strong Southern Baptist Convention. Notice that the statistics by state, division, and region of where Baptists currently exceed 25 percent of the population, almost replicates the former Confederate States of America.

Sheer concentration of numbers and the lack of significant rivals to their religious outlook allow the Baptist churches across much of the South to enforce traditional group values in a way that contrasts with religious beliefs and practices elsewhere. In regions that have greater diversification and more widespread religious pluralism, beliefs and practices are less public, more individually chosen. The ARIS findings may explain the region's "Bible Belt" nickname, a pejorative 20th-century term invented by the iconoclastic Baltimore journalist H. L. Mencken. Southern Christianity is a relatively stable, distinct religion based upon an evangelistic and fundamentalist heritage that involves the acceptance of a literal interpretation of the Bible, as well as an emphasis on an experience of personal conversion. Southern Christianity is emotional, Jesus-centered, and contains a strict moral code but it is also expressed through southern gospel music, Christian country music, and televangelists, as well as through local secular laws against alcohol and obscenity.

Why should the South be so religiously unique? The answer lies in its history, for nowhere else in the nation is history taken so seriously or evoked so often. Many scholars suggest that the dominance of the Baptist religion in the South can only be explained in terms of the "captive religion thesis," that is, the Baptist religion is a faith of a subordinate people struggling against their conquerors. After the South's defeat in the Civil War, the Baptist church was one of the few institutions that remained under Southern control. It assuaged the white populace's feelings of resentment against Northern military occupation. With the old planter aristocracy destroyed, the clergy became the defenders of Southern morals and values, of the "Southern way of life."

Figure 7.11

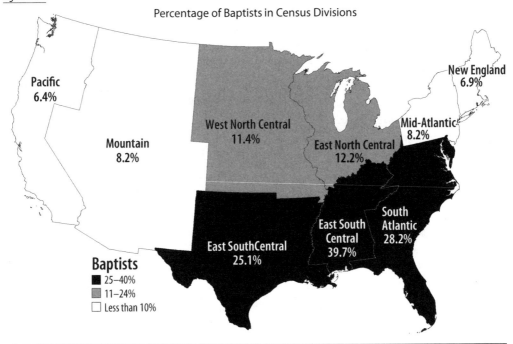

Percentage of Baptists in Census Divisions

Irrespective of race, the Baptist clergy in their writing and preaching have been more influential in community and political affairs in the South than in any other American region. In part this is because the individualistic morality of the Baptists necessitates a close personal relationship between the pastor and the congregant. For the poor white majority and the even more oppressed African Americans, the evangelical focus of the church, with its emphasis on the conversion experience, allowed them to deal with their grinding poverty. The African-American Baptist and Methodist churches were the centers of black social and political life. They were the only institutions over which African Americans held any control.

Until the 1960s, the South was the region most removed from the mainstream of American industrial society. Unlike in the West, few newcomers entered the South, and immigrants from overseas with religious influence were rare in the region. Remarkably, the re-emergence of the "New South" over the last few decades has not altered things very much, as residents of the South are still more church-oriented than people in other sections of the country. Billy Graham, a Southern Baptist preacher from North Carolina, seemed just as potent in the age of videos as he was in an earlier time. The same is true for the clergy from other denominations in the southern evangelical Protestant tradition, such as the Assemblies of God, the Baptist Missionary Association of America, the Church of God (Cleveland, Tennessee), and the Pentecostal Holiness church. In fact, the most important visible contemporary development in American religion has been a resurgence of the revivalist, theologically conservative Protestantism associated with the South and the growing influence of "old-time" religion in other regions. An early symbol of this nationalization of southern religion, which is now taken for granted, was the election in 1976 of Georgia's Jimmy Carter, the first self-professed born-again Christian and Southern Baptist to become President of the United States.

The Catholics and the Northeast

In some ways, the geographical distribution of the country's Catholics is an inversion of the Baptist situation. Instead of being in the South, the heartland of Catholicism lies in the Northeast, particularly the New England States and especially Massachusetts. Unlike Baptists, who are numerically dominant only regionally, Catholics constitute a significant percentage of every region and state. The arrival of Catholics from Europe, mainly between 1840 and 1924, and the more recent entry of Latin Americans built up American Catholicism and created its geographic map. The current distribution shows the effect of recent westward migration as well as immigration, factors of little importance to the Baptist churches. Successive waves of immigration caused the amazing transformation of Massachusetts from a Puritan stronghold to a Catholic-majority state. In other heavily Catholic areas such as Wisconsin, the Southwest, and Louisiana, Catholic concentrations reflect the presence of typically Catholic ethnic groups such as the South Germans, Chicanos, and Cajuns.

The size of a particular group is an important determinant of its members' behavior. From this perspective, we might deduce that the greater the size of the group, the greater will be the variation in religious practice, and the more freedom for individual deviance that will exist because of the difficulty of enforcing social discipline

Figure 7.12

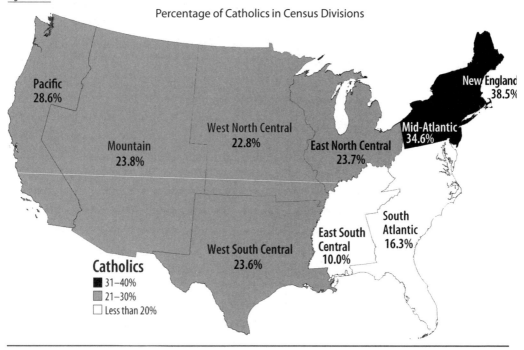

Percentage of Catholics in Census Divisions

among large numbers of people. This scenario has proven particularly true for America's 50 million adult Catholics, who are widely dispersed across the nation. Many have become "nominal" baptized Catholics, who identify themselves as Catholics in surveys but do not currently have contact with parishes. In part this arises as a result of migration to areas where Catholicism is weak institutionally and organizationally, which produces a situation that is also detrimental to church affiliation.

The relationship of America's two largest religious groups, the Catholics and Baptists, who hold the loyalties of nearly half the country's population, is of national importance. The theological gap between the two traditions is wide but the political distance has lessened in recent years. This gap is perhaps best symbolized by the contrast between the fiercely independent local Baptist church in its plain chapel, whose congregation hires its own pastor, and the ornate cathedral run by a clerical hierarchy owing ultimate allegiance to Rome. During the 20th century both organizationally and personally, Catholic-Baptist relationships were marked by caution and reserve. There was little interaction because of their different theologies, governance systems, religious lifestyles, and above all, geographic locations. Aside from their significant numbers in such traditionally Catholic areas as southern Louisiana, South Texas, and South Florida, Catholics were underrepresented in the South. Catholic newcomers to the South are faced with the fact that in many places they are still a small minority and that there is still anti-Catholic sentiment, especially outside the cities. Southern Catholics do not have much political clout, and there are not enough funds for parochial schools, church programs, or personnel. This has meant that southern Catholicism has maintained a less communitarian flavor but has become more ecumenical, innovative and, to some extent, adaptive to local culture. An example of this last trend is that one of the largest American Catholic television ministries is Mother Angelica's Eternal World Network, based in Birmingham, Alabama.

The Lutherans and the Upper Midwest

The Upper Midwest, the old Northwest Territory, is the heartland of a major regional religious culture, Lutheranism. This area largely equates to the West North Central Census Division and the states of Minnesota, Wisconsin, the Dakotas, Nebraska, Iowa, and into Montana. No doubt this geographical clustering helped consolidate the group and prevented switching of denominations. However, migration from rural areas and farm states during recent decades has transformed the overall distribution and increasing numbers of Lutherans are to be found in California, Illinois, and Florida.

This distinct regional cultural milieu emerged after the last of the three waves of Lutheran immigration in American history: First, in 1683, New Sweden was founded in the Delaware Valley. Later, in the 18th century, 60,000 Germans left the Rhineland for Pennsylvania. Then, in the 19th century, a large Scandinavian settlement arrived in the country's northern-tier farmlands. In the countries of northern Europe, Lutheranism was typically the state-established church so initially Lutheran immigrants tended to reproduce their national divisions in the New World. Separate ethnic churches representing Sweden, Denmark, Finland, Iceland, and others were established. Even these later split on doctrinal grounds: By 1900,

Figure 7.13

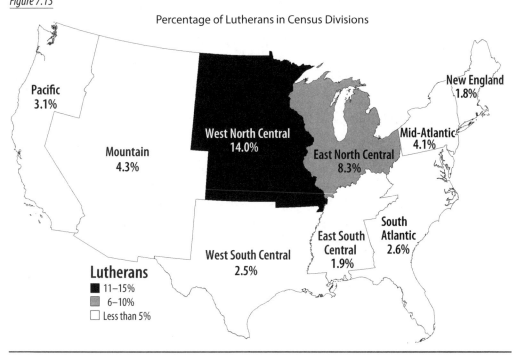

Percentage of Lutherans in Census Divisions

Pacific
3.1%

New England
1.8%

West North Central
14.0%

Mountain
4.3%

East North Central
8.3%

Mid-Atlantic
4.1%

South
Atlantic
2.6%

East South
Central
1.9%

West South Central
2.5%

Lutherans
■ 11–15%
▨ 6–10%
□ Less than 5%

Map graphic courtesy of Catosphere, www.catosphere.com

there were twenty-four separate Lutheran church organizations in America but the 20th century saw Lutherans attempting to bridge ethnic differences and merge their churches. Today, the main divisions arise from the ideological and theological differences between the liberally inclined Evangelical Lutheran Church in America and the conservative Lutheran Church-Missouri Synod. Among the populace, Lutheranism is viewed broadly, as an ethnic or community church: Very few ARIS Lutheran respondents qualified their reply by specifying their particular denomination.

It is difficult to separate what is Lutheran from what is northern European ethnic in the character of the Upper Midwest. In part this is because the region's physical environment of forests, lakes, and severe winters is very close to its population's ancestral homeland in the Nordic countries. This may help to explain why there is so much similarity between the cultural and social environments of the region's rural areas and those of northern Europe. Lutheranism is a moderate, formalistic Christian denomination not given to religious innovation or demonstrativeness hence its allocation to the mainline Christian tradition. It tends to produce sober, serious, industrious people, relatively tolerant but supportive of the political status quo (official statistics also reveal that the states with a high proportion of Lutherans have a low rate of legal abortions). Lutherans take pride in their civic virtues and their strong sense of community, which their religion promotes.

The Mormons of the Mountain West

The Church of Jesus Christ of the Latter-Day Saints, the only truly successful religious group experiment in the American West, constitutes our fourth major religious geographic concentration. Today a majority of Mormons still live in the Mountain states and they are the most clustered religious group in the nation. The essential concentrated western settlement pattern of the group is such that no state east of the Rocky Mountains is even 1 percent Mormon. Mormons tend to congregate with other Mormons. A majority of the population of Utah are Mormons; the greatest dominance by any single religious group over a state.

The fact that the Mormons are the most geographically isolated and uniquely distributed religious group in the nation is no accident. The Mormon migration westward was an attempt to find a "Promised Land" and to establish "a new Zion," that is, to ingrain the "rule of God" on earth for a people with a heritage going back to ancient Israel and archaic America. Moreover, the Mormon leadership, so designated by personal commitment and talent rather than by education or social position, wanted to found a socioeconomic as well as a religious community that would be ruled by revealed principles and run by the priestly servants of God. Their social organization had an egalitarian interpretation of the prophet Isaiah's vision of the desert blooming as a rose (Isaiah 35:1-2). In fact, the Mormons were the only millennial and utopian movement of 19th-century America to survive and flourish. Undoubtedly their geographic isolation and concentration in the Great Basin assisted in their success in building a home in unpopulated Utah for their persecuted group, free from the constraints of "Gentile" influences. Converts were warned to flee the world and "gather" with the Saints to await the Second Coming.

Figure 7.14

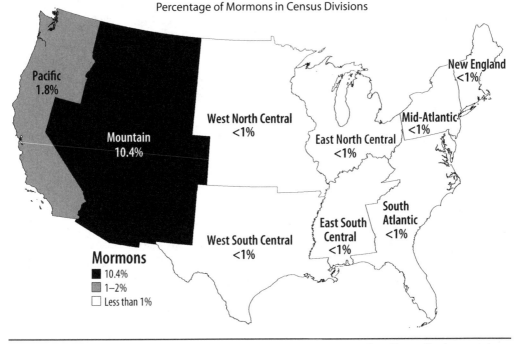

Percentage of Mormons in Census Divisions

The Mormons have always placed an emphasis on recruitment and spreading their message through a massive program of taking Zion to the unconverted and building a network of wards and stakes (that is, bishoprics) all over the world. These consist of meeting houses, welfare storehouses, social-service offices, and temples, established wherever groups of Mormons are located. However, the ARIS data suggest that resistance to the message of the Mormons still persists in regions outside of the West. The 40,000 young male Mormon missionaries who are estimated at any given time to be evangelizing during a two-year commitment to the church appear to be making a significant impact in the United States only west of the Rockies and in Texas. However, despite their abstinence from tobacco, alcohol, tea, and coffee, the Mormons of Salt Lake City are no longer perceived as being on the cutting edge of religious and social experimentation.

The Nones of the Northwest

The West is the fastest-growing section of the country, and so it is worth investigating the manner in which it is different from the rest of the country and whether its difference portends future trends for the nation. The Pacific Northwest states of Oregon and Washington along with the adjoining Mountain states of Colorado, Idaho, Montana, and Wyoming are among the highest scorers in the "No Faith" column in Figure 7.1. The ARIS findings only confirm on a more authoritative basis what has been known for many years—that the area was the most unchurched region in the United States. The western states lead in religious diversity as well as "No Religion" responses and it seems that religious diversity and high levels of irreligion go hand in hand.

The religious "Nones," who are often regarded by sociologists of religion as innovators, are considered unusual in a society like the United States, where nearly everyone has a religious identity. If nonreligious or irreligious behavior is deviant in America, then we can appreciate that such behavior is more likely to go unnoticed or uncommented upon in the West than elsewhere. The residents of the Pacific Northwest are convinced that the area of the last frontier has a culture more tolerant of change and deviance. Some would suggest that the local environment is so heavily influenced by countercultural values that dissent expands to actually encourage the discarding of established religions. One explanation for this phenomenon stresses two points: mobility (that is, migration creates people without ties) and the natural environment. This line of thinking links the "frontier" concept to the effect of land and space on people. Historically, people have moved to the open West to explore new lifestyles and to flee from tradition. Washington State's radical heritage attracted political mavericks and social freethinkers who rejected connections to established institutions (e.g., churches). That the major traditions, such as Catholic and Baptist churches (see Figure 7.5), were weak in the region, and that the smaller traditions and groups were stronger, follows logically.

Nature and a more pristine environment also act as a distraction from organized religion. Many young adults get more personal satisfaction from climbing Mount Rainier or the Cascades, or canoeing on the Columbia River, than from Sunday services. Religious leaders in the area admit that the rich surroundings mean that in the

Figure 7.15

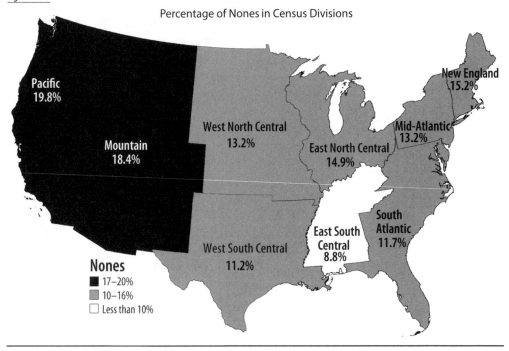

Percentage of Nones in Census Divisions

Pacific 19.8%

Mountain 18.4%

West North Central 13.2%

East North Central 14.9%

New England 15.2%

Mid-Atlantic 13.2%

South Atlantic 11.7%

East South Central 8.8%

West South Central 11.2%

Nones
■ 17–20%
▨ 10–16%
☐ Less than 10%

summer their churches are empty as members flock to the mountains or to Puget Sound to enjoy recreational activities. The spiritual
satisfactions from the scenery and nature outweigh church services,
which lose out in the battle for people's limited leisure time.

Many "Nones" are migrants, and appear to have been raised with
religion. The process of migration often has a disorienting effect on
the individual, which leads to a reassessment of religious loyalties.
Americans have usually migrated for economic reasons, whether to
California during the 1849 gold rush, to the prairies for free land in
the 1880s, or to Detroit for car-production jobs in the 1950s. The
effects of this movement reach out beyond the economic system.
Moving forces the individual to cut established ties with family and
neighbors and to create new ones with strangers. High levels of
migration break down cultural traditions by mixing people from different backgrounds. This process also makes difficult the creation of
new traditions. By disrupting social networks, migration undermines
religious affiliations and outlook. It severs what Peter Berger has
described as "the thin thread of conversation" that links the individual to the religious group.[5] We see here the secularizing influences of pluralism as people switch loyalties in their new community.
In new or growing centers of population, religious organizations are
constantly trying to recruit and retain new members. They cannot
rely on stable social ties of friendship and kinship to integrate new
members. Survey evidence shows that interregional migrants are the
people most likely to switch religious groups or become unaffiliated
as they become exposed to new commitments and "alternative legit-
imations." Thus we would expect the growing regions of the country to have the greatest proportion of religion changers or
"switchers," and the facts bear out this expectation.

The relative lack of older people also explains why the frontier
serves as the breeding ground for the religious experimentation that
is a particular feature of California. The West as mentioned
earlier has been especially hospitable to novel and exotic religions.
The West has cults, or, more politely perhaps, "New Religious
Movements" (NRMs), while the South and Midwest have sects,
enthusiastic offshoots of established churches. As some would see it,
eccentrics of all description go west.

Chapter 13 will show that today especially the relationship between religion and region plays out most obviously in the political realm and can clearly be observed as a factor in state level legislation as well as electoral politics. A good example of this process is that Oregon, the state with the highest level of "No Faith" according to Figure 7.1, is the only one with an assisted suicide law and that this law was approved by popular referendum.

Conversely we should not be surprised to learn that in 2000 the state abortion rate tended to be around one-fourth of the national rate (21.3 per 1,000 women 15-44 years old) in the most "Christian states" of Kentucky (5.3), Mississippi (5.9), South Dakota (5.5), and Utah (6.6).

Whereas popular feeling and regulation can effect access to suicide or abortion, when it comes to actual social behaviors the picture is blurred. For instance, state and regional rates for crime and illegitimate births, which are issues explicitly covered in the Ten Commandments show that the "Bible Belt" is not morally superior according to its own values and desired outcomes compared with areas such as the Pacific Northwest or New England. However, divorce rates did show some religious influence in 2001. They were lowest in "Catholic" Massachusetts (2.4 per 1,000) and Connecticut (2.9) and highest in Nevada (6.8). Yet in "Evangelical" Arkansas (6.6 per 1,000) and Kentucky (5.5) the local divorce rate far exceeded that in Montana (2.6) and even Washington (4.5).[6]

In any society, the dominant religion usually aspires to act as a social control mechanism and engage in social engineering. So the religious characteristics of the people living in a particular locality can help explain rates of political participation, crime, suicide, and divorce but this influence does not extend to all the crucial areas of life. For many important aspects of behavior that also can be measured by social statistics, the "expected" outcomes by state and region are confounded by complex social, demographic, and economic influences and variables. Nevertheless, a fair accounting of the interplay between religious identity and geography in contemporary American society has to recognize that religion is still very much an integral part of local society and culture. It is influential almost everywhere, buttressed by either historic communal ties, the search for spiritual autonomy, or concern for a loved one's safety; reasons vary with locality. Thus it is the differing patterns of religious identification that account for much of the diversity in America by helping to give different regions and states their individual character.

Notes

1. "Christian Faith" is an aggregate of the following traditions: Catholic, Mainline Christian, Baptists, Pentecostal/Holiness, Protestant denominations, Mormon/LDS, Christian Generic. "Other Faiths" is an aggregate of: Jewish, Muslim, Eastern Religions, Other religions & NRMs. "No Faith" is an aggregate of Nones and Don't Know/Refused.

2. New England includes CT, RI, MA, NH, VT, and ME; Middle Atlantic includes NJ, PA and NY; East North Central includes OH, MI, IN, IL and WI; West North Central includes MO,IA,MN,KS,NE,SD and ND; South Atlantic includes FL, GA, SC, NC, VA, WV, DC, MD and DE; East South Central includes AL, MS, TN and KY; West South Central includes LA, TX, AR and OK; Mountain includes NM, AZ, CO, UT, NV, WY, ID and MT; Pacific includes CA, OR and WA. Hawaii and Alaska are not included in ARIS.

3. For a more detailed examination of this issue see the *Religion by Region Series* edited by Mark Silk & Andrew Walsh and published by AltaMira Press. This is a project of the Leonard E. Greenberg Center for the Study of Religion in Public Life at Trinity College, Hartford, CT.

4. Phillip Hammond and David Bromley, eds. *The Future of New Religious Movements*, Mercer University Press, Macon, GA, 1987.

5. Peter L. Berger, *The Sacred Canopy: Elements of a Sociological Theory of Religion*, Doubleday, Garden City, NY, 1967.

6. The authoritative source for social statistics by state and region is U.S. Bureau of the Census, *Statistical Abstract of the United States: 2003*, Washington, DC.

EIGHT

Gender and Socioeconomics

The Religious Factor in the Economy

RELIGION and faith are not only part of people's inner lives, but also influence their social outlook and therefore their prospects and life chances. Religious groups teach their adherents how to behave in this world as well as how to prepare themselves for the next. The balance between how far they focus on "this world" and "the next" has practical outcomes in social and economic behavior, especially in lifestyle and patterns of consumption.

This chapter and the one following will attempt to answer the question: What precise role does religious identification play in economics and the social order? A leading German sociologist, Max Weber, stipulated in a controversial 1903 essay on the Protestant work ethic, *The Protestant Ethic and the Spirit of Capitalism,* that the doctrine and devotionalism of socioreligious groups affected the economic behavior of their adherents. He maintained that a religion supplies a distinctive worldview and cultural values that influence its adherents. This creates a particular bias concerning what is important to individuals in how they spend their time and energies. How much time and thought is given to material ambition in one's life can affect economic attainment and social status within the wider society. In modern American society differences among various religious teachings are important because they apparently induce distinctly differing reactions among people who are subjected to the same stimuli and experiences.

The best and most obvious example of this "religious factor" operating in society and the economy are the millennialist groups and "revolutionist" sects. Their beliefs require reform of human values and behavior that are antagonistic to consumerism and many other

aspects of mainstream contemporary society. Their attitudes and their
social outlook mean they should have low ranking on any social-status scale because they reject many of the key indicators used in assess-
ments of success in America. Such groups, most of which are in the
Protestant denomination tradition and the Pentecostal and Charismatic tradition, are often referred to as sects. A sect is a dissenting
religious group that seeks to preserve its spiritual purity by remaining apart from the world. Its members believe in a moral truth that
is unchanging, universal, and divinely sanctioned. A sect frequently
exercises close control over its members and their personal lives. A
prime example of such a closed community is the Seventh Day
Adventist. Its members can be born in an Adventist hospital, educated in Adventist schools from kindergarten to university, work in
Adventist institutions, buy Adventist food, live in Adventist communities, and end their days in Adventist retirement centers.

Sectarians reject much of the current economic system along with
mainstream ideas of religious respectability as part of their withdrawal from what they consider to be a corrupt and complacent
world. In addition material deprivation and disadvantage, can condition a psychological disposition in individuals to seek certainty and
solace in strict religion. Certainly in the past many sectarians have
responded to their poverty by denouncing what the economy with-
held from them. Their beliefs teach them that human beings are
weak, sinful, and hopeless before God. Asceticism is their lot and
hard work is their only bulwark against escape through pleasures
they cannot, in any event, afford. Sects teach an otherworldly religion and usually reject drinking, gambling, dancing, attending
amusements, and conspicuous consumption. This discipline tends to
make their members desirable employees. Sectarians are often anti-
union but stress ideas like "a fair day's work for a fair day's pay" and
"honesty is the best policy." They reject the greed and values of the
consumer society. The Amish farmer, for example, will disadvantage
himself rather than buy on credit. Jehovah's Witnesses often accept
low pay because they see consumer culture as false and evil. The
Holiness Sects, which began in the late 1800s, teach that the only
real problem is sin, which can be overcome by an encounter with

God. A search for perfection and sanctification orients sectarians to a personalized idea of right and individual achievement within their own nonmaterial value system.

Religious Teachings and Gender Roles

One of the most important influences on the aggregate social and economic circumstances of any particular religious group is its teachings and perspective on the role and status of women. The sociological literature dealing with gender has treated the socioeconomic dependence of women upon marriage, kin, and husbands as one of the hallmarks of traditionalism. Religion is widely recognized as important in creating cultural communities, which in turn directly influence their adherents' attitudes and behavior toward gender roles in society.

The United States features unique social phenomena with two apparently conflicting streams: a relatively religious population living in an advanced post-industrial economy. As a result of these cross-cutting secularization and religious patterns evident in the ARIS findings we should expect to find considerable variation on gender issues among Americans according to the religious bodies with which they identify.

In traditional religious households, women derive their social and economic status through marriage and husbands. Conservative religious beliefs perpetuate traditional gender roles, assigning women to the home and men to the work force. In this model study and work outside the home is forgone in order to concentrate on motherhood and family duties. Thus, groups that stress rigid, traditional divisions of labor tend to limit the socioeconomic opportunities of their female members, thereby lowering the group's average income.

An important factor in the relative socioeconomic status of women within any social group or culture is the extent to which the domestic sphere is defined as women's domain. With greater emphasis on domestic roles for women, women are less likely to be encouraged to increase their education or develop a career. Moreover, marriage and child-bearing are competing for a woman's time, drawing her away from non-domestic roles. Religion is the "carrier" of a normative system. Religious prescriptions about the importance of the family, and particularly about women's primary role in child-bearing and child-rearing, may explain much of the variation among religious groups in educational attainment and labor force participation.

In recent decades, as women have increasingly joined the labor force and worked outside the home, there have been, as was noted in Chapter 5, demographic consequences for marriage, household formation, and child-bearing patterns. At the same time, female economic activity has changed marital decision-making and the household division of labor and, to some extent, has reconstituted sex-role attitudes. Both demographic shifts and the need for two incomes have opened new career and educational opportunities for women. These new options outside the domestic sphere usually conflict with traditional and less egalitarian ideologies of gender differences. Labor-force participation tends to foster liberal views, since women with greater involvement outside the home are more likely to desire roles that conservative theology usually reserves for men. This has important long-term implications for American religion since up until now women have been the backbone of their respective faiths and denominations.

As noted above, religious traditionalism affects women's socioeconomic status directly by discouraging them from getting a higher education and participating in the labor force. Indirectly, it encourages women to marry young and have many children, which in turn make it difficult for women to obtain higher education. Feminists and liberal groups regard access to education as affirming the dignity and autonomy of girls and women. These advocates of modern egalitarian gender roles encourage women to study into their adult years if possible. They focus on education because it is important in complex modern societies in offering entry to well-paid careers and the resulting economic independence.

Educational attainment and the educational profile of men and women

Examination of the educational profiles of men and women across the religious spectrum is important because education is the main vehicle to attain status in modern societies. Variations in educational achievement among women, and between women and men, have crucial socioeconomic consequences for the individuals as well as their families and communities. The ARIS data provide an opportunity to test how far the religious ties are significantly associated with the acquisition of tertiary and higher education of women. In recent decades, political pressure has enhanced women's educational levels and encouraged gender equality in education. Moreover, federal and state policy initiatives have produced increases in overall U.S. high school graduation rates. Individual religious groups differ considerably in the levels of higher education that their adherents attain.[1]

As educational levels have risen nationwide over the past few decades, gender equality in educational attainment has reached new heights. Nevertheless, in most religious groups in the United States, men are still more likely to have completed college. This reflects a generational or historic lag since today more women than men are enrolled in college.

Figure 8.1

Educational Attainment by Religious Tradition—Males
(last grade or school completed)

RELIGIOUS TRADITION	< HIGH SCHOOL GRADUATE	HIGH SCHOOL GRADUATE	SOME COLLEGE	GRADUATED COLLEGE	GRADUATE SCHOOL +	TOTAL*
Catholic	8%	31%	23%	26%	10%	100%
Mainline Christian	5	27	20	31	14	100
Baptist	14	40	21	17	6	100
Christian Generic	10	32	23	24	9	100
Pentecostal/Charismatic	16	40	24	13	4	100
Protestant denominations	12	37	20	22	7	100
Mormon	4	30	33	18	12	100
Jewish	3	13	22	35	26	100
Eastern Religions	10	17	20	30	21	100
Muslim	6	28	13	26	25	100
NRM & Other Religions	13	24	22	15	24	100
No religion	11	32	21	22	12	100
Total U.S. Male Adults	**10**	**31**	**22**	**24**	**11**	**100**

* Some of the row totals do not sum to 100% due to no-response to the education question.

Figure 8.2

Educational Attainment by Religious Tradition—Females
(last grade or school completed)

RELIGIOUS TRADITION	< HIGH SCHOOL GRADUATE	HIGH SCHOOL GRADUATE	SOME COLLEGE	GRADUATED COLLEGE	GRADUATE SCHOOL +	TOTAL*
Catholic	8%	35%	24%	25%	7%	100%
Mainline Christian	5	30	24	27	12	100
Baptist	15	39	22	17	5	100
Christian Generic	8	33	26	23	8	100
Pentecostal/Charismatic	18	39	24	13	4	100
Protestant denominations	11	38	25	19	6	100
Mormon	8	26	35	24	6	100
Jewish	1	19	24	36	18	100
Eastern Religions	6	23	18	41	11	100
Muslim	7	35	18	29	10	100
NRM & Other Religions	10	17	26	23	23	100
No religion	8	31	24	25	10	100
Total U.S. Female Adults	**9**	**33**	**23**	**23**	**8**	**100**

* Some of the row totals do not sum to 100% due to no-response to the education question.

Figures 8.1 and 8.2 confirm that nationally, there are minor differences in educational attainment between men and women. The main difference, although not substantial, is in the highest category of those completing graduate school or obtaining a post-graduate degree, whereby men exceed women.

Across religious groups, however, the educational gaps are wide. Jews have the smallest proportion of poorly educated persons and are also the best-educated group at the top end. A majority of college graduates in the population among both men and women marks American Jews and Eastern religions adherents, who have surpassed the old elite, the Mainline Christians, on this characteristic. Catholics are noticeable because despite being a large group with lots of immigrants they are at the national average educationally, which is an important achievement. In contrast the least educated are Baptists and Pentecostals, who have a plurality of high school graduates.

Overall, it is possible to identify three clusters of "egalitarian" religious groupings with similar educational attainments for both men and women. These were the Jewish, Eastern religions, and Other

Religions/NRM traditions, where both men and women had higher education. On the other hand, Baptists and Pentecostals had the highest proportions of less than a high school education for both men and women. Most other traditions were in the middle range but also had egalitarian profiles. The only tradition with a wide discrepancy between men and women were the Muslims, where men were much more likely to have obtained a post-graduate degree than women.

Gender inequality in higher education

In order to summarize the differences between men and women in higher education, we present in Figure 8.3 male-to-female ratio in the likelihood of graduating from college or obtaining a post-graduate degree (namely the two top categories) ranked by religious group.

The largest gender gaps are found among Muslims, followed by the Protestant denominations. Among these groupings men had substantially more education than women. Gender gaps were found also among the Other Religions/NRM groupings and the Nones but in the opposite direction: Women attained higher educational levels than men.

In Eastern religions, education levels were high for both men and women and the M:F ratios in higher education have an index of 1.00, indicating gender equality in education. In fact there are some surprises, for on this statistic Mormons, Baptists, and Pentecostals are more educationally egalitarian than Jews, Catholics, and Mainline Christians (though of course at lower overall levels of education).

Figure 8.3

Ratio of Males : Females in the Proportion of College Graduates and Post Graduate School by Religious Tradition

RELIGIOUS TRADITION	M : F RATIO IN PROPORTION OF COLLEGE GRADUATE OR MORE
Muslim	1.31
Protestant denominations	1.21
Mainline Christian	1.14
Jewish	1.14
Catholic	1.12
Total U.S. Adult Population	**1.09**
Christian Generic	1.07
Mormon	1.02
Baptist	1.00
Eastern Religions	1.00
Pentecostal/Charismatic	0.99
No religion	0.96
NRM & Other Religions	0.84

Employment Status

Going beyond educational attainment, the ARIS data allow us to explore economic activities of men and women across the religious denominations and thereby the socioeconomic situation of women.

As was mentioned earlier, in certain religions the domestic role is assigned to women, and the provider role is prescribed for men. A religion with this patriarchal outlook contributes to the continued economic dependence of women. As the traditional German expression maintains, the domain of women is "Kinder, Kuche, und Kirche"—children, kitchen, and church.

Participation in the workforce has both economic and social implications. Work has a potential to increase a person's wealth, social interactions, and human capital (experience, seniority, etc.). The analysis of people of working age, namely adults under age 65, presented in Figures 8.4 and 8.5 shows that 76 percent of men and 54 percent of women worked full-time in 2001. Consequently women were far more likely to be not working or working part-time than were men. The data show that religious differences seem to have a greater effect on variation in full-time employment rates between men and women than they do on educational outcomes.

The range among the religious groupings in the proportion in full-time work was only 12 percentage points among males and followed no particular "theological" trend. In contrast the gaps between the religious traditions for females were much wider, on the order of 40 points, and more differentiated. Women in the liberal groupings were more likely to be economically active while the socially conservative and pro-natalist religious traditions had the smallest proportions of full-time women workers.

Turning to the issue of economic inactivity, age plays a major role. While more than 54 percent of economically inactive males and 36 percent of economically inactive females aged 18 to 34 were students, the majority of economically inactive female aged 35 to 49 were homemakers (62 percent). After age 50, economically inactive adults, both males and females, tend to be retired people.

Once education is completed, women face the options of homemaking, part-time work, and full-time career. The data in Figure 8.5, showing labor-force participation for women aged 18 to 64, derive from several competing forces, not just religious orientation. Economic needs, the burden of young children at home, the availability of child care, as well as the local labor market all affect the pattern of employment. Economic necessity generally encourages high rates

Figure 8.4

Employment Status by Religious Tradition
Males aged 18 to 64

RELIGIOUS TRADITION	FULL-TIME	PART-TIME	NOT EMPLOYED	TOTAL*
Catholic	78%	8%	14%	100%
Mainline Christian	80	6	14	100
Baptist	75	7	18	100
Christian Generic	72	11	17	100
Pentecostal/Charismatic	73	10	17	100
Protestant Denominations	72	9	20	100
Mormon	79	8	13	100
Jewish	78	5	17	100
Eastern Religions	66	9	25	100
Muslim	74	14	12	100
NRM & Other Religions	68	12	20	100
No religion	74	10	16	100
U.S. Total Males, Ages 18-64	**76**	**8**	**16**	**100**

* Some of the rows do not sum to 100% due to refusals to the employment
status question.

Table 8.5

Employment Status by Religious Tradition
Females aged 18 to 64

RELIGIOUS TRADITION	FULL-TIME	PART-TIME	NOT EMPLOYED	TOTAL⁵
Catholic	54%	18%	28%	100%
Mainline Christian	56	17	27	100
Baptist	54	13	32	100
Christian Generic	52	16	31	100
Pentecostal/Charismatic	48	17	35	100
Protestant denominations	50	18	32	100
Mormon	34	20	45	100
Jewish	52	21	27	100
Eastern Religions	42	21	37	100
Muslim	20	34	46	100
NRM & Other Religions	60	14	26	100
No religion	57	15	27	100
U.S. Total Females, Ages 18-64	**54**	**16**	**30**	**100**

* Some of the rows do not sum to 100% due to refusals to the employment
status question.

of labor-force participation, especially for unmarried women.

Today the vast majority of women in the prime childbearing years are economically active in some way. However, the proportion of women in full-time employment varies by a factor of three (60 percent Other/NRM; 20 percent for Muslim) between the two polarities among the religious groups shown in Figure 8.5. This large range obviously reflects differences in religious values and the variation in the restrictions imposed on women by the different religions. Muslim women were quite similar to Mormons in their overall participation in the labor force; about 45 percent each of Muslim and Mormon women were not employed. Muslim women were the most likely among women to work part-time while Mormon women were more likely to work full-time.

Gender inequality in the work force

The religious effect is most noticeable when male and female full-time employment rates are compared across the religious traditions as in Figure 8.6. These ratios confirm what Kosmin and Lachman (1993) discovered in 1990, that religious differences had a greater effect on variations in employment than educational attainment between men and women. The variations in full-time employment rates between men and women for Muslims are more than three times as high as the ratio for the Other Religions/NRM category. A clear liberal-conservative continuum again emerges which impacts the labor market and the composition of the national labor force.

Homemakers

Among those women who are not economically active there are differences in the roles they play. In order to illustrate this phenomenon Figure 8.7 focuses on economically inactive females aged 35 to 49. The proportion of women in this age cohort who described themselves as homemakers varies substantially, from 43 percent among the New Reli-

Figure 8.6

Ratio of Males : Females Aged 18 to 64 Years in Full-Time Employment by Religious Tradition

RELIGIOUS TRADITION	M:F RATIO IN FULL-TIME EMPLOYMENT
Muslim	3.69
Mormon	2.30
Eastern Religions	1.57
Pentecostal/Charismatic	1.53
Jewish	1.49
Catholic	1.44
Protestant Denominations	1.44
Mainline Christian	1.43
Total U.S. Adult Population	**1.41**
Baptist	1.38
Christian Generic	1.38
No religion	1.29
NRM & Other Religions	1.13

gions to 82 percent of Muslims and 83 percent of Mormons. Figure 8.7, which shows the proportion of homemakers in the various religious groupings, could be useful to marketers as it shows who is likely to be at home to receive a daytime call or visit. It mirrors the demographic pattern we observed in Chapter 6 with those having the largest families at the top of the chart. The exceptions are the Baptist and Pentecostals, which reflects their racial composition. Both groupings have a high proportion of African-Americans in their ranks and labor force participation rates of black women are higher than the national average.

Figure 8.7

Homemakers by Religious Tradition among Economically Inactive Females Aged 35 to 49
(in percent)

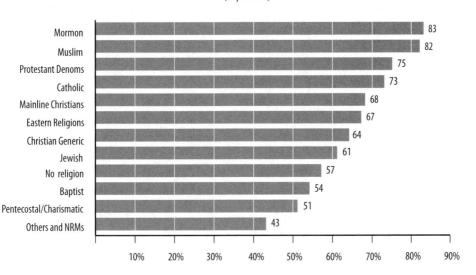

The Liberal-Conservative Continuum

With regard to key socioeconomic indicators such as income, education, employment and home ownership, inequalities and gradients exist between America's religious groups. The religious denominations and traditions tend to fall along a liberal-conservative continuum which is highly correlated with women's socioeconomic attainment. The major clusters appear at either end of the spectrum. The first cluster includes the sects, such as Jehovah's Witnesses, Mormons, and Pentecostals. The opposite extreme includes moderates and liberals, comprised of the non-Christian groups, the Episcopalians, and the Eastern Orthodox. The status rankings are easily explained. The liberal religious groups are more likely to be dual-earner than single-earner households. Over time, economic advantage is transferred to the next generation, which, in turn, can attain higher levels of education and economic prosperity. This analysis suggests that the observed social-status ranking of America's religious denominations is unlikely to change. Max Weber's theory seems to be verified by the ARIS data; different religious doctrines in contemporary America have visible and tangible consequences for adherents' social outlooks and economic behaviors.

However, the socioeconomic implications go beyond aggregate patterns particularly where females are involved. They suggest that individuals, especially women, in some religious groups have greater control over their own lives while others lack personal autonomy. The tendency is for adherents of liberal religions to have autonomy and for conservatives to lack it. Elements of social selection can be both a cause and a result of such religious orientations in a religious market that has a marked degree of switching. In other words people, especially today's women, can exercise the freedom to leave or join groups according to their own desires and psychological needs for personal advancement. In recent decades the burgeoning educational and employment opportunities for women have encouraged such mobility. The end result is to reinforce and perpetuate gender differences in human capital formation between religious groups and traditions that have economic repercussions in terms of family incomes and in social prestige.

Notes

1. Barry Kosmin, Ariela Keysar, and Nava Lerer, "Secular Education and the Religious Profile of Contemporary Black and White Americans", *Journal for the Scientific Study of Religion*, Vol.31 (4), 1992, pp. 523–532.

NINE

Socioeconomic Rankings

Social Prestige

HISTORICALLY, certain religious denominations in America have had higher social status than others. Those with the highest social status have been the mainline liberal churches associated with the oldest wave of immigrants from Britain, such as Episcopalians, the Presbyterians, and the UCC/Congregationalists, a pattern that was first recognized by H. Richard Niebuhr in his 1929 book, *The Social Sources of Denominationalism.*

This link between certain religious groups and high social prestige in a society as open as the United States is not just a matter of birth and family connections. Religious mobility follows social mobility. Upwardly mobile, career-minded individuals seek to join denominations with high social status like the Episcopalian and Presbyterian churches. The voluntary nature of American religion encourages people to "shop around," increasing the likelihood that changes in affiliation coincide with changes in social standing. This status-transmission theory also works in reverse; persons who cannot socially keep up or fit in with the rest of the denomination will move to a congregation of a more compatible class. Among the non-Catholic Christian majority of the nation this often entails switching from a mainline denomination to a more conservative church or to one of the smaller fundamentalist sects.

The Protestant Ethic

The German sociologist Max Weber famously asserted that Protestantism was the locomotive of capitalism. The Weberian school maintains that Puritanism and its evangelical offshoots created a morality that inspired individualism, activism, and pragmatism, and encouraged perseverance and personal effort among its followers. The Calvinist spiritual goal of personal achievement of grace oriented such Protestants towards adopting the goal of personal achievement in economic life as well. Historical research has largely negated this theory but it still has salience as a social force and organizing principle among conservative Protestant denominations and sects.

Yet some commentators have suggested that economic trends in society since the 1950s should have produced secularization. Structural changes in the economy have had a deleterious impact on the "Protestant ethic" and "Puritanism," as enjoyment through consumption has almost become an obligation to Americans. Some would even suggest that corporations through the power of their ubiquitous advertising have taken the traditional role of religion as arbiter of taste. It also could be feasibly argued that in contemporary consumer society, corporations determine group norms, especially for the nation's youth.

Such developments have been contentious issues for conservative religious sects, and lay at the heart of their hostility to modernizing social and economic trends in the first half of the 20th century. They looked back with nostalgia to a less-complicated small-town society close to the original Puritan model. Their leaders regretted the displacement of small business by large-scale corporations and international conglomerates and they criticized the glorification of consumption and readily available credit because it undermined thrift and the belief in deferred gratification.

The conservative advocacy of the traditional Protestant ethic is based not only on the value placed on virtues, but also on the judgment of vices. For instance, conservatives still hold to the Victorian opinion that associated poverty with laziness and alcohol (drugs have since been added to the equation). This can create tension around values, as most fundamentalists and evangelicals also hold to the American business creed, which espouses the value of competition, the dignity of work, the right of the individual in the marketplace, the desirability of material possessions, and the willingness to take risks. Yet they condemn much of the major corporations' material output (along with welfare, government regulations, and labor unions). In recent years they have been particularly upset by "Hollywood" and the advertising of major corporations in the fast-expanding media, clothing, equipment, leisure, and travel industries, which has engendered a hedonistic "fun" morality hostile to traditional Puritan ethics. Nevertheless today their economic critique has become muted in the political arena as they have embraced the Republican Party and come to terms with the consequences of market capitalism (See Chapter 13). One by-product is that the agenda and energy of conservative Christians is now more focused on social issues.

The Data on Social Standing

Elements of the "Protestant ethic" have been absorbed into modern American values as indices of success, "making it," and even the "yuppie lifestyle." Contemporary America in its embrace of educational credentials places considerable emphasis on meritocracy, by which occupations and roles are assigned according to qualifications, such as college diplomas. In 1776 Adam Smith postulated that "an instructed and intelligent people . . . are always more decent and orderly than an ignorant stupid one."[1] The extension of this in the meritocratic atmosphere of the United States in the 1950s, according to Will Herberg, was that "the American believes in progress, in self-improvement and quite fanatically in education."[2] In the spirit of the free market, America also respects and values hard work; people who work full-time are considered more acceptable than, for instance, unemployed people who receive welfare. Property and home ownership are a symbol of a participating and taxpaying member of society with a stake in the market "system." Finally, in a free-market society with open careers and opportunities, financial success is a desirable aspiration and both a tangible and a symbolic token of personal accomplishment.

ARIS provides us with the opportunity to inquire in considerable detail into the actual relationship of social-class factors and the pattern of religious identification. We do this by comparing a range of social indicators relating to "the American dream"—a good education, a secure job, a good income, and a nice home. The four indicators we have chosen are the pattern of employment, the level of educational attainment, the extent of home ownership, and the level of household income. The first two indicators are individual characteristics of respondents. The latter two are household characteristics though in these cases the households are classified by the religious identification of the respondent. Since socioeconomic indicators were collected for all 50,000 households for this analysis, we have taken the opportunity to go beyond the more limited numbers of religious traditions and assemble data on these four social variables relating to the 24 largest religious identification groups in society. The religious groups are listed according to their rank-order position on these four variables and finally on their overall aggregate score on the "socioeconomic index." In this manner we obtain an overall picture of the relative social standing of the religious groups in the country today. Of course, every religious group contains a variety of people from all status levels but the smaller ones are likelier to be unique in character. On the other hand the larger groups are more likely to be normal or closer to the national average because they are subject to the statistical phenomena of the law of large numbers and the bell curve. However, although the differences between some groups and denominations are small, clear patterns and hierarchies of social rankings do emerge.

Ranking by educational attainment

Figure 9.1, like the educational tables presented in the previous chapter, shows that percentages of college graduates vary widely from group to group. The range in college graduation rates is an enormous 60 percentage points between the top and bottom groups. Cultural factors emphasizing the role of higher education and motivating adherents to obtain the post-graduate degrees requisite for professional careers are reflected in the statistics and might explain the variations between the religious groups. Overall, Unitarian-Universalists, an outgrowth of New England's liberal 19th-century theology, achieved the highest educational level, higher than Hindus and Jews. The ranking of certain groups' educational achievements is not random. Jews, for example, do well in measures of education because of a general orientation arising from Jewish intellectual traditions. They place a high value on education, sacrifice to obtain it, and persevere once they enter the system. The exceptions are significant elements in the Orthodox community, including the Hasidim, who are similar to the Protestant fundamentalist sects in their disdain for secular general education.

Figure 9.1

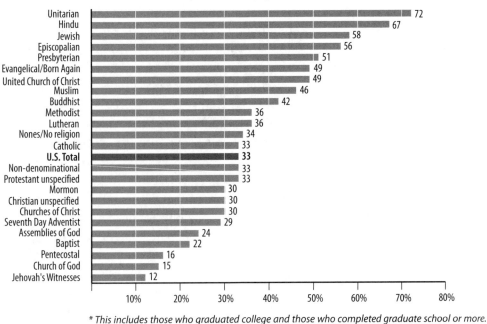

Educational Ranking by Religious Group
(percent of college graduates*)

Religious Group	%
Unitarian	72
Hindu	67
Jewish	58
Episcopalian	56
Presbyterian	51
Evangelical/Born Again	49
United Church of Christ	49
Muslim	46
Buddhist	42
Methodist	36
Lutheran	36
Nones/No religion	34
Catholic	33
U.S. Total	**33**
Non-denominational	33
Protestant unspecified	33
Mormon	30
Christian unspecified	30
Churches of Christ	30
Seventh Day Adventist	29
Assemblies of God	24
Baptist	22
Pentecostal	16
Church of God	15
Jehovah's Witnesses	12

* This includes those who graduated college and those who completed graduate school or more.

The highest-ranked Christians are in the mainline liberal churches. Mainline Protestants do well academically largely because the prestigious institutions within the American educational system are "their system." Many of America's colleges and much of its system of higher education were founded by the various Protestant denominations, and its intellectual and moral coloration was heavily tinted with Calvinism. Most college presidents, trustees, and faculty members were ministers whose appointments depended on their beliefs. Right up to World War II, religion was still prominent in the college and entered the curriculum as moral philosophy that attempted to integrate the entire course of study and instill a common set of social values. Most studies have shown that the differences in occupation and income between groups in American society are largely due to differences in education. However, certain nominally Mainline Protestant or Christian preparatory schools and private colleges have served a social rather than religious purpose. Elite networks and valuable contacts begin in these settings. This kind of socializing is also important in achieving success in many areas of economic life.

An exception to the Protestant traditions' attention to higher secular education is found among fundamentalist Protestants. It is not just a matter of social status. Some are overtly anti-intellectual and hostile to secular education. Others tend to reject worldly knowledge and are suspicious of the claims of science—especially biology and geology and the theories regarding natural selection and age of the world, which can be seen as challenging their beliefs regarding biblical inerrancy. Adherents of such groups prefer to devote themselves to the study of their own sacred texts, which they view as the font of all wisdom. Some argue that secular knowledge is polluting or dangerous to the moral integrity or soul of the individual. However, this association of conservative religious beliefs and poor education is changing. An unexpected finding and new phenomenon is the relatively high proportion of college graduates among self-identified Evangelical and Born-Again respondents as well as Muslims, who stand in sixth and eighth positions respectively in the educational rankings. This trend probably reflects a feature of recent American higher education which is the establishment of new evangelical Christian colleges over the past two decades. This emphasis on producing a new generation of articulate and socioeconomically "successful" members is a new strategy which as we shall show below is beginning to have considerable repercussions in American society in changing the "image" of evangelical and born-again Christians.

It is always heartening to have corroboration of the ARIS findings from a credible source based on robust statistics. One of the few large-scale published annual collections of educational data by religious identification comes from the College Board. It records the average group scores out of a possible 1600 points for those high school seniors who take

Figure 9.2

Average SAT Scores for Top Ten Religious Denominations/Tradition, 2001

Unitarian-Universalist *(Other Religions/NRM)*	1209
Jewish	1161
Quaker *(Mainline Christian)*	1153
Hindu *(Eastern Religions)*	1110
Mennonite *(Protestant denominations)*	1097
Reformed Church *(Mainline Christian)*	1097
Episcopalian *(Mainline Christian)*	1096
Evangelical Lutheran *(Mainline Christian)*	1094
Presbyterian *(Mainline Christian)*	1092
Baha'i *(Eastern Religions)*	1073
National average	**1020**

Source: College Board

the Scholastic Aptitude Tests for college entrance. Figure 9.2 corre-lates very closely with Figure 9.1. The College Board sample is excep-tionally large covering over one million registered students. Such large numbers of candidates ensure robust and valid statistics even for small religious groups. For example the scores in Figure 9.2 for the Unitarians are based on 2,354 cases and for Jews on 27,120 cases.

Ranking by full-time employment

Overall, full-time employment of the adult population aged 18 to 64 did not vary greatly across religious groups. In Figure 9.3 the range between the top and bottom figures is much narrower than for educational attainment, only 16 percentage points. Unitarian and Lutheran adults were the most likely to be employed full-time, whereas those who self-identified as Jehovah's Witnesses and Muslims were the least likely.

Figure 9.3

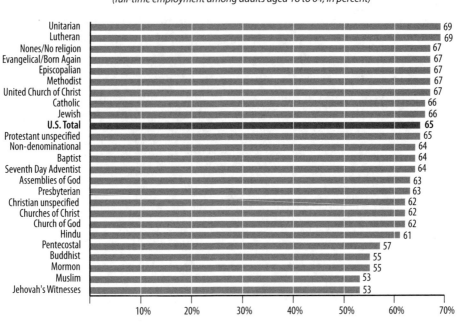

Employment Ranking by Religious Group
(full-time employment among adults aged 18 to 64, in percent)

Religious Group	Percent
Unitarian	69
Lutheran	69
Nones/No religion	67
Evangelical/Born Again	67
Episcopalian	67
Methodist	67
United Church of Christ	67
Catholic	66
Jewish	66
U.S. Total	**65**
Protestant unspecified	65
Non-denominational	64
Baptist	64
Seventh Day Adventist	64
Assemblies of God	63
Presbyterian	63
Christian unspecified	62
Churches of Christ	62
Church of God	62
Hindu	61
Pentecostal	57
Buddhist	55
Mormon	55
Muslim	53
Jehovah's Witnesses	53

The impact on this factor of some groups' beliefs relating to the role and status of women, discussed earlier, means that some groups have more female homemakers in their ranks. Demographics are also a factor. The relatively youthful age structure of Hindus and Buddhists means they have more students in their ranks, which in turn results in fewer economically active adults. The occupational structure is another factor. Groups that have a large proportion of public employees such as teachers, police, or members of the military with early and compulsory retirement ages have reduced numbers of full-time workers. In contrast, groups with larger proportions of self-employed people such as family farmers and small-business owners who can work for as long as they wish will tend to rank higher on this factor.

Income ranking

Figure 9.4 presents the ranking of religious groups according to their median household income in 2000. Since the top income range for ARIS was simply "over $100,000," it is not possible to give an accurate figure for mean average incomes. Instead we report the median income, that is, the total household income that divides the group into two halves. One caution is necessary here: The refusal rate to the ARIS income item was the highest. Overall it was 16 percent and it ranged from 11 percent among Adventists up to 22 percent among Buddhists.

Household income is a function of a number of factors, especially the two previous indices: educational attainment or qualifications. However, the primary factor is the number of earners in the home. Groups with large numbers of dual income households will obviously tend to stand higher on this item. Two well-educated people in full-time employment, the professional couple, will be near the top of any income scale.

Social trends also play their part. In the 1980s a new social trend arose with the growth of a leisure industry geared to the health conscious baby boom/yuppie generation. More people than ever before spent their weekends pursuing recreational activities with high entry costs, such as tennis, skiing, sailing, golf, and horseback riding. As a result upper-middle-class people, especially those without young children, were less likely to be involved in religious activities. Such trends suggest we should not expect high earners to be found in large proportions among the strict religious groups.

Income appears to differentiate religious groups across a wide range. Jews had the highest annual household income, followed by Unitarians, Episcopalians, Evangelicals and Hindus. The income distributions among Hindu households were similar to those of Episcopalians. These rankings tend to mirror those for education. The high standing of Hindus with regard to income suggests many in this segment of the Asian population have apparently succeeded in attaining this aspect of the "American dream." This development is socially significant for the future of American society. Ironically, Eastern religions in their natural environment in Asia have tended to stress passivity, detachment from the world, and contemplation

Figure 9.4

Income Ranking by Religious Group: Median Annual Household Income in 2000
(in U.S. dollars)

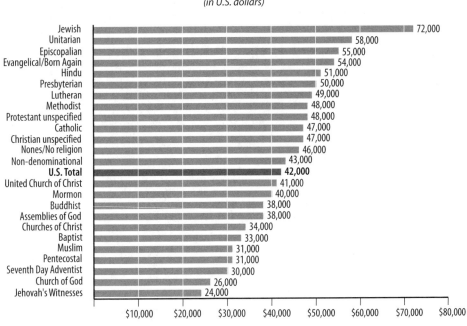

of the inner being, to the detriment of economic development. However, in the past few decades U.S. government policy and immigration preferences have skewed the Asian immigrant population towards the "middle classes" and the professionally qualified. It is noteworthy that as early as 1990 the U.S. Census reported that, overall, Asian median household incomes exceeded white incomes by over $5,000 a year.

One interesting observation is that Jews and Evangelicals are most adept at leveraging their educational advantage into high income since they both stand higher on the income ranking than the educational one. As with most social indicators, race affects the results. Asian and white incomes are much higher than black or Hispanic incomes in the United States. Thus, any religious group's median average is affected by the proportion of its adherents who are black or Hispanic (see Chapter 14). For some groups such as Catholics, Baptists, Muslims and Pentecostals this factor is of considerable importance in their overall position.

Household size also affects per-capita income and spending power. Indeed, we know that for many of the high-income groups at the top of Figure 9.4, household size is comparatively low; therefore, it is possible to argue that the real economic difference between Jews, Unitarians, and Episcopalians as compared with Baptists, Pentecostals, and Holiness adherents is actually wider than it appears. On the other hand the high-income groups tend to be concentrated in the larger metropolitan areas where the cost of living, and especially of housing, is high, so the gap in terms of discretionary income may be overstated.

Figure 9.5 is worthy of attention not only for the greater detail it provides. It shows that most religious groups' income profiles are skewed to one polarity or another; i.e., they are not a matter of chance. Liberals and modernists embrace the economic opportunities of the free market more. The liberal and modernist groups tend to have more affluent households and fewer poor ones while the strict religious groups have the inverse situation. This suggests our earlier comments about sectarians were correct.

Figure 9.5

Household Annual Income in 2000 by Religious Tradition/Group of the Respondent*

(in percent)

RELIGIOUS GROUP	UNDER $25,000	$25,000-49,999	$50,000-74,999	$75,000-99,999	$100,000+	DON'T KNOW/ REFUSED	TOTAL
Catholic	20.4%	24.9%	17.9%	10.7%	12.9%	13.1%	100%
Mainline Christians	20.2	25.6	17.2	10.8	12.9	13.2	100
Methodist	23.2	26.3	15.8	10.3	10.6	13.9	100
Lutheran	20.0	24.3	18.9	12.0	12.7	12.2	100
Presbyterian	15.6	28.0	17.3	11.9	14.4	12.8	100
Episcopalian	17.0	23.2	18.3	10.8	18.0	12.7	100
United Church of Christ	21.2	27.7	15.3	6.7	14.7	14.5	100
Baptist	31.8	27.4	14.7	6.9	6.3	12.9	100
Christian Generic	21.2	26.9	17.3	8.5	10.6	15.6	100
Christian unspecified	21.1	27.5	17.2	8.5	10.7	15.1	100
Protestant unspecified	22.6	23.1	16.2	8.5	10.0	19.6	100
Evangelical/Born Again	16.1	22.8	24.6	12.8	11.0	12.7	100
Non-denominational	18.9	33.0	17.8	7.5	11.3	11.5	100
Pentecostal/Charismatic	34.1	28.5	14.2	6.6	3.6	12.9	100
Assemblies of God	23.9	29.3	17.1	6.1	8.2	15.4	100
Church of God	42.0	23.1	13.5	4.9	3.1	13.3	100
Pentecostal unspecified	33.5	29.7	14.6	6.5	3.3	12.5	100
Protestant Denominations	30.8	27.0	13.2	7.9	6.2	14.9	100
Churches of Christ	29.4	25.4	13.5	9.4	5.8	16.6	100
Jehovah's Witnesses	37.9	27.2	12.8	6.9	2.7	12.5	100
Seventh Day Adventist	32.7	27.8	8.1	8.1	12.2	11.1	100
Mormon	21.8	31.2	18.7	9.0	7.7	11.7	100
Jewish	10.6	18.1	13.0	8.9	29.6	19.6	100
Eastern Religions	24.9	25.4	16.2	4.4	11.6	17.6	100
Buddhist	29.4	24.6	12.4	4.4	7.5	21.7	100
Hindu	17.4	25.5	22.1	4.6	18.3	12.0	100
Muslim	36.1	21.9	9.8	7.1	11.0	14.2	100
NRM & Other Religions	26.4	23.5	14.2	10.6	13.8	11.4	100
Unitarian-Universalist	18.4	21.0	15.4	12.1	21.4	11.5	100
Nones/No religion	23.2	25.1	16.6	8.8	13.2	13.1	100
Total U.S. Households	**23.0**	**25.1**	**15.9**	**8.9**	**10.9**	**16.3**	**100**

Note: Rows may not add to 100 percent due to rounding.

Ranking by home ownership

Home ownership is a desirable goal in American society. It provides a secure investment, social standing in the community, and a sense of belonging to a locality. Owning your own home is not directly affected by income; it appears to be more closely related to age, area of residence, and religious affiliation, though the last factor may be strongly connected to the first two. Since it is linked to thrift, home ownership may be thought to have some ties to the "Protestant ethic." It could also be that property ownership is attractive to those seeking social status and who are not able to obtain it professionally or by other forms of consumption. Property has symbolic as well as intrinsic value. It is also real wealth that can be inherited by children and family members.

Figure 9.6 shows that rates of home ownership (including with a mortgage) vary widely across the groups with a range of 44 percentage points between the top and the bottom groups. The Mainline Christians and other groups in the Protestant traditions have the highest rates of home ownership, particularly those groups that are attractive to the elderly or to residents of rural areas. Presbyterians, Methodists and Lutherans have home ownership rates of 80 percent or more. Some groups that stood high on the previous ranking indices are much lower down on this one. In part this is because many urban dwellers, especially in the large metropolitan centers, are renters. This is particularly true for Jews, Unitarians, and Catholics all of whom have surprisingly low rates of home ownership (72 to 73 percent) and are concentrated in cities.

Note that mainly non-Christian groups such as Buddhists and Hindus, groups that rank high in terms of education and mid-range on full-time employment and income have the lowest rates of home ownership. They tend to concentrate in coastal states such as California, New York, and Florida and metropolitan areas where property prices are high and where it is difficult for young people to get on the property ladder. Interestingly, Muslims and Hindus showed similar low levels of home ownership despite their different income levels. This seems to suggest that adherents of these religious groups are not yet fully integrated or participating members of an American society, which considers owning one's own home as the achievement of the American dream. More predictably, sects with low overall social ranking on most indices, such as the Jehovah's Witnesses and Pentecostals, also have low rates of home ownership. This is where racial composition is a factor. Religious groups with a large black constituency are affected by the disadvantaged situation of blacks in society. For instance, black incomes are still considerably lower than white and Asian incomes, and presumably as a result only half of black households own their home while around three in four white households do.

Figure 9.6

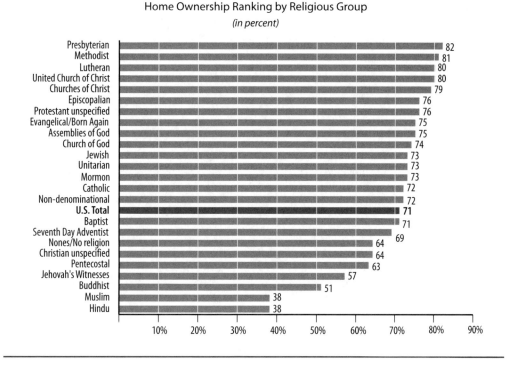

Home Ownership Ranking by Religious Group
(in percent)

Social Ranking and the Religious Pecking Order

Figure 9.7 is a composite of the 24 religious groups' scores on the four socioeconomic indices associated with aggregate "social standing" in American society. The lower the total scores the higher the ranking or relative position. The internal composition of the religious groups affects all four variables. Race and gender have a major impact, and factors such as age and the number of generations of the respondent's family that have lived in this country affect the figures as well.

Figure 9.7

Rankings by Religious Group on Socioeconomic Indicators

	HIGHER EDUCATION	EMPLOY-MENT	INCOME	HOME OWNERSHIP	TOTAL POINTS	POSITION
Unitarian-Universalist	1	1	2	12	**16**	1
Episcopalian	4	5	3	6	18	2
Evangelical/Born Again	6	4	4	8	22	3
Lutheran	11	2	7	3	23	4
Jewish	3	9	1	11	24	5
Methodist	10	6	8	2	26	6
Presbyterian	5	15	6	1	27	7
UCC/Congregational	7	7	14	4	32	8
Protestant unspecified	15	10	9	7	41	9
Catholic	13	8	10	14	45	10
No religion	12	3	12	18	45	11
Hindu	2	19	5	**24**	50	12
Non-denominational	14	11	13	15	53	13
Assemblies of God	20	14	17	9	60	14
Christian unspecified	17	16	11	19	63	15
Churches of Christ	18	17	23	5	63	16
Mormon	16	22	15	13	66	17
Baptist	21	12	19	16	68	18
Buddhist	9	21	16	22	68	19
Church of God	23	18	18	10	69	20
Seventh Day Adventists	19	13	22	17	71	21
Muslim	8	23	20	23	74	22
Pentecostal	22	20	21	20	83	23
Jehovah's Witnesses	**24**	**24**	**24**	21	**93**	**24**

The first position is held by Unitarian-Universalists, a group with a "Yankee pedigree" and a long history of high status and prestige in American society. Theirs is a very liberal religion both in theological and social outlook that is known for embracing modernism. The second position is held by the Episcopalians, another of the historically high-status Protestant "establishment" denominations. Both groups are urban, upper middle-class populations historically prominent and over-represented in the nation's political and cultural life. A newcomer group in both senses of the term then follows. This is the Evangelical/Born-Again Christian group which is composed of individuals who responded to ARIS by self-defining with these theological categories rather than with any of the traditional denominational labels. The Lutherans, a large group within the Mainline tradition, stand just ahead of the Jews. The Jewish ranking is unsurprising since it has been shown that on many demographic and social indicators Jews are very similar to Mainline Christian groups among whom they are positioned in this table.

The social-standing figures demonstrate that large, variegated groups of diverse origins such as Catholics and Nones have similar middle-range social standing. One surprise is the poor showing of Mormons. However, the explanation, as possibly with the Lutherans, is regional concentration, though in the Mormon case it is detrimental. Data from the U.S. Bureau of Economic Analysis on personal income per capita in the Mountain states support the ARIS findings: according to this indicator, Mormon-Majority Utah was ranked number 46, and Idaho, which contains a Mormon plurality, stood at number 40.

The lowest social rankings were held by the groups in the Holiness tradition or sects as well as the Muslims. Since piety and religiosity are increasingly associated with lower-middle-class families, conservative Protestantism is flourishing. The explanatory theory for this is that less-well-off classes tend to be found at the conservative end of the religious spectrum because people facing uncertainty and instability in their lives, whether social or economic, look towards religious groups with more structure and fewer interpretative options, i.e., toward the fundamentalist denominations. It has been suggested that the better off middle and upper classes like to *do* their religion and attend worship services while the lower classes are more inclined to *feel* it. This theory accounts for the fact that expressive religions such as Pentecostalism are regarded as a "haven for the dispossessed." In this formulation, certain religious traditions can be seen as a channel for frustration resulting from socioeconomic inequalities.

In the light of what is often believed about the relationship between religion and social values, the results in Figure 9.7 might seem paradoxical. In the religious divide between conservatives and liberals, the higher social-status groups tend to be concentrated at the liberal end of the spectrum, with the important exception of the black churches. In the political realm (see Chapter 13), the adherents of the successful modernist liberal and secular groups and their institutions generally tend to be most critical of the *status quo* and more amenable to economic and social reform and welfare-state ideas. In contrast, the strongest supporters of the Republican Party and the free-enterprise system are the theologically conservative, evangelical, and fundamentalist groups, whose followers do not appear to be very successful socioeconomically. The exception to the rule is, of course, the self-identified "Evangelicals" who have emerged as a high-status group. They are affluent and well-educated and presumably articulate and self-confident. Their place near the top of the pecking order which up to now has been dominated by liberal and modernist groups is a significant event for American religion and society.

Notes

1. Adam Smith, *The Wealth of Nations*, 1776, Book V, Chapter 1, Part 3, Article II.
2. Will Herberg, *Protestant, Catholic, Jew: An Essay in American Religious Sociology*, Doubleday, Garden City, NY, 1955.

TEN

Patterns of Consumption of Modern Technologies

Market Research

SO FAR it has been demonstrated that many religious groups form cultural communities with distinct levels of social status and income in part due to their different levels of acceptance of modernism and material values. But how far do these differences translate into different patterns of consumption apart from obvious areas affected by religious doctrine such as diet, for example the food and beverage rules of Jews, Mormons, Muslims and Adventists? Do religious groups vary in their purchases of technologies and products related to home entertainment? One might expect them to do so because these products are associated with consumer choice, individual choice, informality, and personal expression. Certainly two small groups, the Amish sect of the Mennonite Church and the Hasidic sects of Judaism abjure watching television. In the Amish case it is a consequence of their non-use of electricity, while Hasidim reject TV and the internet because of their potentially immoral or unwelcome content.

ARIS thus provided the opportunity for some unique market research into religious segmentation in the marketplace. We chose to focus on the new technologies that are such a prominent symbol of 21st-century society and are now so available and important in the modern economy. A sub-sample of one-third of ARIS respondents received a CENTRIS omnibus questionnaire with questions on their households' ownership or use of modern technologies in early 2001. TV ownership was found to be ubiquitous across all the religious groups and traditions large enough to analyze properly. Cable television was received by a majority (50 to 60 percent) of all groups, with the exception of Seventh Day Adventists, where only 39 percent of households had it. Several other items which were then relatively new products on the market were investigated. These were thought to relate to both discretionary spending and "buy in" to the fashion for home entertainment. The findings for the five product items chosen are presented in Figure 10.1.

In 2001 around one in four American household subscribed to satellite TV. Subscriptions were lowest at 15 percent among Evangelicals and non-denominational Christians. This might suggest a conservative religious skew, except that the adherents of Assemblies of God in the Pentecostal tradition were more likely customers along with the "Protestants" and Muslims. High rates of subscribership to satellite TV among these groups might be explained by geography. Assemblies of God and Pentecostals tend to live in rural areas where satellite viewership is more common. They may also prefer satellite TV because it offers a wider range of "religious" programming than cable TV offers. Satellite TV's offering native language and Middle Eastern channels is another possible explanation. Large screen TVs were most popular among Muslims (20 percent) and least popular among Adventists (5 percent) and Evangelicals (3 percent).

Video games have received adverse publicity for their supposedly harmful influence on children due to both their sometimes antisocial and violent content and their habit-forming nature. However, though again levels of ownership were low, there was no pattern of rejection across the theological spectrum. These games were most popular among Muslim households (19 percent) and least popular in UCC and Jewish homes (5 percent). As regards recent video purchase, the content of videos can of course vary from the educational to the erotic. Mormons (12 percent) were the most frequent purchasers while again Jewish households (2 percent) were the least likely purchasers. This suggests that an age bias or the presence of children in the home was more important than religious outlook for many of these products.

Finally DVD ownership, for which content can again vary but is most likely to be movies, was most popular among Hindus (18 percent) and least popular among Adventists (2 percent). In the Hindu case this probably reflects the popularity of the "Bollywood" market niche in this community. Overall these patterns on home entertainment suggest that none of the religious groups covered operated an outright ban on these products or saw this new lifestyle development as a moral threat to its adherents.

Figure 10.1

Patterns of Entertainment Technology Consumption among
Selected Religious Groups

(percent of households by respondent's religious identification)

	SATELLITE TV	LARGE SCREEN TV	VIDEO GAME SYSTEM	VIDEO CASSETTE OWNERSHIP IN PAST 30 DAYS	DVD
Assemblies of God	28%	10%	15%	8%	6%
Baptist	23	13	12	9	6
Buddhist	19	14	14	11	14
Catholic	25	15	13	9	9
Christian	25	14	15	10	10
Church of God	23	11	15	10	5
Churches of Christ	19	11	8	7	5
UCC/Congregational	19	8	5	6	6
Episcopalian	24	11	7	6	6
Evangelical	15	3	6	4	6
Hindu	27	7	7	3	18
Jehovah's Witnesses	21	8	9	9	5
Jewish	19	9	5	2	6
Lutheran	24	11	10	8	7
Methodist	24	12	9	6	6
Mormon	20	9	10	12	7
Muslim	28	20	19	7	16
Non-denominational	15	8	7	8	6
Pentecostal	23	11	13	10	7
Presbyterian	21	12	7	7	5
Protestant	28	13	10	8	7
Seventh Day Adventists	17	5	7	5	2
No religion	24	12	12	8	10
U.S. Total	**24**	**13**	**12**	**8**	**8**

Figure 10.2 relates to a battery of product items used as a measure of the take-up on innovation in the field of communications technology. Personal computer ownership in 2001 was held by around one in five American households but it was noticeably higher

among Muslims (31 percent), Buddhists (29 percent) and Hindus (25 percent). Internet access is closely related to PC ownership so again Muslims and Buddhists were the leading users. Once more this suggests a bias towards younger people and those with overseas ties because of the internet's ability to maintain contact with relatives abroad. Multiple telephone ownership was led by Jews followed by Mormons and non-denominational Christians then other groups that stood high on the income rankings.

Figure 10.2

Patterns of Innovation in Communications among Selected Religious Groups 2001

(percent of households by respondent's religious identification)

	PC OWNERSHIP	INTERNET ACCESS	MORE THAN 1 TELEPHONE IN THE HOME
Assemblies of God	19%	15%	17%
Baptist	15	12	17
Buddhist	29	20	23
Catholic	20	16	20
Christian	22	18	22
Church of God	15	10	14
Churches of Christ	17	12	16
Congregational	15	12	15
Episcopalian	18	16	22
Evangelical	14	12	21
Hindu	25	18	15
Jehovah's Witnesses	17	12	17
Jewish	16	15	31
Lutheran	19	16	19
Methodist	17	14	18
Mormon	21	16	24
Muslim	31	23	19
Non-denominational	16	11	24
Pentecostal	17	13	18
Presbyterian	17	15	19
Protestant	19	16	15
Seventh Day Adventists	19	13	14
No religion	21	18	21
U.S. Total	**20**	**16**	**19**

Overall the analysis of the data on patterns of communications technology consumption like home entertainment devices suggests that religion is not a significant factor in this realm so that for example, Catholic and No Religion patterns are almost identical across the tables. Differences that are found on income and education are not reproduced in the area of technology consumption. This is an important finding since it suggests that none of the religious groups feels this is an arena for values conflict or believes it needs to take an anti-modernist stance over these 21st-century products. This trend seems to reinforce the notion mentioned earlier that because technology is now regarded as neutral and not inherently destructive of humanity and religious values conservative religious groups no longer concentrate their societal critique on economic issues and materialism as such but on the social consequences of "bad usage" of technology.

One reason may be the recognition that these technologies can be used and successfully adopted for evangelism and religious education. Just as in a previous generation TV came to be seen as a useful medium for evangelism the potential of these new technologies has been quickly identified by the clergy. Most congregations now have websites and email communications with their memberships that may well alter their cultural, interpersonal, and social dynamics. In fact there has been a whole-hearted embrace of the new technologies by most conservative religious groups. This phenomenon has been aided by the pricing policy for these products, which are obviously aimed at a mass market and are not viewed as luxury items. The new devices are amenable to personal or parental controls so that the actual content of the home entertainment and new media devices can be narrow-cast to make it compatible with religious groups' beliefs and values norms. This makes many religiously minded people less suspicious than they were in the past in relation to broadcast media such as Hollywood movies and network TV, which they believed were alien and antagonistic to their world views. In fact a major development in the American media, entertainment, and music industries is the recognition of the economic significance of the "Evangelical Christian market" along with those of other religious sub-cultures.

ELEVEN

Religious Affiliation and Recruitment

The National Picture

A KEY concern for all streams of organized religion is the pattern of religious affiliation or membership—who formally belongs or who does not belong but could or should. Despite recent innovations using new communications technology such as TV evangelism, American religion generally delivers its product locally through congregations. Their structure tends to follow the historic format established in the colonial era by the Protestant sects, namely, neighborhood groups of worshippers. In sociological terms congregations provide social solidarity in units of manageable size that deliver a community with a sense of belonging more intimate than the city or state yet larger than the extended family.

Today as in the past, local houses of worship provide significant social and welfare services and often act as community centers. In addition to religious services and traditional lifecycle rituals, they offer a variety of services and programs to their members, and sometimes to non-congregants, such as day care, nurseries, meals for shut-ins, homeless shelters, youth activities, programs for the elderly, and cultural or leisure events. Yet congregations vary in governance and operation according to the ecclesiology and role of the clergy in each particular religious group. To use a commercial analogy, some congregations are branch offices, some are franchises, and some are independent enterprises. As we noted in Chapter 3, the definition of membership varies across groups and traditions. Nevertheless ARIS found that most of the American public feels confident enough to decide when asked: *Is anyone in your household currently a member of a church, temple, or mosque?*

It is important to realize that the unit of analysis here is the individual and the household in relation to the religious group with which they identify. It is a study of affiliation patterns among the American public. All the congregations in the religious group or tradition are aggregated together. It is not an analysis of congregations of various sizes or styles.

Every religious denomination that wants to increase or even maintain its membership has to seek out and recruit new members and it relies on its local congregations for this service. Moreover, congregations are an essential part of what is variously described as the independent, voluntary, or non-profit sector of society. Yet in practice they work in a competitive environment in their struggle for souls. Along with every other center of voluntary activity, they must compete for the time, attention and resources of the public. Practicalities require them to adopt a strategy to attract funds either by attracting generous high-income or wealthy people, or by engaging sufficient numbers of members.

In recent years some churches and ministers have responded to this imperative by becoming more businesslike in their attention to social trends as a guide to successful recruitment, outreach, and missionary activities. This has been especially true among evangelical Protestants, who have often hired polling organizations to provide them with market research data. The evangelicals saw a major opportunity in America's recent demographic changes. One was the result of the demographic trend towards longevity and the resulting emergence of a large population of elderly people. The other was the large baby boom generation and particularly that segment that migrated to the sun-belt and the "exurbs." The latter are dense communities of subdivisions in recently transformed but heretofore rural counties that are too far from metro areas to be properly termed suburbs. A cohort of entrepreneurial evangelical pastors came to similar conclusions as the sociologist Ernst Troeltsch, who suggested that if a religion wants to grow, it needs "cultural fit" and a willingness to accommodate the needs of its market.

The prime market for any religious group is people who identify with its brand but have not yet purchased its "products." Membership rates—which reflect the ability to recruit from among the constituency of group identifiers—vary considerably across religious groups. For example, while 75 percent of all identifying Mormons belong to a church, only 53 percent of "Jews by religion" belong to a synagogue; among Eastern religions temple membership rates are even lower at 36 percent of all identifiers.

Therefore of special interest to religious groups must be those who self-identify with a particular religious group and consider themselves adherents of the faith or denomination but do not (yet) belong to any of its religious institutions. The goal is to strengthen the group by bringing such people into the fold so that they can become active and participating members. One of the most important sociological findings of ARIS was that although 81 percent of American adults identify with a religious group only just over half live in households where somebody is currently a member of a religious body. This means that in theory around one-third of the national population consists of potential recruits to religious congregations.

One favorite tool of "church growth" professionals, in order to target potential members, is to compare the demographic profiles of members versus non-members. For instance, if a particular group's non-members tend to be young, male, and non-white, then special outreach programs can be customized to reach them. This information is just as valuable as geographic or residential information about potential members in helping various groups that wish to expand and get their messages out.

This chapter provides a demographic analysis of membership patterns for all of the nation's religious groups showing who are the members and non-members of religious institutions. It analyzes these populations using a variety of demographic and socioeconomic characteristics: age, gender, ethnicity, education level, employment status and geography. However we must be careful not to overemphasize the "selling" component of congregations. They are places for worship, not just for relief and protection or for making social contacts.

We begin with general comparisons of those currently affiliated and those unaffiliated with organized religion among the entire national adult population. In the next chapter we will zero in on nine major religious identification groups—Catholics, Baptists, Methodists, Lutherans, Presbyterians, Pentecostals, Episcopalians,

Mormons, and Jews—to see how the process of affiliation operates in each. The research question posed is a very practical one: How do members differ from non-member adherents?

The figures that follow present statistics on a single social variable or characteristic. Each shows the proportions and population estimates for the number of adults who are members and the number of non-members, whom we term "potential members." The latter group consists of people who though identifying with a religious group in 2001 also reported that neither they nor anybody in their home was affiliated with one.

Age

Often religious affiliation is induced by a desire to have episodic personal and family lifecycle events such as baptism, marriage and funerals under religious auspices. In some groups congregational membership is necessary for these rituals. As a result membership tends to correlate with age. Families with children join religious congregations more than never-married persons, who are on average younger, and once they join they tend to remain members. As expected those least likely to be members are younger adults, under

Figure 11.1

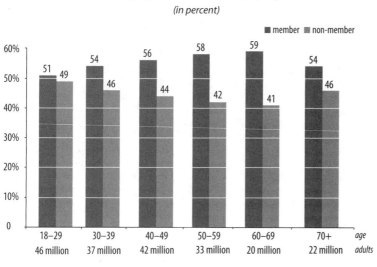

Congregational Membership by Age
(in percent)

■ member ■ non-member

age 30. Most of them have not yet married nor do they have children they wish to socialize or educate. Nevertheless they are an attractive if elusive large target group for religious leaders who wish to find new members.

Another feature of membership patterns is that as people become older they tend to drop out of activities. As shown in Figure 11.1, nationally congregational membership peaks among adults aged 60 to 69 years old, but falls after age 70. Nevertheless the most noticeable feature of Figure 11.1 is the generally flat nature of this statistic. The range in the proportion of members across the various age cohorts is quite narrow, only eight percentage points wide.

Congregational membership peaks among adults aged 60 to 69 years old, but falls after age 70.

Marital status

As shown in Chapter 5, marital status is very much correlated with religious outlook and identification since it relates to religious notions of morality. Marital status is also highly correlated with age. In fact, the pattern of congregational membership of single, never-married persons in Figure 11.2 is a mirror picture of adults aged 18 to 29 in Figure 11.1, whereas the pattern of widowed is the mirror picture of the oldest age group, those over 70 years of age.

Figure 11.2

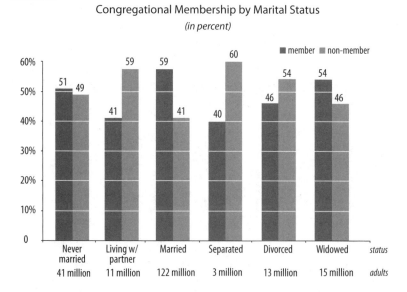

Congregational Membership by Marital Status
(in percent)

Given traditional religious views of marriage it is perhaps not surprising to find that the two marital status groups that stand out as polar opposites are married adults and two sub-categories of single adults—the separated and those who live with a partner. That divorcees are more likely to be members than are the separated is unexpected. One might suppose that the large Catholic population affects this statistic since, in theory, practicing Catholics should not divorce but remain separated. However, we can assert that non-marriage and disruption of marriages tends to depress congregational membership. This makes psychological as well as theological sense. Since most people marry in a religious ceremony, the breaking of the marriage tie and vows might be thought to result negatively on ties to religious institutions. While indeed most married adults report congregational membership, and most of those who are divorced or living ("in sin") with a partner do not belong to religious institutions, once again the "membership gap" at 19 percentage points might not be as wide as some religionists have predicted.

Gender

In order to try to control for the other factors we have noted, the analysis of gender differences is limited to single-person households, in which the connection between gender and membership is unclouded by the presence of other adults of either sex. Males living alone are far less likely than females living alone to hold congregational membership. Almost two-thirds of them do not belong to religious institutions. Males who live alone tend to be never-married young males while the females are more likely to be older and widowed. Nevertheless the gender gap, at 15 points, is wider than the gaps for age or between some marital status categories.

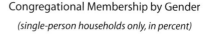

Figure 11.3

Congregational Membership by Gender

(single-person households only, in percent)

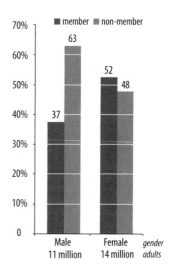

Race and ethnicity

Figure 11.4 shows vast differences (up to 28 percentage points) in the likelihood of people from various ethnic or racial backgrounds belonging to a religious congregation. For example, if you knew nothing about a person except that she or he was black, you could predict that the individual was highly likely to live in a household where somebody was a member of a congregation, since over two-thirds of African-American homes are religiously affiliated. Asians are at the other extreme on this statistic, with only 39 percent living in households in which somebody is a member of a congregation. The white population is just above the national average in terms of congregational membership (54 percent). Among Hispanics and Native Americans the proportions are similar, but for both groups members are in a minority.

Figure 11.4

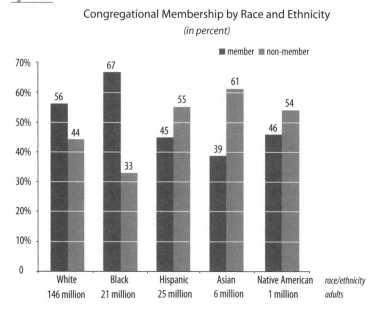

Congregational Membership by Race and Ethnicity
(in percent)

Figure 11.4 confirms a number of common observations made in the literature about American religion. African-Americans score highest on most measures of religiosity. The Asian and Hispanic

patterns suggest that the tendency for immigrants to remain uncon-
nected with mainstream society also applies in the religious sphere,
though age factors and economic issues may come into play as they
may well do with Native Americans.

Geography

Given the persistence of distinct cultural regions in the U.S., geography is a clear predictor of congregational membership. As seen in
Figure 11.5, there are major differences among the various areas of
the country. Congregational membership was highest, at 66 percent,
in the East South Central Census Division, part of the traditional
southern extension of the Bible Belt, and lowest in the Pacific Census Division at 43 percent. This low rate of congregational membership was widespread in a large unit with over 30 million adults.
Non-membership is highly correlated with the prevalence of Nones

Figure 11.5

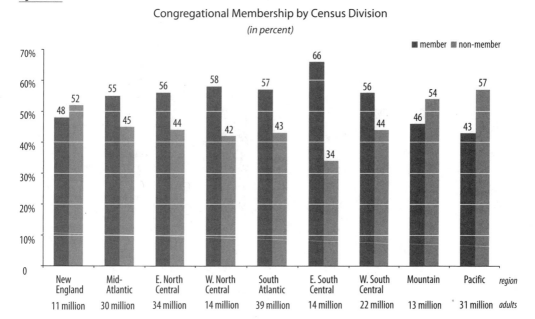

Congregational Membership by Census Division
(in percent)

Note: New England includes CT, RI, MA, NH, VT, and ME; Middle Atlantic includes NJ, PA and NY; East North
Central includes OH, MI, IN, IL and WI; West North Central includes MO, IA, MN, KS, NE, SD and ND; South
Atlantic includes FL, GA, SC, NC, VA, WV, DC, MD and DE; East South Central includes AL, MS, TN and KY; West
South Central includes LA, TX, AR and OK; Mountain includes NM, AZ, CO, UT, NV, WY, ID and MT; Pacific
includes CA, OR and WA. Hawaii and Alaska are not included in ARIS.

in the area. This suggests that, in the aggregate, non-affiliation with organized religion may be part of a linear process leading towards identification with the "no religion" bloc.

Educational level

Anti-religious writers such as Karl Marx have often contended that faith and belief is "the opiate of the masses." If that were true then congregational membership should be more prevalent among the less-educated segments of society. Our data contradict that contention. Figure 11.6 shows a strong linear relationship, whereby the higher the level of education, the greater the likelihood of residing in a household with congregational membership.

Figure 11.6

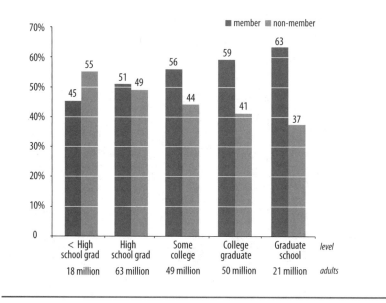

Congregational Membership by Level of Education
(in percent)

College graduates and those who have post-graduate education are far more likely to belong to a household with congregational membership than those with less than high school education. Although the universities and the campuses may not be regarded as the most fertile field for organized American religion, it appears that the alumni of these academic institutions certainly are. This trend warns us to be cautious in our conclusions about the meaning of religious affiliation. Belonging to a church or synagogue has always had more than a purely religious significance in American society. Congregational membership also has links to social prestige and respectability in many local communities and can be said to be part and parcel of the American social and economic system. Nonetheless, higher education does not appear to alienate people from involvement with religion.

Annual household income

Another indicator of socioeconomic status is household income. Figure 11.7 compares the annual household income profiles of members and non-members. The income gaps between households with and without congregational membership were found at the two extremes. Non-member households dominated among the poor with under $25,000, while member households had a higher share at the higher income levels. In all, over 44 percent of members compared with only 34 percent of non-members had over $50,000 in annual income in 2000.

Figure 11.7

Household Income of Members and Non-Members
(U.S. national total)

INCOME LEVEL	TOTAL	NON-MEMBERS	MEMBERS	RATIO UNAFFILIATED PER 100 MEMBERS
Number of Households (in millions)	105.0	50.0	55.0	91 : 100
Under $25,000	19.5%	22.2%	17.1%	130 : 100
$25,000-49,999	24.5	24.5	24.7	99 : 100
$50,000-99,000	26.9	22.8	30.5	75 : 100
$100,000 and over	12.4	11.1	13.7	81 : 100
Don't Know/Refused	16.6	19.4	14.1	
Total	**100.0**	**100.0**	**100.0**	

Note: Totals may not add to 100 percent due to rounding.

Interestingly, members in congregations were also more likely to report their annual income than non-members. Alongside the educational data, this finding might suggest that higher social status persons are more likely to claim and hold membership in religious congregations. Since congregational membership inevitably costs money because it involves activities that require fees or payments for participation including the giving of charity, these findings are not surprising. Nevertheless, economics cannot be the whole reason for this pattern given that the highest income category in Figure 11.7 is less religiously affiliated than the one below it. The figures clearly point towards poorer households as the potential clients for religious groups that wish to recruit new members.

Presence and number of children in the household

Overall, households who hold congregational membership were more likely to have children. Moreover, they also tend to have bigger families. As shown in Figure 11.8, in 24 percent of the households who hold congregational membership there were two or more children compared with 17 percent of non-member households with two or more children. This validates earlier findings that showed conservative religious groups, which tend to have higher membership ratios, tended to adopt a pro-natalist ethos.

Figure 11.8

Number of Children in the Household of Members and Non-members

NUMBER OF CHILDREN	NON-MEMBERS	MEMBERS	TOTAL
Number of Households (in millions)	50.0	55.0	105.0
0	66%	61%	64%
1	15	15	15
2	11	15	13
3 or more	6	9	7
Don't Know/Refused	2	<1	1
Total	**100**	**100**	**100**

Congregational Membership among Mixed Religion Families

One clear marketing challenge for many religious institutions today is the new phenomenon of the mixed religious identification family analyzed in Chapter 6. An obvious question is: Are mixed religion and interfaith families less likely to belong to a congregation? One might hypothesize that the parents in such families are on average less religious, as evidenced by their willingness to marry outside their religious tradition or group. Or, even if they are religious, they might simply defer decision-making on affiliation because of the difficulty of making a choice.

As we have previously shown, nationally 54 percent of adults reported that someone in their household was a member of a congregation but we have also noted that families with young children are much more likely to be affiliated. For example, 66 percent of Methodists in general, compared with 77 percent of Methodists with children under age 18, are church members; likewise 68 percent of Pentecostals in general, compared with 80 percent of Pentecostals with children under age 18, belong to a church.

In addition household membership varies by religious group since some are more successful than others in their ability to affiliate their potential market. The research question explored here is: how do intact families with children behave regarding congregational membership? Are same-religion families more or less likely to belong to some groups than mixed families?

Generally, the above hypothesis seems to be correct. Regardless of the religious composition of the family, 65 percent of all same-religion families with children belong to a church or temple, but only 56 percent of mixed religion families belong to a church or temple. Yet this relationship varies by religious group, and interestingly the relationship does not always go in the same direction. Figure 11.9 reveals that for most religious groups, families with endogamous parents, where both parents share the same religious identification, have a higher rate of membership in religious congregations. In some cases, for example among Baptists, Methodists, and Lutherans,[1] the gaps are over 20 percentage points. However, in a few religious groups the contrary happens. Mixed families where there is one

Presbyterian parent are more likely to belong to a congregation than endogamous or both-parent Presbyterian families.

As one would expect, partners with no religion are the exception to the rule. Obviously it is more likely that the family will belong to a religious institution if one partner identifies with a religious group than if neither identifies.

Figure 11.9

Comparison of Household Congregational Membership Rates for Families with Children by the Religious Identification of the Respondent Parent in Intact Mixed and Endogamous Households

(selected religious groups)

RELIGIOUS GROUP OF RESPONDENT	MIXED RELIGION FAMILIES	ENDOGAMOUS FAMILIES
Mormon	72%	85%
Presbyterian	72	68
Episcopalian	62	79
Lutheran	58	87
Methodist/Wesleyan	58	80
Catholic	57	67
Christian	56	70
Protestant	53	64
Baptist	51	77
No religion	49	10
Pentecostal/Charismatic	48	80
U.S. Total	**56**	**65**

Reflections on Religious Affiliation

In earlier chapters we discovered how religions differ by the social class and status of their adherents. The findings discussed in this chapter tend to reinforce the notion that the interaction between social status and religious outlook operates similarly in the overall generic pattern of religious affiliation in the United States. Historically a relationship between social position and religion has been found in most Western societies, whereby those who have done best in society generally are the most likely to be committed to and involved in organized religion. The respectable members of the community, the middle classes, attend church as part of their lifestyle. Historically America differed from most other western societies in that urban working-class people were also religious in sentiment and belief but as we have seen most surprisingly the poorest among them today tend not become congregational members.

The clear distinction the ARIS data make between identifiers and actual members is an important practical contribution to the study of American religion. It offers a glimpse into the characteristics of that immense potential market—namely the one-in-four Americans who self-identify with a religious group but are not currently affiliated. Used intelligently these findings have the potential to assist those who wish to operate in the religious market to recruit further members.

Note

1. We use the religious identification of the respondent parent to identify the religious classification of the family, given the equal probability to be questioned.

TWELVE

Membership Patterns among Specific Religious Groups

Catholics, Baptists, Methodists, Lutherans, Presbyterians, Pentecostals, Episcopalians, Mormons, and Jews

DEMOGRAPHY, geography and social class variables appear to influence the overall pattern of congregational membership yet as has been shown in an earlier chapter the different religious groups clearly have "niche markets." Therefore, it should be illuminating to investigate the variation in recruitment patterns among their potential constituencies for nine major religious groups.[1] As we shall discover there are clear differences to be seen, especially among the main Christian traditions as regards current patterns of affiliation that traditional analytical approaches using an institutional framework often fail to distinguish.

It is important to realize that affiliation criteria, who is a member and who is not, differ widely among religious groups. Some are inclusive and some are exclusive regarding congregational membership. ARIS involved a self-assessment on behalf of the household unit by the individual adult respondent (see Chapter 3). Cumulatively, such responses might not reflect official records as reported by the various denominations. Moreover, the profiles presented here are aggregate national figures and do not present information on key explanatory factors such as the effects of congregational size, the role of clergy, and local customs. Rather the statistics that follow present overall comparisons among segments of the population within each religious group according to age, education, marital status, and region of residence.

Catholics

While the age pattern for Catholic members and non-members was similar to American adults in general, marital status (Figure 12.3) presented a different pattern. Most noticeable is the low membership rate among separated Catholics, a small minority, accounting for approximately 900,000 adults. Married Catholics were by far more likely to belong to a church than married Americans in general, so they represent the most traditional Catholic adherents.

Figure 12.1

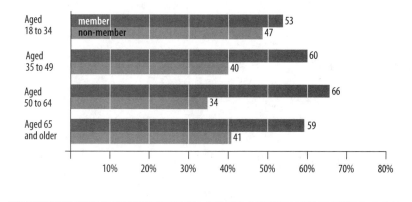

Age of Respondent by Congregational Membership
(Catholic identifiers, in percent)

The linear relationship between education and congregational membership was stronger among Catholics than all Americans and the membership gaps were bigger. This poses a recruitment issue for the Catholic Church since the category of high school graduate or less is the largest in terms of size and offers the best potential recruitment pool for Catholic parishes.

Figure 12.2

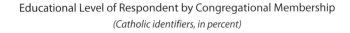

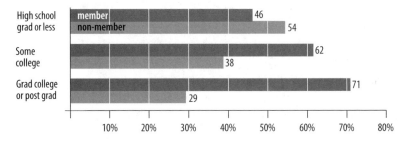

Educational Level of Respondent by Congregational Membership
(Catholic identifiers, in percent)

Figure 12.3

Marital Status of Respondent by Congregational Membership
(Catholic identifiers, in percent)

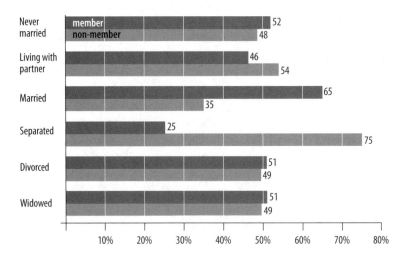

The country can be divided into two areas for Catholic congregational membership. Catholics in the historic regions of settlement in the Northeast and the Midwest (North Central) were far more likely to claim to belong to a parish church than those in the West and the South. This again points to new migrants as a potential recruitment pool in the sunbelt states.

Figure 12.4

Region of Residency of Respondent by Congregational Membership
(Catholic identifiers, in percent)

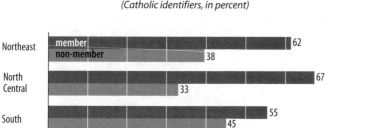

Baptists

Baptist membership rates failed to correlate with age even more than the overall national one. Regardless of age group, affiliation remained high at about 69 percent. Marital status (Figure 12.7) did make a difference, whereby divorced and separated adults were less likely to live in household, with congregational membership.

Figure 12.5

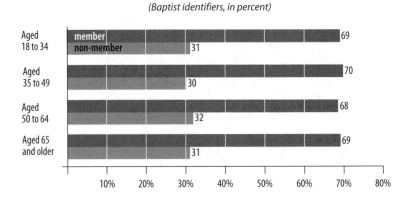

Age of Respondent by Congregational Membership
(Baptist identifiers, in percent)

Despite smaller gaps in membership between educational levels among Baptists compared to Catholics, the high membership rate among adults who graduated college or obtained post-graduate degrees was striking.

Figure 12.6

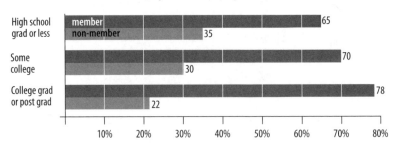

Educational Level of Respondent by Congregational Membership
(Baptist identifiers, in percent)

Figure 12.7

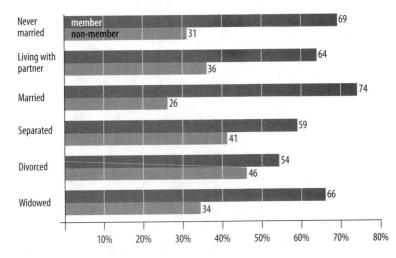

Marital Status of Respondent by Congregational Membership
(Baptist identifiers, in percent)

Regional gaps were not big among Baptists, though the congregational membership rate was highest in the Baptist heartland of the South.

Figure 12.8

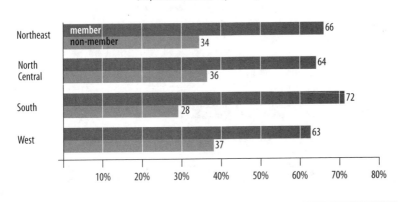

Region of Residency of Respondent by Congregational Membership
(Baptist identifiers, in percent)

Methodists

The Methodist age pattern is quite unusual with the youngest age group exhibiting the highest level of congregational membership at a membership rate similar to that of young Baptists. Younger Methodists are a much smaller cohort than the older ones. It seems those who have stayed loyal to Methodism among the younger are more "enthusiastic" and more affiliated, which may reflect the strong youth programs in many Methodist congregations.

Figure 12.9

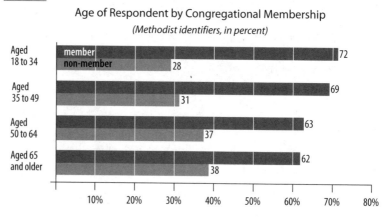

Age of Respondent by Congregational Membership
(Methodist identifiers, in percent)

Membership rates differed quite substantially by educational level among Methodists. High congregational membership rates for college graduates and post-graduates were similar to those among Baptists.

Figure 12.10

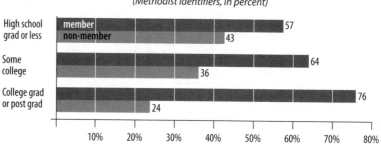

Educational Level of Respondent by Congregational Membership
(Methodist identifiers, in percent)

Again, the membership rate among separated Methodists was far lower than any other marital status group. Married adults did not have the highest congregational membership—the membership rate of single Methodists exceeded 70 percent both for the never married and surprisingly also those living with a partner "without benefit of clergy." In part these statistics must be related to the massive generational erosion of Methodists we reported in Chapter 5.

Figure 12.11

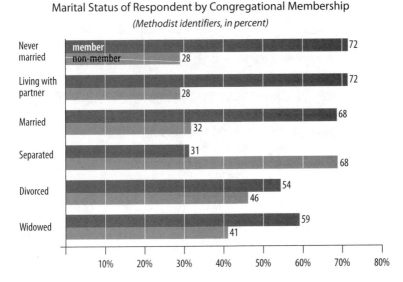

Marital Status of Respondent by Congregational Membership
(Methodist identifiers, in percent)

Regional variation among Methodists follows the national pattern.

Figure 12.12

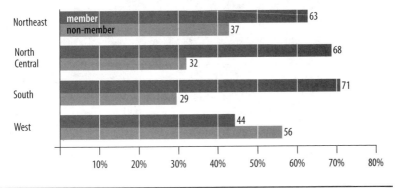

Region of Residency of Respondent by Congregational Membership
(Methodist identifiers, in percent)

Lutherans

Overall congregational membership among Lutherans was high at 68 percent. Differences by age group were similar to those of Americans in general. Membership peaked for those aged 50 to 64 and then dropped off sharply for the oldest cohort.

Figure 12.13

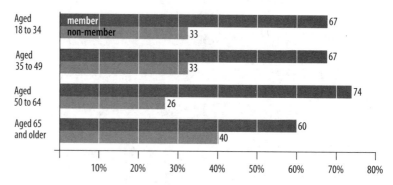

Age of Respondent by Congregational Membership
(Lutheran identifiers, in percent)

Educational patterns among Lutherans resembled the general population, although congregational membership rates were higher.

Figure 12.14

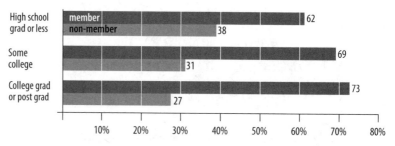

Educational Level of Respondent by Congregational Membership
(Lutheran identifiers, in percent)

Membership rates for the various marital statuses were again similar to those of Americans in general.

Figure 12.15

Marital Status of Respondent by Congregational Membership
(Lutheran identifiers, in percent)

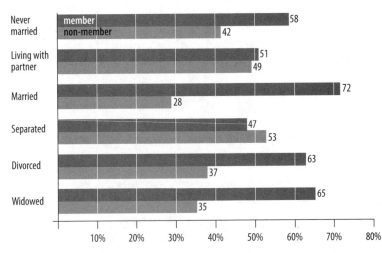

As with other religious groups, the region of greatest concentration—in this case the Midwest—had the highest affiliation rate.

Figure 12.16

Region of Residency of Respondent by Congregational Membership
(Lutheran identifiers, in percent)

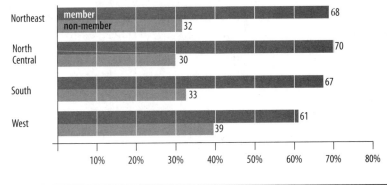

Presbyterians

As mentioned in Chapter 3, the extrapolation of ARIS estimates of overall Presbyterian membership rates is very close to the church's own published data. This makes this analysis of particular interest as it approximates "reality" more closely than for some other more disparate groups examined here. Presbyterian congregants mirrored Methodists in age structure, but the cohort gaps are even wider. Almost one million Presbyterian adults were aged 18 to 34, and their congregational membership rate exceeded that of all the other age groups.

Figure 12.17

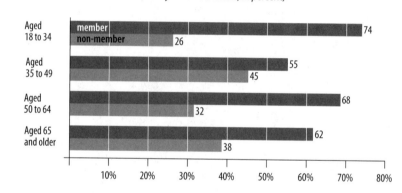

Age of Respondent by Congregational Membership
(Presbyterian identifiers, in percent)

Congregational membership was skewed educationally for Presbyterians. Adults who graduated college or who obtained post graduate degrees were by far more likely to reside in households with congregational membership.

Figure 12.18

Educational Level of Respondent by Congregational Membership
(Presbyterian identifiers, in percent)

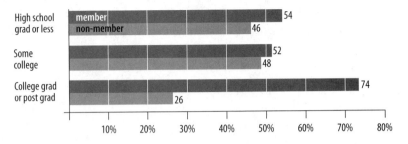

Due to statistically insignificant numbers of Presbyterians who were separated or living with a partner, we chose not to show the marital status chart.

Presbyterians in the Northeast exhibited the highest congregational membership rate compared with residents in the other three main geographical regions.

Figure 12.19

Region of Residency of Respondent by Congregational Membership
(Presbyterian identifiers, in percent)

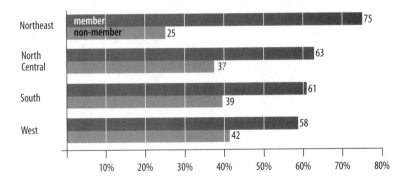

Pentecostals/Charismatics

The following statistics relate to respondents who stated "Pente-costal" or "Charismatic" in response to the primary ARIS question and do not include those identifying with specific denominations such as Assemblies of God or Church of God. Young Pentecostals had higher congregational membership than the average with a rate of 68 percent. This pattern is noteworthy. Overall the oldest group, adults over age 65, represented a small group among Pentecostals. Thus overall membership in Pentecostal congregations was boosted by their many young followers.

Figure 12.20

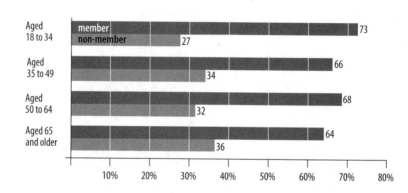

Age of Respondent by Congregational Membership
(Pentecostal identifiers, in percent)

Congregational membership of Pentecostals at the different edu-cational levels resembled that of Lutherans. Congregational mem-bership increased with more education.

Figure 12.21

Educational Level of Respondent by Congregational Membership
(Pentecostal identifiers, in percent)

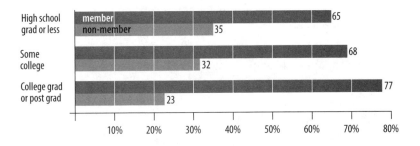

Once again a lack of sufficient cases prevents us from showing the marital status chart.

Congregational membership among Pentecostals is slightly higher in the Midwest (North Central) and in the Northeast.

Figure 12.22

Region of Residency of Respondent by Congregational Membership
(Pentecostal identifiers, in percent)

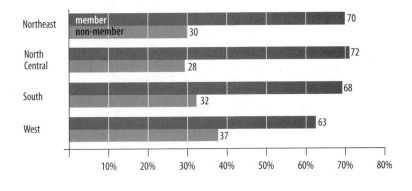

Episcopalians

Extrapolated ARIS membership estimates and the official data of
the Protestant Episcopal Church coincide quite closely in a similar
way to the Presbyterian case. Membership patterns by age among
Episcopalians resembled those of Catholics peaking at age 50 to 64
years, but at higher levels. The overall congregational membership
rate of Episcopalians at 64 percent is slightly higher than the Catholic
rate of 59 percent.

Figure 12.23

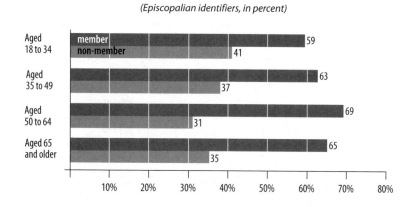

Age of Respondent by Congregational Membership
(Episcopalian identifiers, in percent)

Membership by educational level of Episcopalians also resembled
that of Catholics. The large gaps were between the two extreme
groups, the high school graduates versus college graduates. College
graduates among Episcopalians represented the largest educational
group and their high congregational membership rate contributed to
the overall higher membership rate, compared to Catholics.

Figure 12.24

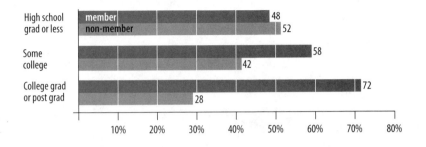

Educational Level of Respondent by Congregational Membership
(Episcopalian identifiers, in percent)

Again, a lack of sufficient cases from some marital status groups precludes us from presenting a marital status chart.

The similarities between Catholics and Episcopalians stopped when it came to geography. The region that stood out with a higher congregational membership for Episcopalians was the Northeast, while in the other regions differences were minor.

Figure 12.25

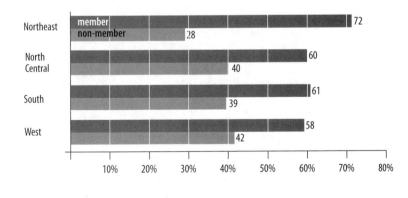

Region of Residency of Respondent by Congregational Membership
(Episcopalian identifiers, in percent)

Jews

This refers to Jews by religion, and does not represent the entire etho-cultural American Jewish population. Overall, synagogue and temple membership rates among Jews were low, but flat in terms of age cohorts.

Figure 12.26

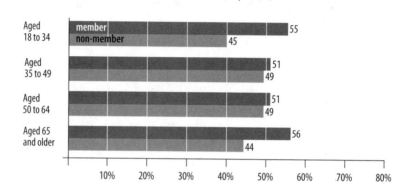

Age of Respondent by Congregational Membership
(Jewish identifiers, in percent)

Synagogue membership tended to rise with an increase in educational level among Jews. This familiar pattern is probably associated with household income since synagogue membership is dependent on fees rather than voluntary offerings, and these tend to be higher than for other religious groups.

Figure 12.27

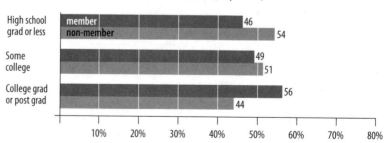

Educational Level of Respondent by Congregational Membership
(Jewish identifiers, in percent)

Among Jews in the Northeast and the South, about half of all households belong to a synagogue. Membership is particularly low in the West while in contrast about two-thirds of Jews who reside in communities in the Midwest live in households with synagogue membership.

Figure 12.28

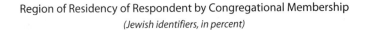

Region of Residency of Respondent by Congregational Membership
(Jewish identifiers, in percent)

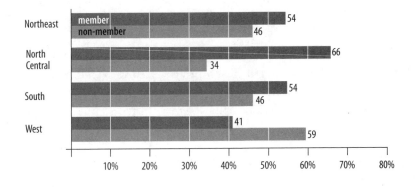

Mormons

The Mormons are a small population but they tend to be homogeneous in their demographic characteristics. For instance due to early marriage age and a high proportion of married adults, there were not enough respondents in the Mormon sample in the various other marital status categories to warrant a report. Mormons are also concentrated geographically. Most of the respondents resided in the West in Utah and neighboring states. Therefore, we restrict the comparisons between members of the Church of Jesus Christ of the Latter day Saints and non-members to the age and educational level variables.

Mormons have among the highest rates of church membership in the U.S. The only age group of Mormons that stood out with above average church membership was adults aged 35 to 49. The family orientation and emphasis on child-bearing in their church probably explains this pattern.

Figure 12.29

Age of Respondent by Congregational Membership
(Mormon identifiers, in percent)

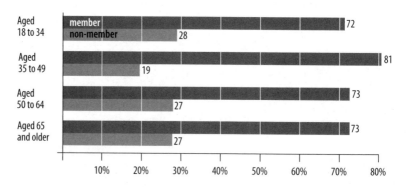

Interestingly, there were wide differences in Mormons' membership rates by education. Adults at the lowest educational level, high school graduates or less were far less likely than college graduates to reside in households with congregational membership.

Figure 12.30

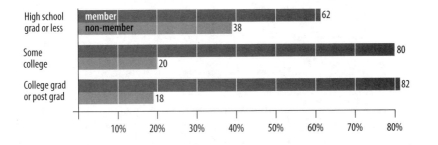

Educational Level of Respondent by Congregational Membership
(Mormon identifiers, in percent)

The unique geography of Mormonism was described in Chapter 7.

Reflections on Congregational Membership

This analysis examined the record of a number of religious groups in recruiting their potential constituency of identifiers into current members of congregations. Some groups do seem to be successfully reversing the national trends, recorded in the previous chapter, in their ability to recruit and mobilize different segments of the population. In other words, they are creating a specific market niche. In earlier chapters we discovered how the various religious groups differ by the social class and status of their adherents. In this chapter, we find that congregational membership is a badge of social standing in some groups more than others. For instance the "educational gap" between the membership rates of the most and least educated among the "more ethnic" religious groups such as Jews and Lutherans is only 10 or 11 percentage points. It is 12 or 13 points among the Pentecostals and Baptists, but rises to 20 points among Mormons and Presbyterians, and reaches 24 and 25 points respectively among Episcopalians and Catholics.

The process by which this happens is well known to observers of social life. A local religious congregation is not just a collection of people who pray together; it is a neighborhood-based surrogate community which shows similarities of occupation and lifestyle among the membership. The individual congregants choose a particular church on the basis of their compatibility with its other members—that is, the social atmosphere and the belief they will "fit in" and make friends. This feeling is of course modulated by other personal characteristics such as their ethnic backgrounds and residential choices. It is a social process that favors the "small" congregation over the larger one. So a religious group that has lots of small congregations or "boutiques" should be better at affiliating its potential constituency of adherents. This suggests that the Catholic Church disadvantages itself because canon law prescribes a parish system that produces large congregations that are in theory forced to worship locally and cannot "shop around." This creates a more bureaucratic, rather than market-oriented, system. ARIS data suggest that consumer resistance or self-exclusion is most common among poor rather than privileged Catholics.

The success of the mega-churches, especially the non-denominational ones, seems to undermine this thesis. They are known for having highly segmented demographics and they tend to be a regional phenomenon of the South and West. We may well be comparing two different styles or types of religion with distinct market niches. The ethnic or "communitarian" Catholics (and Lutherans and Jews) of the East who are usually born into the faith, as well as African-Americans with their unique congregational format and style, form distinct models of congregation. This model can be contrasted with the "associational" model developed by the white evangelicals of the sun-belt. Their congregations, particularly the mega-churches, are composed of autonomous religious shoppers. It is well to remember that in a large and complex free market conflicting trends can occur, and rival brands and outlets can operate and flourish simultaneously.

The intervening variable ARIS did not and could not deal with or measure is the human factor—the role of clergy and ministry. In the realm of religion the reputation and character of the "sales force" at both the local and national levels seems crucial in attracting and retaining worshippers. Charisma has always been an important factor in religious and spiritual life but it is as hard to measure as it is to manufacture.

Notes

1. ARIS aggregates together the various denominational bodies among some Protestant churches such as Baptists, Lutherans, and Pentecostals so the value of these statistics for specific denominations is limited. We have also deliberately not sorted them by race.

THIRTEEN

Religion and Political Party Preference

IN RECENT years, religious belief and behavior have become increasingly important in party politics. Post-election analysis of the November 2004 presidential vote in particular dwelt on the relationship between political behavior and the religion of voters because "values" was identified by some polls as a key issue influencing the electorate. However, the relationship between politics and religion has developed much differently in the United States than in the other leading democracies of the world.

Since the end of World War II, Christian Democratic political parties sponsored by church organizations and religious groups have played major roles in Italy, Germany, Belgium, and the Netherlands. Recently, former Communist states like Poland and Hungary have witnessed similar phenomena. Outside Europe the non-Christian democracies have also produced religious parties; the Hindu Bharatiya Janata Party in India, several Orthodox Jewish parties in Israel, and the Buddhist Komeito party in Japan, among others. Without an established church as in Britain and the Scandinavian countries or religiously organized political parties of the type mentioned above, America and its political landscape have nonetheless resonated with religious rhetoric, particularly in the last few decades.

The emergence of religion as a factor in American politics is due in part to cultural divisions that are increasingly evident in society. These have tended to overshadow the divisions of the past that were based on economic standing—haves vs. have-nots, rich vs. poor, white collar vs. blue collar. Politics today is in large part a function of culture when the issues at the heart of political debate seem to be around God, guns, abortion, and foremost in the 2004 election, civil unions and gay marriage. No one cultural issue will contend with the economy or national security as the most important issue facing the nation but together cultural issues drive the thinking and calculations of candidates, parties, and voters. And at the heart of American culture is religion.

The escalation of religious references in public debate relates to the most troubling social and legislative issues of our time: abortion, euthanasia, the death penalty, medical research and biological ethics, sexuality, patriotism, church-state relations, public education, and the moral status of the family. In many if not most of our religious denominations, social liberals and social conservatives are divided over values, over whether to return to traditional behavior patterns or to adapt to changing behavior patterns. Ultimately, decisions are based upon personal determination of morality and lifestyles.

Political Party Preference

As part of ARIS a large nationally representative sub-sample of over 34,000 American adults (age 18 or older) in the continental U.S. (i.e., excluding Alaska and Hawaii) were asked the following question: *Generally speaking, do you usually think of yourself as a Republican, a Democrat, or an independent?* The pattern of responses is shown in Figure 13.1. They revealed that American adults in general are almost equally distributed into three political camps, Democrats, Republicans, and independents, with a slight edge to the Democrats.

The goal of this chapter is to examine and explore the interrelationship between religion and the current pattern of political party preferences.

Figure 13.1

Political Party Preference: All Adults

Generally speaking, do you usually think of yourself as . . . ?

(weighted)

PARTY PREFERENCE	# OF RESPONDENTS	# IN POPULATION	PERCENT
Democrat	10,447	66,555,000	32.0%
Independent	10,468	61,979,000	29.8
Republican	10,426	61,771,000	29.7
Other	575	3,120,000	1.5
Don't Know	1,001	5,824,000	2.8
Refused	1,377	8,527,000	4.1
Total	**34,294**	**207,983,000**	**100.0**

Figure 13.2

Political Party Preference: Registered Voters Only

Generally speaking, do you usually think of yourself as ... ?

(weighted)

PARTY PREFERENCE	# OF RESPONDENTS	# IN POPULATION	PERCENT
Democrat	8,863	57,045,000	34.2%
Republican	9,135	54,883,000	32.9
Independent	7,626	45,894,000	27.5
Other	323	1,772,000	1.1
Don't Know	494	3,016,000	1.8
Refused	659	4,225,000	2.5
Total	**27,100**	**166,836,000**	**100.0**

Figure 13.1 relates to the whole adult population of 208 million. It shows that party preferences are almost equally divided among the three possible options but with 8 percent unwilling to commit. Figure 13.2 covers the 80 percent of all adults who report being registered voters. It presents the political preferences of those people who really matter to the parties, that is, the registered voters. They appear more definite in their political opinions than the total population since they contain proportionately fewer Don't Knows and Refuseds. Among registered voters Democrats and Republicans score almost the same—one-third to each party—but the party gap favoring the Democrats narrows slightly. The independents slide to third place among registered voters. Still, independents represent almost 46 million votes. This is a large number that can determine which party ultimately wins an election.

Voter registration is not an automatic process in the U.S. and the procedure varies by state. Age and citizenship criteria are common to all states under federal law but otherwise it is a voluntary act that fits in with the idea that it is a civic duty rather than a right. A difference between the U.S. and the other liberal democracies is that voter registration is generally lower among qualifying Americans and electoral turnout is lower as well. One explanation is the more frequent number of elections in the U.S. and the larger number of public offices that are elected and on the ballot. Another factor is the primary system, whereby the "real election" in some states and districts that have "safe seats" is the internal party contest among

Republican or Democrat voters. This means that the make-up of the political parties' own electorates has important consequences for national politics because they are grand coalitions of interest groups with wide and differing social, economic, and cultural agendas.

One of the popular criticisms of American politics is that there is a very constricted choice of party options compared with the range that exists in other multiparty Western democratic societies. Few other democratic countries offer a choice between just two main political parties. Moreover, most of these countries have forms of proportional representation that serve to encourage the formation of parties and political fragmentation. Yet the United States has largely operated a two-party system of Republicans and Democrats for over 150 years. The pattern of local and national party preference and the social composition of their supporters have changed over time. For example, today's Republicans, certainly in the South, are not the direct descendants of the party of Lincoln. However, there is an element of "tribal loyalty" to many Americans' party preference. It bears some resemblance to their support for sports teams or their religious identification in that they are born into families with a tradition of loyalty to one party.

Party preference does not tend to change frequently. This preference is often reinforced by the influence of friends, neighbors, fellow workers, and co-religionists. This relationship operates in both directions. It is not always that political opinions make people Democrats or Republicans but rather that their self-identification with a social grouping leads them to identify with a party preference that in turn leads them to adopt the political ideology that underpins its values and policies.

Communities of thought and opinion as well as social communities emerge in this process. The end result is that we speak of "red" and "blue" states and regions. Paradoxically, the electoral system of primaries and general elections aids this process since it allows on occasion for the individual voter to express dissatisfaction with a particular candidate or party faction and to split the ticket. This option avoids the need for the voter to renounce his or her primal loyalty. In this vast and populous nation each political party is a coalition of interests and factions that would constitute separate political parties

in most other democratic societies. The 50 states vary in their political histories and styles as well as the issues that differentiate the parties. Thus the Republican Party of New Jersey is different from that
of Texas and the Democratic Party in Oregon is not an exact replica
of that in Louisiana and neither are their supporters.

As stated earlier, contemporary American party politics is increasingly a contest about cultural values about which many people feel
passionately. This is not to say that ethical and moral values did not
matter in the past; they obviously did in the 1860s when the issue
of slavery led to civil war. Yet since that conflict, with the exception
of Prohibition and civil rights, most of the nation's divisive political
issues have not been as closely tied emotionally to people's religious
beliefs and values as are many hot button issues today. Current political controversies about abortion, stem cells, gay marriage, the teaching of evolution and intelligent design, school prayer, and school
vouchers seem particularly capable of both dividing groups and coa-
lescing sides. These issues possess a powerful emotional resonance
and the capacity to produce an intensity of passion on both sides of
the debate.

However, the two parties are coalitions, especially at the national
level. Both parties have their liberal and conservative wings, though
the Democrats have more liberals and the Republicans more conservatives. The balance between liberal and conservative ideologies
is the real locomotive of American politics. Even this dualism is complicated by, for instance, the frequent crossover between economic
and social liberalism. A person can support civil rights or choice
regarding abortion but also believe in lower taxation and reduced
government entitlements. Even this pattern is mediated by race,
region, and increasingly gender. Except perhaps in presidential elections, conservative or liberal opinion does not automatically translate into support for the Republican or Democratic Parties.

Nevertheless, over the past decade an intellectual climate has
emerged that perceives issues that explicitly relate to economics and
politics as part of a secular liberal agenda and issues of personal
morality and behavior as part of the conservative "Judeo-Christian"
agenda. Increasingly, religious identification is acknowledged as an

important factor in political party preference. Every four years journalists and pundits show a renewed interest in the religious beliefs and opinions of both the electorate and the candidates. Few of these observers, however, have sufficient reliable information to carry out their task. For that, a large-scale, nationally representative sample such as ARIS is required.

Politics and Religious-Secular Outlook

Political party and outlook

The crucial question is whether people's religious-secular outlook correlates with their political party preference? Does a secular outlook predict a more liberal, i.e., Democratic political inclination, and does a religious outlook predict a more conservative, i.e., Republican preference? Without claiming causality, Figure 13.3, showing political party preference by outlook, illustrates the utility and importance of the concept of outlook and its correlation with political party preferences.

Figure 13.3

The Pattern of Political Party Preferences within Religious or Secular Outlook Types

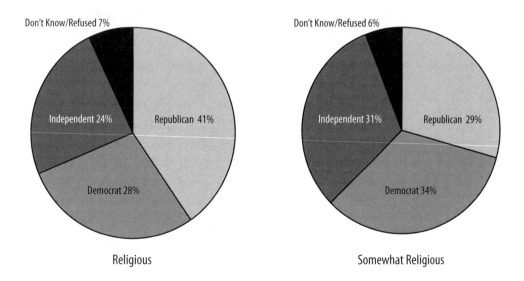

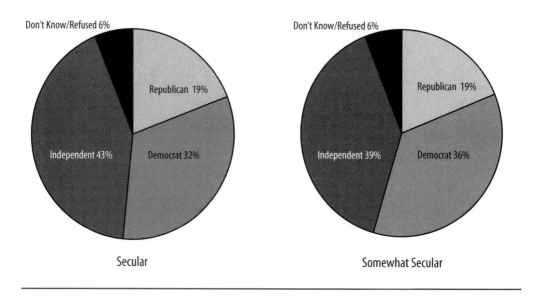

Secular

Somewhat Secular

Among those with a religious outlook there is a clear plurality of Republicans over Democrats, 41 percent to 28 percent. Among the somewhat religious the plurality lies with the Democrats with the independents slightly outnumbering the Republicans. Among the two types of secular outlook independents hold a plurality. The proportion favoring the independent political preference is stronger among the secular than the somewhat secular. Interestingly the proportion favoring the Republican Party is exactly the same, 19 percent for both secularist types. Another interesting feature is that the proportion of Don't Knows and Refuseds to answer the question about politics is the same across all four types of outlook.

When we reverse the analysis and look at the composition of the parties' supporters in terms of cultural outlook in Figure 13.4 we find that almost half of the Republicans regard their outlook as "religious" as opposed to only 29 percent of adults who self-identify as independents. Overall more Democrats and political independents opt for the middle ground of "somewhat religious" than for the "religious" category. Thus the pattern for independents is closer to that of the Democrats than the Republicans. The Republicans have a plurality of "religious" rather than "somewhat religious." They are also the least likely to describe themselves either as "secular" or "somewhat

Figure 13.4

The Religious or Secular Outlook Profile of the Supporters of the Political Parties
(Base: Adult Population 208 million, N = 12,447; in percent))

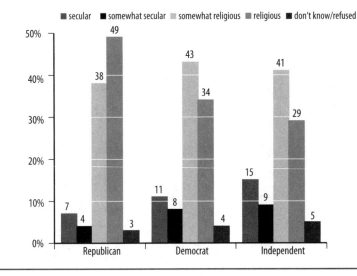

secular." Only one in nine Republicans has a secularist outlook as compared with one in five Democrats and one in four independents.

Political independents are the most likely to be secular in orientation. Almost one in every four adults that self-identifies as independent regards him or herself as secular. Moreover most of these independents categorically describe themselves as "secular" rather than "somewhat secular."

The key finding here is that it is Democrats and not independents who emerge as the more "centrist" group in U.S. politics on the religious-secular outlook scale. It appears that the independents grouping which is furthest away from Republican "values."

Belief in God

Overall 87 percent of adult Americans either "agree somewhat" or "agree strongly" that God exists. It is important to note that this number is higher than the combined scores of "religious" and "somewhat religious" Americans (75 percent) shown in Figure 3.1. This obviously means that some with a secularist cultural outlook also believe God exists.

Figure 13.5

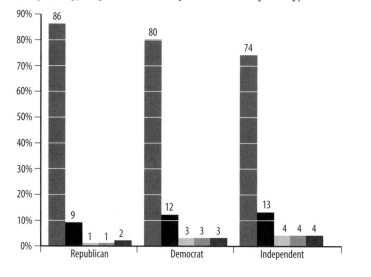

Agree with the Statement: God Exists
(Base: Adult population 208 million; in percent)

■ agree strongly ■ agree somewhat ▨ disagree somewhat ▨ disagree strongly ■ don't know/refused

How does this key expression of cultural outlook play out across the political spectrum? Republicans express the strongest belief in God—95 percent agree that God exists with 86 percent agreeing "strongly." Only 2 percent of Republicans express a disbelief in God. Among Democrats 92 percent agree that God exists with 80 percent agreeing "strongly." Independents are more likely to be skeptics than the supporters of the two main parties, although they also are predominantly believers with 74 percent agreeing "strongly" that God exists. However, once again we find that it is the Democrats who are positioned almost exactly in the center between the Republicans and the independents.

Since there is no agreed definition of the powers or attributes of God in the previous question we posed, it is necessary to probe further and ascertain if there is any difference in the intensity or quality of the belief in God and how that relates to politics. We asked if people agreed (strongly or somewhat) or disagreed (strongly or somewhat) with the statement: *God performs miracles.*

Figure 13.6

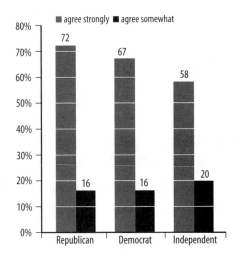

Agree with the Statement: God Performs Miracles
(Base: Adult population 208 million; in percent)

Figure 13.6 shows that performing miracles appears to be an agreed attribute of the God most Americans believe exists. Their God is an active agent in the world. From this perspective one can assert that contemporary Americans' vision of God is a more normative, monotheistic one. This is somewhat closer to that of the Pilgrim Fathers than that of the Founding Fathers of the Republic, many of whom were deists and pictured the Almighty as much less active in human affairs and as the "great clockmaker."

Republicans are the group most likely to take the "biblical" position, with 88 percent agreeing God performs miracles (the vast majority of those agreeing strongly). Among Democrats 83 percent agree on the miraculous powers of God as do more than three in four independents, who are again the most skeptical group with the lowest level of overall agreement as well the highest proportion only "agreeing somewhat." These findings show that once again the Democrats emerge as the middle group on this religious item.

Religious or secular outlook and voter registration

Overall, 80 percent of adult Americans were registered to vote in 2001. If, as we maintain, the focus of current political debate is primarily on values and is thus essentially a "culture war" are there differences in the rates of voter registration and therefore likelihood to vote among the culture types?

Figure 13.7

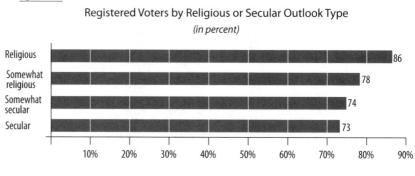

Registered Voters by Religious or Secular Outlook Type
(in percent)

Religious Americans are the most likely to register to vote with 86 percent registered voters and the secular the least likely at 73 percent. This high civic engagement among religious adults has consequences since their voices are more likely to be heard by parties and politicians. Part of the reason for the lower political involvement of secularists is that they tend to be drawn from sections of the population with generally lower than average rates of voter registration such as the young, single people, and immigrants.

Religious tradition and voter registration

Now that we see that those holding a "religious" outlook are more likely to be registered to vote in elections there is a natural follow-up question. Do all people who identify with different religious groups behave similarly with regard to this civic duty? Namely, are Catholics, Protestants, Jews, Muslims, Eastern religions and others equally likely to register to vote?

As Figure 13.8 illustrates, the majority of religious traditions fall within the range of 78 to 85 percent registered voters. However,

Mainline Christians stand out with 88 percent registered voters. At the other end of the spectrum are Muslims with only 44 percent of adults registered to vote. Jehovah's Witnesses, one of the groups that we have often included among "Protestant denominations," are shown separately here because they are a natural outlier group. This is the direct result of their faith prohibiting participation in the political realm. Their score in this table serves to illustrate the overall validity of the ARIS data on this item.

Figure 13.8

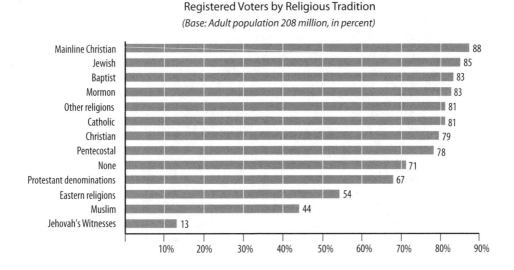

Registered Voters by Religious Tradition
(Base: Adult population 208 million, in percent)

These patterns of voter registration have social as well as political implications. The groups scoring lower on this factor tend to be those most removed from the national or cultural mainstream. Many of the Protestant sects, besides the Jehovah's Witnesses, maintained minimum civil engagement in the broader society during the 1920s and 1930s and were ambivalent about involvement in the body politic. This table shows that there are still vestiges of this tradition of disengagement. The "Nones" are largely composed of those with a secular outlook. As we have previously noted, they are also a group which is by definition somewhat estranged from the cultural mainstream of a largely religious people. The Muslim and Eastern religions' low rates of registration involve factors other than faith, such as their higher than average proportion of immigrants and their younger age profiles.

Nevertheless the use of voter registration as an index of political involvement and as a proxy indicator of engagement in the mainstream of national life is highlighted by an analysis of the religious identification pattern among elected national politicians and appointed Supreme Court justices. Since the founding of the Republic the overwhelming majority of Presidents and Supreme Court Justices have been adherents of the Mainline Christian churches and denominations.[1] Even in 2004 Mainline Christians are considerably over-represented among those elected to the United States Senate with 51 out of 100 senators, including 13 Presbyterians. Other traditions that are found at the top of Figure 13.8, Jews, Baptists, and Mormons are also over-represented in the United States Congress. At the other end of the spectrum are the newcomers who form the bulk of those found in the Eastern religions and Muslim categories and have yet to acculturate and fully integrate into American society and the political system.

Political Party Preferences

The basis for segmenting the population into the thirteen religious traditions shown in Figure 2.2 is theology and associated moral and philosophical positions on the nature of mankind. We should thus expect differences in how those who identify with various belief systems and views of the world approach the political realm. Who then is most likely to be a Republican? Who is most likely to prefer the Democratic Party? And who is most likely to veer towards being politically independent?

Figures 13.9 to 13.11 show as expected that in the aggregate religious groups vary in the political preferences of their adherents. Some bodies lean heavily toward either Democrats or Republicans, while others have no strong tendency either way.

The most pro-Republican group by far is the Mormons. Mormons are one of the smaller groups so on statistical grounds alone one would expect more homogeneity. In addition, Mormonism gives its adherents a totality of experience and in exchange elicits above-average commitment to its ideals and lifestyle. Mormons are also geographically concentrated in Utah and the states surrounding the Great Basin. While the LDS Church avoids endorsing candidates or taking part in party politics it takes positions on issues such as the Equal Rights Amendment that it considers threatening to its worldview. The political result is clear in Utah where Mormons are a numerical majority of the population. In terms of political office, five out of six members of Utah's Congressional delegation are both Mormon and Republican.

Figure 13.9

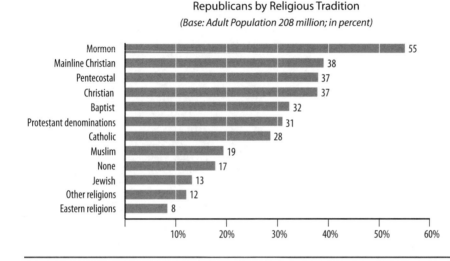

Republicans by Religious Tradition
(Base: Adult Population 208 million; in percent)

Two other features are noteworthy in Figure 13.9. The top groups in terms of Republican support are the various Protestant tradition groups. This was a feature of American politics throughout the 20th century. In contrast, the lowest levels of support for the Republican Party are to be found among the five Non-Christian groups. Interestingly, Catholics, the nation's largest religious group, can be found in the middle of the chart between the Protestants and the non-Christians.

History and the socioeconomic profile of Mainline Christians explains much of their preference for the Republican Party. However, the bias towards the Republicans by the Christian/evangelical category and among Pentecostals probably lies in the fact that some believe loosening constraints on business and the free market is a divine imperative. Some pastors teach that unobstructed capitalism is biblically based. They also correlate godliness and economic prosperity seeing a cause-and-effect relationship between personal righteousness and material comfort.

Figure 13.10

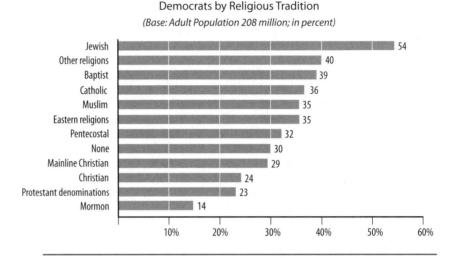

Democrats by Religious Tradition
(Base: Adult Population 208 million; in percent)

Figure 13.10 on Democratic Party support is largely an inversion of the previous chart describing Republicans. Whereas Mormons (55 percent) lead other religious groups in politically preferring Republicans, they are the last group (14 percent) in their preference for Democrats. In Figure 13.10, followers of another small religious tradition, Jews, replicate the Mormons in Figure 13.9. Jews lead the religious categories in preferring Democrats (54 percent) and are third least likely to support Republicans (only 13 percent).

However, not all religious traditions exhibit such clear-cut party preferences. For instance, 38 percent of Mainline Christians prefer Republicans and 29 percent prefer Democrats. Similarly, 37 percent of Pentecostals lean toward Republicans and 32 percent toward Democrats. Among Baptists it is 32 percent for Republicans and 39 percent for Democrats. However, as with Pentecostals this apparent balance hides an imbalance along the racial divide between white and black that we will consider in Chapter 14. Catholics, who have been the anchor of the Democratic Party coalition since the Civil

War, are now more balanced between the parties but they still show a significant Democrat bias. To some extent this continuing preference is due to the growth in the proportion of Hispanics in the ranks of Catholic identifiers.

Americans have a third political option and that is to identify or register with neither party. Thus, a third preference, political independence, emerges. This non-party preference accounts for 30 percent of the population and ranges between 22 percent and 43 percent across all religious groups. Non-Christians, aside from Jews, seem most likely to take this position. In fact this chart tends to mirror Figure 13.8 on voter registration. It is obvious that among the "Nones" who do not identify with any religious group there is a strong strain of independence and a reluctance to join or identify with any institution. In contrast we discover that Baptists and Pentecostals are the least likely to be independents and so the most likely to be politically partisan or involved among the religious groupings.

Figure 13.11

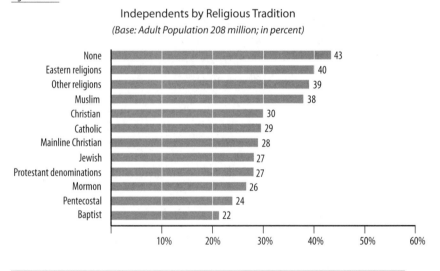

Independents by Religious Tradition
(Base: Adult Population 208 million; in percent)

The statistics presented in Figures 13.9 to 13.11 are noteworthy but they deal with self-identifiers only. This identification is a rather loose association for many people who are merely nominal members of religious groups. These nominal members probably have been baptized and may seek lifecycle events such as marriage or burial within these churches and faiths but they are not regular worshippers and therefore not under the direct and continuous influence of its teachings. In order to gauge properly the direct influence of religion on contemporary American politics, we will have to examine the pattern of congregational membership.

Figure 13.12

Congregational Membership by Political Party
Is anyone in your household currently a member of a church, temple or mosque?
(Base: Adult population 208 million; in percent)

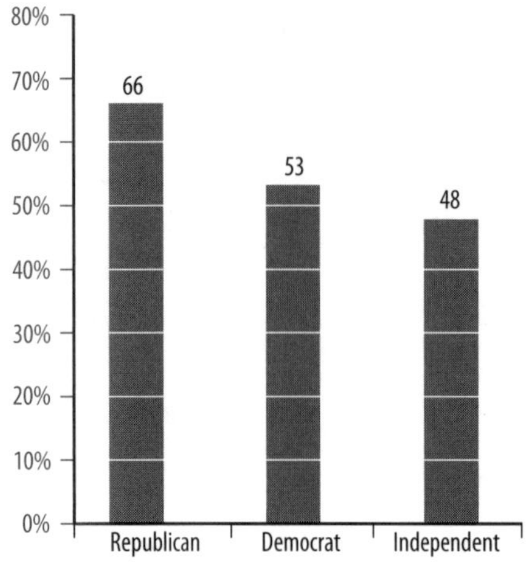

The Religious Vote

As expected, Figure 13.12 shows quite clearly that Republicans are more likely to be affiliated with religious institutions. About two-thirds of them live in households where somebody is a member of a church, temple, or mosque. Figure 13.12 also illustrates the differences in religious behavior among adults of different political inclinations. Democrats and independents alike are split almost 50:50 between members and non-members of religious congregations. Though the Democrats are again the middle group on this index they are much further from the Republicans and closer to the independents than they were on earlier charts.

The political party preferences of religiously affiliated voters

We now explore the pattern of political party preferences of registered voters who are actually members of religious institutions. By focusing on registered voters we capture those respondents who are more likely to vote and determine the outcome of elections. We also minimize the potential bias that can arise from incomplete coverage of the target population. For example, ARIS 2001 was conducted in English. Thus, non-English-speaking adults are not represented. We believe that this is less of a problem when focusing on registered voters because they are more likely than members of the general population to be English speakers.

Do the patterns of political party preferences of congregational members differ from those of the larger population of identifiers? We can assume that self-reporting "members" are both regular attendees at worship services and the bulk of the constituency that takes the faith seriously. That in turn leads to the assumption that some of the aggregate differences in political party preference among members of the various religious groupings probably can be laid at the door of religion. Unfortunately, due to inadequate sample sizes for statistical analysis, three groups, Muslims, Eastern Religions, and Other Religions/New Religious Movements, have to be omitted from the following charts, so these cover only nine categories of religious groupings.

Figure 13.13

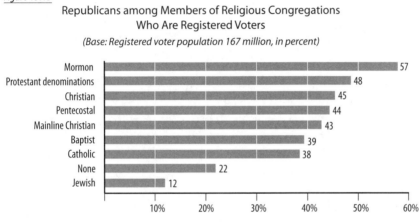

Republicans among Members of Religious Congregations
Who Are Registered Voters

(Base: Registered voter population 167 million, in percent)

A comparison of the pattern of Republican support between the preferences of identifiers in Figure 13.9 and members in Figure 13.13 shows that the affiliated voters are more Republican than the larger population of identifiers across all groups. Mormons still rank highest among Republicans, which is not surprising, since such a high proportion hold church membership. For most groups the change in focus to the subset of members produces a swing to the Republicans. The most politically significant finding here is for Catholics, the nation's largest religious group. Catholics who report that they are church members, which in this case we presume means practicing Catholics, are much more likely to be Republicans (38 percent) than the larger body of Catholic identifiers (28 percent).

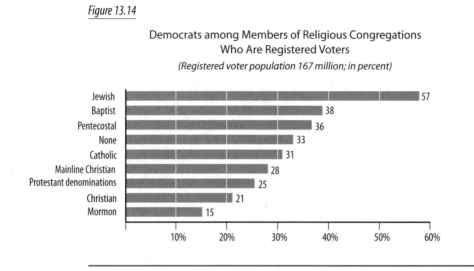

Figure 13.14

Democrats among Members of Religious Congregations
Who Are Registered Voters
(Registered voter population 167 million; in percent)

There are fewer marked differences between members and identifiers with regard to the Democratic Party (see Figures 13.10 and
13.14) compared with the Republicans. The most Democrat-leaning
group, the Jews, consolidate their support slightly when only synagogue members are reporting. Most noteworthy is the fall in support
for the Democrats among affiliated Catholics compared with all adult
Catholic identifiers.

Figure 13.15

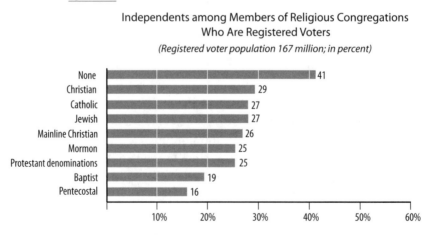

Independents among Members of Religious Congregations
Who Are Registered Voters
(Registered voter population 167 million; in percent)

Figure 13.15 illustrates a sociological rule. Joiners—in this case people who have registered as voters and are motivated to join a religious congregation—are less likely to take a neutral party posture, i.e., to be independent. The exceptions are the "Nones" who in this case are a subset of the large No Religion population. Most of these "affiliated Nones" are in mixed religious identification households. Nevertheless they mirror the overall "Nones" profile with a plurality of political independents and considerably more support for Democrats than for Republicans.

The Catholic vote

In terms of sheer size, the most important religious group in the U.S. is the Catholic population, with 51 million identifiers. However, we have already noted that this potential voting bloc has undergone dynamic change in recent decades in its pattern of party preferences. The difference in party preferences between members or practicing Catholics (who both identify with the Church and participate in parish life) compared with "cultural Catholics" (who self-identify as Catholic but do not say they are currently members) is striking, especially when Hispanic Catholics, who now comprise one-third of the nation's Catholics, are separated out in Figure 13.16. Among registered voters, non-Hispanic practicing Catholics, favor Republicans over Democrats by 13 points (41 percent to 28 percent) but among the cultural non-Hispanic Catholic voters, this is reversed and Democrats are favored over Republicans by 8 points (36 percent to 28 percent). Even among Hispanics, who are largely an urban and lower-income population, the practicing versus cultural Catholic political divide also occurs. Practicing Catholic Hispanics favor Republicans by 8 points and are 15 points less likely to support Democrats than cultural-Catholic Hispanic voters.

The current context of polarized public religious discourse has obviously rent apart the long established non-Hispanic Catholic community (the number of non-white non-Hispanics—mainly Asians and blacks—is insignificant as a proportion of this population). The emergence of this population of cultural Catholics reflects the vestige of eroded connections to upbringing, family, or ethnic community. The cultural Catholics who identify but don't affiliate are the wild card in any assessment of the role of Catholicism in contemporary American politics. ARIS is the first empirical study to offer an opportunity to measure the consequences for voting between cultural and practicing Catholics.

Figure 13.16

The Catholic Vote
(in percent)

	POPULATION	REPUBLICAN	DEMOCRAT	INDEPENDENT	OTHER
All Adult Identifiers	51.0 million	28%	36%	29%	6%
Catholic Electorate	41.6 million				
(Baptized)					
Hispanic	14.2 million	18	47	27	8
Non-Hispanic	36.7 million	31	33	30	6
Church Members	27.2 million				
(Practicing)					
Hispanic Voters	5.3 million	24	46	24	6
Non-Hispanic Voters	21.9 million	41	28	28	3
Unaffiliated	14.4 million				
(Cultural Catholics)					
Hispanic Voters	4.8 million	16	61	16	7
Non-Hispanic Voters	9.6 million	28	36	32	4

All rows total 100%

The fact that practicing Catholics are now so Republican in party orientation shows that a political era has ended. Throughout the 20th century Catholics, like Jews, were more likely than white Protestants to support an expanded role for government to help the deprived in order to produce a "just society." It is probable that this Catholic concern for community contrasted with the Protestant emphasis on individualism and this difference propelled them into the Democratic and Republican parties respectively. We can now observe that the commonality of cultural outlook on values has largely ended this party divide among church-going non-Hispanic whites.

Figure 13.17

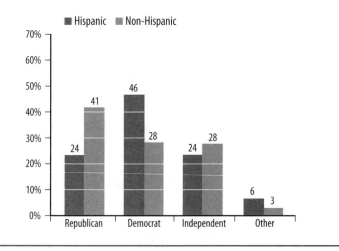

Catholic Church Members Who Are Registered Voters:
Political Party Preferences

Figure 13.18

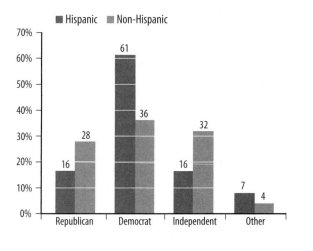

Unaffiliated Catholics Who Are Registered Voters:
Political Party Preferences

The Race and Ethnicity Factor in Religion and Politics

Today it is often assumed that the interrelationship between religion and politics operates differently among minority populations in the U.S. than among the white majority. However, there have been few attempts to demonstrate this assumption empirically due to the lack of representative national studies of sufficient size. Fortunately ARIS has the ability to fill this void because of its large number of respondents. We can look at the current situation among three minorities: African Americans, and the two fast-growing, largely immigrant populations of Hispanics and Asians.

African Americans

African Americans are unique in both religion and politics. They are politically important because they comprise almost 11 percent of the adult population and 81 percent are registered to vote. Their religious profile in Figure 13.19 shows that they are mainly Christians in the Protestant traditions.

The majority of them—Baptists, Methodists, and Pentecostals—identify with the historically black churches, which have been the main political instruments of their communities for generations. Only a minority of African Americans belong to the multiracial (but white-dominated) Catholic and Mainline churches and Protestant denominations. Blacks are the most religious population in American society on most indicators of religiosity (see Chapter 14), and this is reflected in the proportion of "Nones" in Figure 13.19 at 11 percent which is below the national average.

In terms of party preference African Americans are predominantly Democrats. They have uniquely low rates of Republican sympathies across all religious groups. Hardly any vestige of the early 20th-century support for the Republican Party remains. Religion seems therefore to play little part in their political preferences. The only exceptions are the low level of political interest among some adherents of Protestant sects such as the Jehovah's Witnesses, which have a high proportion of black members, and the common national pattern of a high independent preference among the "Nones."

African Americans are the exception to the contemporary political phenomenon that theological conservatism and high rates of religiosity are associated with support for the Republican Party. Black Americans, though conservative even on some social issues, have always stressed the need for social justice and racial equality and inclusion, which they associate with Democratic Party policies. In fact most elected black officials are Democrats, including all 43 members of the Congressional Black Caucus, and several are prominent Protestant ministers and pastors.

Figure 13.19

Political Party Preferences of African Americans by Major Religious Traditions
(in percent)

RELIGIOUS GROUPING	PERCENT OF POPULATION	REPUBLICAN	DEMOCRAT	INDEPENDENT	OTHER & DK/RF
Baptist*	46%	5%	72%	18%	5%
Christian/Evangelical/ Non-denominational	10	9	59	23	8
Methodist*	7	4	70	21	5
Pentecostal/Holiness*	7	8	63	23	7
Catholic	7	2	76	17	4
Protestant Denoms & Sects	4	2	39	25	34
Mainline Christian	3	8	70	18	3
None	11	4	45	40	11
Total**	95	5	65	22	8

* Historically black churches and denominations.

** The remaining 5 percent of the population comprises refusals and those in other religious traditions.

Hispanics

Hispanics are now the largest minority population, comprising 12 percent of the adult population. Their religious profile is unique because the majority is Catholic. However, this majority is less overwhelming than is sometimes imagined. Around 25 percent identify with Other Christian groups and there is a considerable proportion of "Nones" (13 percent).

Since many are new immigrants, only 70 percent are registered voters so the full impact of the recent rise in Hispanic numbers is not yet evident. Nevertheless their political party preferences are already of importance. The most striking point about Hispanic politics is that it does not mirror the African-American pattern. Among all adults the distribution of party preferences is 40 percent Democrat, 20 percent Republican, and 31 percent independent.

Figure 13.20 provides the distributions of party political preferences for various religious groups: Catholics, no religion, and other Christians, based on almost 2,000 adults who identified themselves as Hispanics.

Figure 13.20

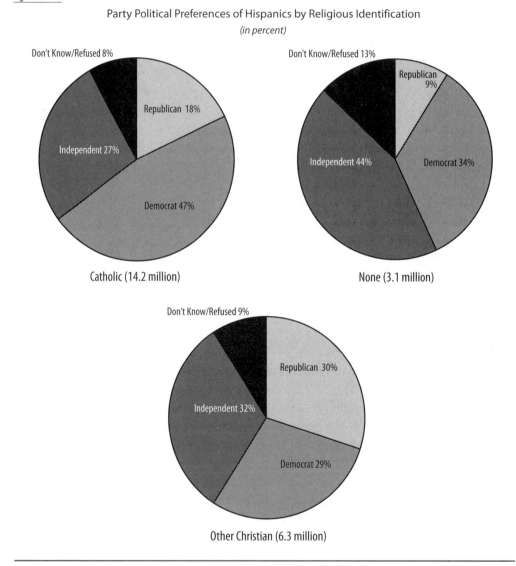

Party Political Preferences of Hispanics by Religious Identification
(in percent)

Catholic Hispanics, the majority, are the most likely (47 percent) to think of themselves as Democrats. On the other hand, Other Christians are the most likely to identify as Republicans (30 percent). We thus find that Hispanics follow the "white" pattern whereby identification with Protestantism is associated with more support for the Republican party. Yet as we have already noted religiosity among Catholic Hispanics is also associated with increased support for the Republicans.

As expected, Hispanics who profess no religion are by far more likely to be independent politically, 44 percent of them compared with only 27 percent of Catholic Hispanics. The very low level of support for the Republicans among Hispanic "Nones" is a significant finding. The refusal rate on party political preferences is similar among the three groups at 3 percent, while "don't know" is more prevalent among those who profess no religion.

Asian Americans

Asian Americans are a minority composed of many different national origins—Chinese, Japanese, Korean, Filipino, Indian, Vietnamese, Thai, and others. In terms of their religious identification, adult Asians are almost evenly divided among four major groupings, Eastern Religions, No-Religion, Catholic, and Other Christians, as shown in Figure 13.21. The ARIS data do not include Hawaii, where there is an Asian majority and where Eastern religions are more predominant.

Religion seems to play a major role in political party preferences among Asian Americans. The Catholics strongly prefer Democrats over Republicans while other Christians are almost evenly balanced between the two parties. AsianAmericans who profess Eastern Religions show similar rates of Democratic preferences as the two Christian groups but are unique in their shunning of the Republicans. In this pattern they reflect the parties' standing in the state of Hawaii, where Eastern religions–Asian Americans are the majority of voters.

The "Nones" in Figure 13.21 have two Democrats for every Republican but they are even more independent in preference than "Nones" nationally. One caveat is necessary here. Only 54 percent of these Asian Americans are registered to vote. This probably reflects their newcomer status and, as has been mentioned, the fact that Hawaiians are not included in ARIS.

Figure 13.21

Political Party Preferences of Asian Americans by Religious Identification
(in percent)

RELIGIOUS GROUPING	PERCENT OF POPULATION	REPUBLICAN	DEMOCRAT	INDEPENDENT	OTHER/ DK/RF
Catholic	20%	21%	35%	35%	8%
Other Christians	23	35	38	25	2
Eastern Religions	22	6	37	33	23
None	22	13	25	50	12
Total	**87***	**20**	**33**	**36**	**11**

* The remaining 13 percent of the population comprises refusals and those in other religious traditions.

Conclusions

If, as some commentators suggest, values relating to family, morality, and faith come to dominate state and national elections and political debate in the United States, then the more relevant religious patterns will be for explaining party politics and election results.

Most people's political and religious loyalties are established early in adult life and do not fluctuate easily from year to year. So the ARIS data have a considerable "shelf life" and will be useful and informative for elections for many years. There are strong and complex correlations between religion and political affiliation. In politics, independents are often seen as occupying a "swing" position in between Republicans and Democrats. They are perceived as in the middle of the road between conservatism and liberalism. Yet in terms of religious outlook, it is the Democrats who occupy the middle position. The Republicans are, for the most part, religious, and independents are largely secular. Democrats are most likely to call themselves "somewhat religious."

But religious outlook is only one dimension of religion. Another crucial dimension is behavior, which we measure by household membership in a religious congregation. Some people who have a religious outlook may not belong to a congregation, while some secular people may actually be members of a congregation. Membership in a religious congregation is associated with being a Republican. Non-membership is associated with being an independent. Democrats, again, are in the middle.

At a high level of abstraction, this continuum makes perfect sense. Many people who have a religious outlook and who belong to a religious congregation are drawn to the Republican Party because they agree with its social conservatism on issues such as traditional notions of marriage, abortion, homosexuality, and the death penalty. At the other end of the spectrum, it is not surprising that people who have a secular outlook and people who do not belong to a religious congregation would also reject any political affiliation. In the middle is the "big tent" of the Democratic Party, which embraces people with a wide range of political—and religious—beliefs. The humorist Will Rogers once quipped: "I'm not a member of any organized political party. I'm a Democrat!"

Not all people who have a religious outlook and belong to congregations are socially conservative. While most blacks describe themselves as religious, and are members of congregations, they are the most loyal Democrats of any ethnic group. Jews also are likely to be Democrats, even if they are members of religious congregations. Jehovah's Witnesses are another exception to the rule. Although they are highly religious, they are politically independent because their religion prohibits them from participation in politics. Surprisingly, too, the religious right is harder to spot than commonly thought. Evangelicals and members of Protestant denominations are far less committed to the Republicans than black church members are to the Democratic Party.

While these cases appear to weaken the link between religion and political preference, paradoxically they can be seen to strengthen the link when placed in a broader context. Religion is not one-dimensional. That is why it is impossible to use the degree of religious outlook by itself as a predictor of political preference. It is crucial to know the religious group or denomination with which a person is associated. And since religion is tied up with race and ethnicity in complex ways that are rooted in history, those characteristics too help predict political leanings and voting patterns. Congregational membership and active church going are important factors which when associated with party affiliation seem to turn private belief into civic participation with public consequences.

What are the practical implications of these findings? The clearest message for Democrats and Republicans is that independents are unlikely to be won over in large numbers by messages with strong religious content since independents are the most secular segment of the electorate. Given their socioeconomic profile, independents are likely to be found in the middle ground on most economic and political issues, but not on faith issues.

For Republicans, religious appeals can energize the base while appealing to the socially conservative and religious "Reagan Democrats." If political debate can be framed primarily as a "culture war" this will be to the advantage of the Republican Party. Republicans have a natural edge in that those with a religious outlook, particularly Protestants, not only tend to be Republican but have the highest propensity to vote in national elections.

Democrats, in contrast, can use religious appeals to retain the support of wavering Reagan Democrats, but should not expect that religion will boost their support among other, more secular Democratic constituencies. Indeed, Democrats are better off when the battleground moves away from religion—as President Clinton's adviser, James Carville, observed when he said, "It's the economy, stupid."

The intersection of religion and politics has been fascinating to observe since the earliest days of the Republic. What adds to the fascination is that social and economic issues and interests are constantly shifting though the pace of change varies between different generations and epochs. Certainly the truisms of a generation ago no longer hold for the early years of the 21st century, so up-to-date, broad-based research such as ARIS is worthy of close scrutiny and study by political scientists and tacticians alike.

Note

1. For further details see Kosmin and Lachman, *One Nation Under God : Religion in Contemporary American Society*, p.253.

FOURTEEN

Race and Ethnicity in Religious Identification

HISTORICALLY in the U.S, differences in religion have added to the cultural distinctiveness of the nation's racial and ethnic populations. To what extent this situation is still true in the early 21st century will now be examined. All the ARIS respondents were asked to self-identify with the official U.S. census categories of racial and ethnic groups. We begin this chapter by looking at the ethnic composition of each major religious tradition and group. Then we will show how ethnic minorities differ not only from the so-called, white non-Hispanic majority but also from each other. However, at the outset it has to be made clear that the following data relate to the larger population of all adult identifiers and not just the current memberships of the various groups.

In 2001, there were a number of sets of religious traditions and groups that could be identified according to their racial composition. The first was overwhelmingly dominated by white non-Hispanic adherents. This featured the Mainline Christians (with the excerption of the Methodists), Mormons, and Jews. Another set, such as Jehovah's Witnesses, Baptists and Muslims, had a large proportion of black non-Hispanic or African-American adherents. A third set composed of Catholics, Evangelicals, and Pentecostals had a substantial proportion of Hispanics, while the fourth set comprising the Eastern religions and to a lesser extent Muslims had a plurality of Asians. A sixth set looks quite similar to the overall national adult population in its racial/ethnic composition. This included the No Religion, New Religious Movements, and the unspecified Christians, as well as the Non-denominational Christians.

Figure 14.1

Race and Ethnic Make-Up of Religious Traditions and Groups

(weighted estimate, in percent)

	WHITE	BLACK	ASIAN	HISPANIC	OTHER	TOTAL
U.S. Total Adults	**70%**	**10%**	**3%**	**12%**	**5%**	**100%**
RELIGIOUS TRADITION/GROUP						
Catholic	64	3	3	29	2	100
Mainline Christians	90	6	1	2	1	100
Methodist	86	11	1	1	1	100
Lutheran	96	1	0	1	1	100
Presbyterian	91	3	2	3	1	100
Episcopalian	89	9	1	0	1	100
United Church of Christ	93	0	0	5	2	100
Baptist	64	29	1	3	2	100
Christian Generic	71	10	3	12	3	100
Christian unspecified	67	12	3	14	3	100
Protestant unspecified	87	4	0	6	3	100
Evangelical/Born Again	77	3	0	20	0	100
Non-denominational	73	11	1	13	2	100
Pentecostal/Charismatic	65	20	1	12	3	100
Assemblies of God	80	5	5	8	2	100
Church of God	84	12	0	4	0	100
Pentecostal unspecified	58	22	0	17	3	100
Protestant Denominations	71	15	1	11	2	100
Churches of Christ	89	6	1	2	2	100
Jehovah's Witnesses	46	37	0	14	3	100
Seventh Day Adventist	67	26	0	7	0	100
Mormon	91	0	0	8	1	100
Jewish	92	1	1	5	1	100
Eastern Religions	20	3	67	6	4	100
Buddhist	32	4	61	2	1	100
Muslim	15	27	34	10	14	100
NRM & Other Religions	70	8	2	11	9	100
Nones/No religion	73	8	5	11	4	100

Note: Rows may not total 100 percent due to rounding.

Figure 14.1 shows that one of the most conspicuous social differences between and among religious groups remains their ethnic and racial makeup. A logical corollary of this situation is that the religious profiles of America's racial and ethnic groups also demonstrate high degrees of differentiation. So we shall now examine the religious profile of each ethnic group using an array of key religious variables.

Native Americans

Our first example is the original and oldest ethnic group in America, Native Americans or American Indians, included under "Other" in Figure 14.1. Today they are both the smallest ethnic/racial minority and the one whose religious profile is probably least known. However, due to the sheer number of respondents to ARIS 2001, we have a unique opportunity to provide representative national data based on a substantial sample of 680 household cases.

America's "Indians" have been the object of Christian missionary activities since the beginning of European colonization of the continent. The first Bible published in America was produced in the Algonquin language. From 1819 on, the annual congressional appropriation for Indian education and agriculture directly funded mission schools, hospitals, and orphanages. Not until well into the 20th century did U.S. government aid to mission schools end. Figure 14.2 sets out the current position as regards the religious aspect of the cultural integration or assimilation of this minority into the national pattern and correspondingly away from its ancient nature and spirit beliefs, embodied by the shaman.

Religious identification

The largest religious traditions among Native Americans were Baptist and Catholics, comprising together about one-third of the adult population. This pattern can be explained by geography, since a great number of Native Americans live in either Oklahoma or the Southwest. Baptists and Catholics are, of course, also the two largest religious groups among the Americans generally. However what is exceptional among Native Americans is that they are much more likely than others to identify with No Religion (19 percent) and Other Religions (6 percent). If one adds in the four percent of refusals these figures reveal that around one-in-three Native Americans did not subscribe to mainstream forms of religion despite the fact that they have been the target of Christian missionary activity for several hundred years.

Figure 14.2

Religious Identification of Adult Native Americans
(weighted estimates, 680 respondents)

RELIGIOUS TRADITION	ESTIMATED ADULT POPULATION	PERCENT
Baptist	261,000	20.4%
Nones	247,000	19.3
Catholic	174,000	13.6
Christian Generic	166,000	13.0
Pentecostal/Charismatic	104,000	8.1
Mainline Christian	102,000	8.0
NRM & Other Religions	82,000	6.4
Protestant Denominations	39,000	3.0
Remainder Traditions	54,000	4.1
Don't Know/Refused	51,000	4.0
Total	**1,280,000**	**100.0**

Note: Column does not total 100 percent due to rounding.

Religious belonging

Given the information shown above it is perhaps unsurprising that Native Americans fall below the national average on congregational membership. Overall 46 percent of Native Americans resided in households where somebody was a member of a religious congregation or institution.

Religious or secular outlook

Only 10 percent of Native Americans described themselves either as "secular" or "somewhat secular," while the great majority (77 percent) preferred to describe themselves as religious or somewhat religious as illustrated in Figure 14.3. However, a substantial proportion of Native Americans, 13 percent, did not respond to this question and this "refusal rate" was particularly marked compared with other ethnic groups.

Figure 14.3

Religious or Secular Outlook: Native American Adults

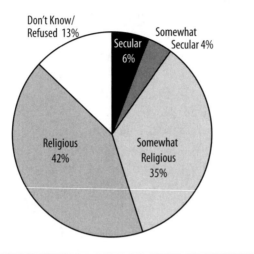

Religious attitudes: belief in God

Whereas three-in-four Native American adults regarded themselves as religious in some way an even greater majority (87 percent) believed that God exists.

Overall the four sets of religious data examined above suggest that Native Americans still maintain their own religious patterns and that these set them apart from the national norms analyzed in earlier chapters.

Asian Americans

The growth of the nation's Asian-origin population was restricted by immigration bans until 1965. However it expanded rapidly during the 1980s and 1990s. As a result it includes a larger number of first generation Americans than the other minorities. In recent years the countries of origin of this burgeoning minority have also diversified; today it is composed of many different national groups including Chinese, Japanese, Korean, Filipino, Indian, Pakistani, Vietnamese, Thai and others. This is a varied and fast changing population, in which many of the newcomers have little cultural connection to earlier immigrants who were mainly of Japanese and Chinese origin.

Religious identification

In terms of their religious identification as shown in Figure 14.4, adult Asian Americans in 2001 were almost evenly divided among four groupings: Eastern Religions, No-Religion, Catholic, and other Christians (Christian generic, Baptist and Mainline Christian) with each having just over 20 percent. However, the ARIS data do not include Hawaii, where Asian Americans are a majority and Eastern religions are more predominant; this would add another 400,000 persons to that category. This addition would still leave adherents of the Eastern religions tradition smaller in proportion to the combined Christian faith groups comprising all Catholics and Protestants at around 40 percent of the total. A Christian plurality might be unexpected at first glance but it reflects the self-selection process in international migration. People who decide to emigrate to the U.S. tend to be those who find American society compatible with their lifestyle and aspirations. This automatically creates a Christian bias since the baptized elements of Asian-American societies and those who attended Christian mission schools tend to be most westernized. This trend is particularly evident among Korean immigrants.

Figure 14.4

Religious Identification of Adult Asian Americans
(weighted estimates, 611 respondents)

RELIGIOUS TRADITION	ESTIMATED ADULT POPULATION	PERCENT
None	1,388,000	22.0
Eastern Religions	1,375,000	21.5
Catholic	1,263,000	20.0
Christian Generic	713,000	11.3
Muslim	493,000	7.8
Mainline Christian	377,000	6.0
Baptist	267,000	4.2
Remainder Traditions	132,000	2.0
Don't Know/Refused	313,000	5.0
Total	**6,304,000**	**100.0**

Note: Column does not total 100 percent due to rounding.

The large No Religion component among the Asian-American minority population is also a unique feature. It reflects in part the geographical settlement pattern. Asian Americans tend to settle in the "irreligious" West (35 percent in California) since they come from across the Pacific. Other contributing factors associated with a preference for the "None" category are the youthful age structure and high proportion of Asian Americans with postgraduate education.

Religious belonging

A notable feature of religion among Asian Americans is their low rate of membership in religious institutions. According to ARIS 2001 only 39 percent of Asian-American adults resided in households where somebody belongs to church or a temple. This statistic reflects and is a direct outcome of the religious profile of this minority with its large proportion of Nones and Eastern religions, which have no tradition of congregational activity on the typical American pattern.

Religious or secular outlook

As illustrated in Figure 14.5, almost one-third of Asian Americans regarded themselves as "secular" or "somewhat secular." In addition the 28 percent of Asian American adults who regarded themselves as "religious" was by far the lowest proportion among racial and ethnic groups in the U.S.

Figure 14.5

Religious or Secular Outlook: Asian-American Adults

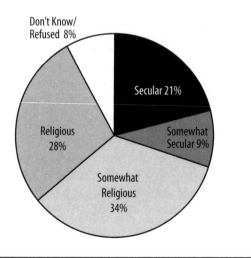

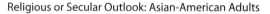

Religious attitudes: belief in God

Despite the tendency towards a secular outlook, most Asian Americans believe that God exists: 59 percent "agree strongly," 22 percent "agree somewhat," whereas only 4 percent "disagree somewhat" and 5 percent "disagree strongly."

The ARIS findings indicate that the Asian-American minority exhibits a diverse pattern with regard to religious identification. Asians are also unique in being far more irreligious and secularized on a number of measures than the rest of the nation.

African Americans

Religious identification

Much of the literature on American history and social science tends to emphasize the unique qualities of the African-American religious heritage and the "racial divide" in religion. In terms of social outcomes this was long true and it reflected the aphorism that the most segregated time in America was Sunday morning. However, from a theological standpoint African Americans self-identify overwhelmingly as Christians in the Protestant traditions and conservative mold of "Middle America." The most noticeable feature of the African-American religious identification profile in Figure 14.6 is that almost half this population self-identifies with the Baptist tradition. This religious bias is the inheritance of a regional culture that is held in common with white Southerners.

Unfortunately the imprecision of the replies of most respondents to the religious identification question means we are unable to specify categorically whether respondents identified with historically black churches. This means that in Figure 14.6 the category of Mainline Christians includes Methodists, who identify the United Methodist Church along with adherents of the AME and AME Zion Churches. However the results which show a concentration in the Baptist, Methodist, and Pentecostal denominations—the religious heartland of the historically black churches—strongly suggests that religious segregation remains the preference for a majority of this minority. Thus we must assume that only a minority of African-

Americans belong to the multiracial (but white-dominated) Catholic or Protestant denominations.

Another statistic in Figure 14.6 is socially significant. The very low rate of refusal to the main ARIS identification question among African-American respondents (2.4 percent), compared with the national average (5.4 percent), can be viewed as an indicator of the important place of religion for this minority and its culture.

Figure 14.6

Religious Identification of Adult African Americans
(weighted estimates, 4,245 respondents)

RELIGIOUS TRADITION	ESTIMATED ADULT POPULATION	PERCENT
Baptist	9,963,000	45.9
None	2,327,000	10.7
Mainline Christian	2,246,000	10.4
Christian Generic	2,240,000	10.3
Pentecostal/Charismatic	1,552,000	7.2
Catholic	1,429,000	6.6
Protestant Denominations	899,000	4.1
Muslim	236,000	1.1
NRM & Other Religions	150,000	0.7
Remainder Traditions	120,000	0.5
Don't Know/Refused	524,000	2.4
Total	**21,685,000**	**100.0**

Note: Column does not total 100 percent due to rounding.

Religious belonging

African Americans were the population most likely to belong to religious institutions—67 percent live in households where somebody belongs to a religious congregation. As stated in Chapter 11, the black churches in particular have long served as more than houses of worship for their communities; they have active social, economical, educational, and political roles. A 2000 survey of African-American churches coordinated by the Interdenominational Theological Center reported that 86 percent of the congregations provided assistance to families in need and 76 percent conducted voter registration.[1]

Religious or secular outlook

African-American respondents are the most religious segment of American society on most indicators of religiosity. Figure 14.7 illustrates that almost half of them claimed a "religious" outlook and another 33 percent a "somewhat religious" outlook.

Figure 14.7

Religious or Secular Outlook: African-American Adults

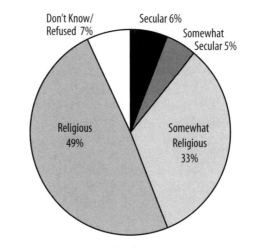

Figure 14.8 provides a further insight into the pattern of African-Americans' outlook across the major Christian traditions as well as among those who profess no religion.

Figure 14.8

Religious or Secular Outlook: African-American Adults
by Selected Religious Traditions

RELIGIOUS TRADITIONS	RELIGIOUS	SOMEWHAT RELIGIOUS	SECULAR/ SOMEWHAT SECULAR	REFUSED/ DON'T KNOW	TOTAL
Pentecostal	68%	21%	2%	8%	100%
Mainline Christian	62	30	7	2	100
Christian Generic	56	29	7	8	100
Baptist	53	37	7	3	100
None	15	31	36	18	100
Total	**49**	**33**	**11**	**7**	**100**

Note: Some rows may not total 100 percent due to rounding.

Two distinct patterns emerge regarding African-Americans' outlook. First, those who profess a religion are quite homogeneous, although the Pentecostals are those most likely to regard themselves as "religious." Second, African Americans who profess no religion are distinctively different. They are more likely to regard themselves as secular in some way and much less likely to profess a religious outlook, and more like to refuse to answer the question.

Religious attitudes: belief in God

One of the most striking findings of ARIS 2001 is the almost universal belief in God among its large sample of African Americans. When asked: *Do you agree that God exists?* 90 percent "agree strongly," 5 percent "agree somewhat," while only 1 percent "disagree somewhat" and 1 percent "disagree strongly."

It is interesting to note that although 13 percent of African-American adults did not identify with a religious group (i.e. those replying "None" or refusing to answer), only 2 percent of the population challenged the existence of God.

Hispanics

Religious identification

The Hispanic population is a cultural category composed of Americans originating in societies that use the Spanish language or have a Spanish or Latin American heritage. This group includes members who would otherwise be classified with the "racial" groups—white, black, Asian, or Native American. This diverse population grew considerably in the last decade of the 20th century to become the nation's largest officially recognized minority population. Overall, in the 2000 Census, 35.3 million people were identified as Hispanics; of these, 23 million were adults and the rest were 17 years old or younger. This was a considerable rise from the 1990 Hispanic total of 23 million of whom almost 14.6 million were adults.

The ARIS 2001 had almost 3,000 adult Hispanics.[2] The key question in this survey, *What is your religion, if any?* yielded over 60 different religious groups and bodies. However, for analytic reasons Figure 14.9 shows only the religious groupings which were chosen by at least 30 adult Hispanics in the 2001 sample.

Given the fast rate of growth due mainly to immigration from an ever-widening number of Latin American countries we should expect some dynamic changes over the past decade. Because of this, Figure 14.9 describes the religious identification of American Hispanics at two points in time, 1990 and 2001. Fortunately the use of identical methodologies in the two national surveys under examination allows for the exploration of trends and changes. Figure 14.9 not only provides the most comprehensive contemporary profile of religious identification among adult American Hispanics but also records the nature of recent changes.

Catholicism was the dominant religion among Hispanics in 2001. Figure 14.9 shows the number of adult Hispanic Catholics rose from about 9.6 million in 1990 to over 13 million in 2001. However, despite the sharp increase in absolute numbers, one of the most important findings was the drop in the proportion of Hispanics who were Catholic. In 1990, 66 percent of adult Hispanics identified themselves as Catholics but in 2001 only 57 percent of them did so. In contrast, the proportion of non-Catholic Christians remained steady from 1990 to 2001 at around one-quarter of adult Hispanics.

Clearly the most important recent trend was the rapid growth in the no-religion group, which was the second largest preference group among Hispanics in 2001. In 1990, fewer than one million adult Hispanics self-identified as professing no religion, or as atheist, agnostic or secular but almost 3 million opted for these self-classifications in 2001. Consequently their proportion of the Hispanic population grew from 6 percent to 13 percent.

This pattern, of growth in the No Religion group, parallels national trends referred to in earlier chapters. ARIS 2001 documented the great increase both in absolute numbers as well as in percentages of the adults who do not subscribe to any religion. Nationally, 14 percent of American adults prefer to be identified as atheist, agnostic, humanist,[3] secular or having no religion.

Another trend revealed by Figure 14.9 was an increase in the unspecified Christian population and a decrease in the unspecified Protestant population in 2001; again a feature that affected both Hispanics and the general population. Similarly, the percentage of Hispanic Baptists decreased during the past decade despite an increase in total numbers.

Last, since 1990 there has been a substantial increase in the number of adults who refused to reply to the question about their religious preference. This general pattern is reflected among Hispanics
as well. While less than 1 percent refused to reveal their religious
identification in 1990, almost 3 percent refused to answer in 2001.
Yet that refusal rate is still below the 5.4 percent refusal rate in the
general adult population.

Further analysis of the survey data finds that many Hispanics who
left the Catholic Church opted for no religion at all whereas it had
been thought that the vast majority of ex-Catholics became Protestants, and in particular Pentecostals. It is often assumed that the
decline in Catholics' share of the Hispanic population is mirrored by
an equally large increase in the share of Pentecostals. In fact ARIS
2001 showed that although the number of Pentecostal Hispanics
doubled between 1990 and 2001, their share of the overall Hispanic
population increased only modestly from 3 percent to 4 percent.

Figure 14.9

Self-Described Religious Identification of U.S. Adult Hispanics, 1990–2001
(weighted estimates)

	1990		2001	
	NUMBER	PERCENT	NUMBER	PERCENT
Catholic	9,608,000	66%	13,090,000	57%
Baptist	1,077,000	7	1,148,000	5
Christian (unspecified)	757,000	5	1,837,000	8
Pentecostals[4]	438,000	3	918,000	4
Protestant (unspecified)	366,000	3	230,000	1
Methodist/Wesleyan	250,000	2	229,000	1
Jehovah's Witnesses	244,000	2	229,000	1
Other Christian[5]	584,000	4	1,149,000	5
No religion[6]	926,000	6	2,985,000	13
Other religion[7]	270,000	2	459,000	2
Don't Know/Refused	124,000	<1	689,000	3
Total	**14,597,000***	**100**	**22,963,000****	**100**

* Total adult population is drawn from Census 1990. Number in each religion calculated from distribution of religious identification in NSRI 1990.

**Total adult population is drawn from Census 2000. Number in each religion calcu-
lated from distribution of religious identification in ARIS 2001.

Note: Some totals may not add to 100 percent due to rounding.

Religious belonging

Congregational membership or the rate of "belonging" to a religious institution is lower among Hispanics at only 45 percent compared with the national average of 54 percent. Still, membership varies greatly by religious tradition just as it does in the overall American population. Figure 14.10 shows the varied pattern of religious institutional membership among Hispanics. Protestants were clearly far more likely to reside in households where somebody is a member of a church. It may seem odd that 19 percent of Hispanics who profess no religion answered positively to the question about household religious affiliation. However, usually someone else in the household who professed a religious adherence was a church member.[8] In fact, in the general population as well, 19 percent of people who profess no religion similarly reported a congregational membership for their household. However, this similarity in religious institutional membership between Hispanics and non-Hispanics does not hold for Catholics. While 59 percent of identifying American Catholics, in general, report household membership in a church, only 46 percent of identifying Hispanic Catholics do so.

Figure 14.10

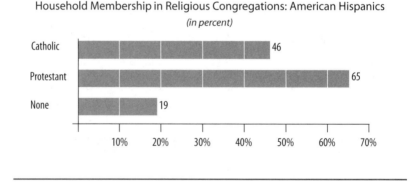

Household Membership in Religious Congregations: American Hispanics
(in percent)

Religious or secular outlook

Do American Hispanics regard their outlook on life to be essentially religious or secular? Whereas three-quarters of Americans in general see themselves in some way as religious (37 percent regard themselves as "religious," and 38 percent as "somewhat religious"), Hispanics are far more likely to opt for the less certain category. So while 30 percent of Hispanics regard themselves as "religious," 45 percent regard themselves as "somewhat religious."

In addition Hispanic responses varied according to their religious identification. Figure 14.11 provides a picture of the major differences between Catholic and Protestant Hispanics as well as the unique outlook of those who identify with No Religion. Almost half of Protestant Hispanics regard themselves as "religious." Yet only 28 percent of Catholic Hispanics regard themselves as "religious." Catholics are much more likely to lean toward the more ambivalent term "somewhat religious." More than half of Catholics chose that category, compared with only 37 percent of Protestants. The main finding then is the particularly strong religious outlook among Protestant Hispanics. However, if we combine the two categories, "somewhat religious" and "religious," there is hardly any difference between the outlooks of Catholics and Protestants.

In contrast the worldview of Hispanics who profess No Religion is clearly secular. Half of them regard themselves as either "secular" or "somewhat secular." Naturally, the dominant group, 42 percent, consider themselves as "secular," and only 8 percent as "somewhat secular." This pattern was very close to the national situation. Generally American adults who professed no religion also had a secular outlook; 39 percent regarded themselves as "secular," and 12 percent as "somewhat secular."

Figure 14.11

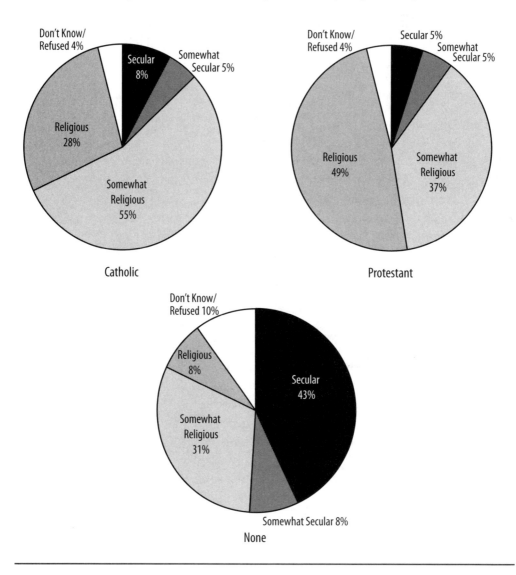

Religious or Secular Outlook: Hispanic Adults by Religious Group

Religious attitudes: belief in God

Belief in God is an important gauge of an individual's overall religious attitude. Figure 14.12 offers a glance at the views of American Hispanics as to whether God exists according to the three main Hispanic religious preference groupings.

Catholic and Protestant Hispanics alike believe strongly that God exists. However, once again Protestants are more certain in their opinions and are more likely to express a stronger religious worldview than Catholic Hispanics.

The No Religion group, however, is unsurprisingly more skeptical about the divine and only 53 percent of them "agree strongly" with the statement and almost a third say that they only "agree somewhat" that God exists. Although these patterns are typical among people who subscribe to no religion,[9] they are certainly atypical among Hispanics in general. Nevertheless, even 85 percent of No Religion Hispanics seem to agree that "God exists." This suggests that the "Nones" category contained people who, although having no ties to organized religion, are not necessarily non-believers.

Figure 14.12

Belief that God Exists among Hispanics by Religious Grouping
Do you agree or disagree that God exists?
(in percent)

AGREE/DISAGREE	RELIGIOUS GROUP			
	CATHOLIC	PROTESTANT	NONE	TOTAL
Disagree strongly	2%	2%	4%	2%
Disagree somewhat	1	2	5	2
Agree somewhat	11	4	32	12
Agree strongly	84	91	53	80
Don't Know/Refused	2	1	6	4
Total	**100**	**100**	**100**	**100**
Number of adults *(in millions)*	13.1	5.8	3.0	23.0

One of the main conclusions suggested by the ARIS data regarding the Hispanic population is the weakness of this minority's ties to institutional religion, as manifested by below-average church affiliation and the growing proportion of Hispanics in the No Religion group. Further analysis has revealed that young people and new immigrants are particularly "unchurched." Nevertheless, lack of belonging does not mean lack of belief or lack of a "religious outlook." In fact Hispanics who professed no religion are more likely to believe in God than other members of the general public who profess no religion. Interestingly, Hispanic Protestants are typical Protestants and they most resembled the overall American population in terms of their higher level of church membership and stronger religious beliefs.

The White Majority

The majority population of the nation according to the official census categories is the white non-Hispanic population, which numbered over 145 million adults and 70 percent of the national adult population in 2000. Therefore, inevitably in statistical terms the characteristics of this population dominate the overall social patterns of American society. In addition the historical dominance of this population group in the nation's cultural and political realms means that its patterns and special characteristics are particularly important.

Religious identification

A comparison of Figure 14.13 and the national profile provided in Chapter 2 (Figure 2.2) shows that the most notable difference is in the share of Mainline Christians. This religious tradition associated with the historically dominant "WASP" establishment culture remains much stronger among the white non-Hispanic population— 22 percent compared with 17 percent among all Americans. Jews and Mormons also have a somewhat higher share among white non-Hispanics, whereas Catholics and Baptists have a smaller share. As we have already noted, the latter feature is due to the high proportion of black Baptists and the large Hispanic contingent among Catholics. Unsurprisingly the proportion of Muslims and adherents of the Eastern religions is also lower among white Americans.

Figure 14.13

Religious Identification of Non-Hispanic White Adults
(weighted estimates)

	ESTIMATED ADULT POPULATION IN MILLIONS	PERCENT
U.S. Total Adults	**146.0**	**100.0%**
RELIGIOUS TRADITION		
Catholic	33.1	22.7
Mainline Christians	32.0	21.9
Methodist	12.0	8.2
Lutheran	9.2	6.3
Presbyterian	5.1	3.5
Episcopalian	3.0	2.1
United Church of Christ	1.3	0.9
Baptist	21.7	14.9
Christian Generic	16.1	11.0
Christian unspecified	9.3	6.4
Protestant unspecified	4.0	2.7
Evangelical/Born Again	0.8	0.5
Non-denominational	1.8	1.2
Pentecostal/Charismatic	5.1	3.5
Assemblies of God	0.9	0.6
Church of God	0.8	0.5
Pentecostal unspecified	2.6	1.8
Protestant Denominations	4.3	2.9
Churches of Christ	2.3	1.6
Jehovah's Witnesses	0.6	0.4
Seventh Day Adventist	0.5	0.3
Mormon	2.5	1.7
Jewish	2.6	1.8
Eastern Religions	0.4	0.3
Buddhist	0.3	0.2
Muslim	0.2	0.1
NRM & Other Religions	1.2	0.8
Nones/No religion	21.5	14.7

Religious belonging

Overall, 56 percent of white non-Hispanic adults reside in house-holds where someone belongs to a religious institution. This is also the national percentage. Due to the large sample size of the ARIS white non-Hispanic sample, we are able to compare ten of the religious traditions. As illustrated in Figure 14.14, household member-ship for whites varied greatly by religion. At the top were Mormons with a 74 percent membership rate and at the bottom were the New Religious Movements with only a 36 percent membership rate.

Figure 14.14

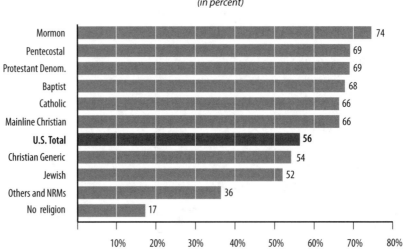

Household Membership in Religious Congregations by Religious Tradition: White Non-Hispanics *

(in percent)

Religious Tradition	Percent
Mormon	74
Pentecostal	69
Protestant Denom.	69
Baptist	68
Catholic	66
Mainline Christian	66
U.S. Total	**56**
Christian Generic	54
Jewish	52
Others and NRMs	36
No religion	17

* Percentage of those who identify with each religion who live in a household in which someone is a member of a religious institution.

As mentioned earlier, since this religious indicator represents a household attribute, the membership rate among adults who profess No Religion may be explained by mixed-religion households where somebody else in the household, who does profess a religion, is affil-iated with a religious institution.

Religious or secular outlook

Figure 14.15 shows that overall, 17 percent of white adults regard their outlook as "secular" or "somewhat secular." This is slightly above the national average, but as we show in Figure 14.16 the likelihood of having a secular or a religious outlook varies greatly by religious group.

Figure 14.15

Religious or Secular Outlook: White Non-Hispanic Adults

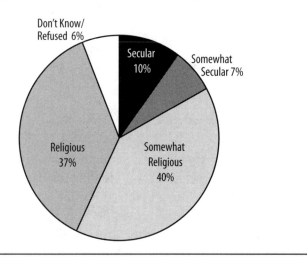

The advantage of comparing religious denominations for each racial and ethnic group is that this type of analysis allows measurement of the independent role of religion controlling for racial-ethnic composition. As shown in Figure 14.16, among white non-Hispanics, the Mormons, those identifying with the Protestant denominations, and Pentecostals had the strongest religious outlook. At the other end, still among white non-Hispanic adults, those who identified with non-Christian traditions—No Religion, Jews, and New Religious Movements or Other Religions were the most likely to have a secular outlook and to refuse to answer.

Figure 14.16

Religious or Secular Outlook by Religious Tradition: White Non-Hispanic Adults
(in percent)

RELIGIOUS TRADITION	RELIGIOUS	SOMEWHAT RELIGIOUS	SECULAR/ SOMEWHAT SECULAR	REFUSED/ DON'T KNOW	TOTAL
Catholic	35%	50%	12%	3%	100%
Mainline Christian	39	49	10	2	100
Baptist	54	38	5	2	100
Pentecostal	64	27	5	4	100
Protestant Denominations	68	25	5	2	100
Mormon	69	17	9	5	100
Christian Generic	45	38	12	5	100
Jewish	10	41	43	6	100
NRM & Other Religions	25	21	40	14	100
None	8	27	53	11	100
Total	**37**	**40**	**17**	**6**	**100**

Note: Categories may not total to 100% due to rounding.

As expected, the gaps between the religious traditions are larger on the "religious" option than in the "somewhat religious" category. The range of high to low percentages for the more certain response, "religious," was more than 60 points (the largest difference being between the Mormon and the No Religion categories), compared with only 33 points between the Mormon and Catholic respondents who chose the middle of the road option "somewhat religious."

Religious attitudes: belief in God

An overwhelming majority (89 percent) of white non-Hispanic Americans believe that God exists—77 percent "agree strongly," 12 percent "agree somewhat," 2 percent "disagree somewhat" and 3 percent "disagree strongly" with the statement. Therefore, we might expect less variability by religious tradition on this indicator. Figure 14.17 shows this was true for all those in the various majority Christian traditions but not for those outside them with the exception of the small population of white Muslims.

White adherents of the Eastern religions are less strongly theistic than the followers of this tradition in general. Another contrast is the white "Nones" are more certain than minority "Nones" who tend to prefer the "agree somewhat" response option.

Figure 14.17

Belief that God Exists among Non-Hispanic White Adults
(in percent)

	DISAGREE STRONGLY	DISAGREE SOMEWHAT	AGREE SOMEWHAT	AGREE STRONGLY
U.S. Total Adults	**3%**	**2%**	**12%**	**77%**
RELIGIOUS TRADITION/GROUP				
Catholic	1	1	12	84
Mainline Christian	1	1	12	83
Methodist	0	1	11	84
Lutheran	2	2	12	83
Presbyterian	0	0	15	81
Episcopalian	0	2	15	80
United Church of Christ	1	1	10	84
Baptist	0	0	5	93
Christian Generic	0	1	9	86
Christian unspecified	0	1	8	89
Protestant unspecified	1	2	14	76
Evangelical/Born Again	0	0	1	99
Non-denominational	0	0	10	85
Pentecostal/Charismatic	1	0	4	95
Assemblies of God	2	0	2	96
Church of God	0	0	13	86
Pentecostal unspecified	1	0	3	96
Protestant Denominations	0	0	3	95
Churches of Christ	0	0	4	94
Jehovah's Witnesses	0	0	0	98
Seventh Day Adventist	0	0	0	100
Mormon	0	1	6	93
Jewish	5	8	24	54
Eastern Religions	7	14	20	58
Buddhist	9	15	26	48
Muslim	0	0	8	92
NRM & Other Religions	7	4	19	56
None/No religion	13	11	22	54

Conclusion

This excursion into the influence of minority or majority status on responses to questions concerning religious identification, belonging, belief, and behavior demonstrates that the various racial and ethnic groups in U.S. society are very different in terms of their patterns of attachment to religious traditions and that they have unique and differing patterns of religiosity.

Yet our research demonstrates that religious identification is even stronger than race, ethnicity, or language as a predictor of religious belief or outlook. For instance, white and black Baptists and Pentecostals are largely alike in belief and outlook, though of course blacks are more likely than whites to identify with these traditions in the first place. True there are often racial or ethnic differences in worship styles within the same tradition and congregations tend to be racially homogeneous as a result of the persistence of residential segregation and class differences. Yet there is no evidence of significant and consistent statistical differences in belief or outlook within the major religious traditions—Catholics, Baptists, Pentecostals or Nones—according to whether they are white, black, brown, red, or whether they speak English or Spanish.

Notes

1. Dash Michael and Christine Chapman, *Leadership and Life in Black Churches,* Interdenominational Theological Center, Atlanta, GA, 2004.

2. For a full report on the Hispanic population see: *Religious Identification Among Hispanics in the United States—The PARAL Study, 2002,* by Ariela Keysar, Barry A. Kosmin and Egon Mayer, The Graduate Center of the City University of New York and Brooklyn College.

3. None of American Hispanics in 2001 self-identified as Humanist.

4. Pentecostals include: Holiness, Charismatic, Assemblies of God, Church of God. In 2001 they also include: Four Square Gospel, and Full Gospel.

5. Other Christian groups include: Episcopalian/Anglican, Evangelical, Eastern Orthodox, Mormon/Latter-Day Saints, Lutheran, Nazarene, Presbyterian, Seventh Day Adventist, Church of Christ, Congregational, Apostle, Disciples of Christ, Quaker, Christian Reform, Non-denominational, and Independent Christian Church. In 2001 they also include: Brethren, and Covenant.

6. Includes Atheist, Agnostic, and Secular.

7. Other religion groups include: Buddhist, Hindu, Jewish, Moslem, Taoist, Baha'i, Unitarian, Humanist, Spiritualist, Eckankar, Rastafarian, Scientologist, other (unclassified). In 2001 they also include: Wiccan, Pagan, Druid, Indian religion, and Santeria.

8. The question is phrased: *Is anyone in your household currently a member of a church, temple, synagogue, or mosque?*

9. Among Americans in general who profess no religion: 22 percent "agree somewhat" that God exists and 45 percent "agree strongly."

FIFTEEN

A Profile of the American Muslim Population

POLITICAL events over recent years have drawn interest and attention to the country's Muslim population. Yet accurate and detailed knowledge about its size and social characteristics has been lacking. ARIS collected data on all religious groups, so among the respondents interviewed, 219 reported their religion as Muslim or Islam when asked: *What is your religion, if any?* Although not a large sub-sample from a statistical viewpoint, it is an unusually large number for this hard-to-reach minority in a nationally representative survey. The ARIS data on Muslims presented here and in previous chapters are also unique because they can be compared with other religious groups and traditions and are statistically weighted to represent the U.S. adult population as a whole. Given the intense interest and numerous inquiries we have received concerning Muslims we have assembled here some key statistics from earlier chapters in order to give a focused and more robust picture of the adherents of this faith than previously available on the national level.

Population Size

The Muslim population estimate in Chapter 2 (Figure 2.1) which shows 1,104,000 Muslim adults is based on all those who self-identified with the Muslim tradition; it is not sorted by whether they are Sunni, Shia, or Nation of Islam. The population total is smaller than the figures in circulation in much of the media before the ARIS findings were released.[1] Yet it is twice the number reported in the earlier NSRI survey in 1990. Allowing for the survey sampling error of plus/minus 0.5 percent, the ARIS 2001 figure may be adjusted upwards to 1 percent of Americans. Thus the maximum of this range gives a national figure for adult U.S. Muslims of 2.2 million and a total national population (including children) of just under 3 million. By comparison, the earlier NSRI 1990 found that 0.3 percent of adult respondents adhered to Islam.

There are a number of logical and technical arguments for the accuracy of the ARIS 2001 findings. Its numbers are accepted by experts as the only estimates which are based on objective scientific measurement.[2] Nevertheless certain inherent difficulties have to be acknowledged in counting this religious tradition. Some have to do with terminology. Others relate to varying levels of cooperation with surveys, which require sample weighting and efforts to adjust for specific problems stemming from the undercounting of recent immigrants to the United States.

The confusion of Arabs with Muslims

Considerable confusion exists in many circles about the Arab American and Muslim populations. Ethnic and religious categories are often misused. Put simply the problem is that in reality the majority of Arab-Americans are not Muslims and the majority of Muslims are not Arab-Americans.[3]

This counter-intuitive fact may seem strange to those who are not aware of the nation's religious and immigration history. Yet recent research by the Arab-American Institute confirms the 1990 NSRI as well as ARIS 2001 findings in this regard.

The Arab-American Population

Unfortunately, the term Arab American, as an ethnic category, is not counted directly by the U.S. Census.[4] Country of birth and ancestry data produce a population of just under 1,200,000.[5] The Arab American Institute (AAI) claims there are 3.5 million Americans who have some Arab heritage, the majority of whom are Lebanese.

More noteworthy for our purposes than the actual numbers is that the AAI also reports that 75 percent of Arab-Americans are Christian while only 25 percent are Muslim, i.e., around 850,000.[6]

Most Muslim experts claim that around 1 in 4 American Muslims are of Arab origin. If we use this AAI estimate of 850,000 Arab-American Muslims and multiply by four, the total Muslim population logically cannot be more than 3.4 million—which, in fact, is close to the upper range of the extrapolated ARIS 2001 estimate of 2.8 million including children.

The above AAI figures also appear to point to the fact that even recent immigrants from Egypt, Jordan, and Iraq are disproportionately Christian. This is not surprising. From a sociological perspective we should expect the most westernized populations from these countries to be most attracted to settle in the U.S. Moreover, Arab Christians such as Egyptian Copts, Lebanese Maronites, and Iraqi Chaldeans and Assyrians, who appear in the ARIS data in the Catholic and Orthodox totals, have long suffered from an identity crisis and insecurity in the strife-torn Middle East.

A similar pattern can be assumed to have occurred among immigrants from Iran, a non-Arab country. This explains why the religious minorities of Iran such as Christians, Jews, Baha'i, Zoroastrians and agnostics happen to be strongly represented among Americans of Iranian descent. It stands to reason that few strict believers in the Shiite Muslim faith would leave the Islamic Republic of Iran to dwell in "infidel" America.

Sample Weighting, the "Undercounting" Phenomenon, and Sampling Error

The sample weighting techniques employed by ARIS 2001 (see Methodological Appendix) try to adjust for the known reluctance of certain sections of the population to be surveyed. This adjustment effectively recreates the sample to reflect the size and known characteristics of the American population according to the findings of the 2000 U.S. National Census.

Obviously there is undercounting of religious minorities beyond our ability to weight the data on demographic variables. Among recent immigrants from dictatorships and fractured societies, language problems and a fear of answering personal questions about religion and other sensitive topics tend to reduce the level of cooperation with surveys in the United States.

The undercounting phenomenon[7] and the possibility of higher than average refusal rates explain the population figures of the ARIS report in Figure 15.1. They allow for the possibility that the real proportion of Muslims in the U.S. population may lie in the upper range of the maximum sampling error and could be twice what the survey found: 1 percent rather than 0.5 percent. Nevertheless, there are limits to how far one can go in the upward adjustment process of any particular religious group, given a finite U.S. population, without reducing the size of other religious groups.

In the case of a small minority religious tradition such as Muslim, the only way to scientifically measure the size and characteristics of the population and improve the level of precision of the figures over and above the data provided in Figures 15.1 and 15.2 and elsewhere in this volume is to sample an even larger number of representative households than the 50,281 covered by ARIS 2001. This limitation on the ability to provide detailed information on minority religious groups should be taken into consideration in planning any future national survey of religious identification in the United States.

Non-Christian Religious Groups

To put the misconceptions about the U.S. Muslim population numbers in a wider perspective, it is necessary to remember that the American public traditionally has had a poor understanding of the actual demographic composition of the American population.[8] People tend to greatly overestimate the size of minority groups. In fact, the smaller the minority is in size, the greater the exaggeration: a factor of 2 for Hispanics, a factor of 4 for Asians and a factor of nearly 10 for American Indians.

This innumeracy is understandable and particularly strong in the area of religion, where as we have seen the U.S. Census does not venture to count the population. Yet to date, no scientific national survey has found the non-Christian religious groups to account for more than 4 percent of the American population. The ARIS 2001 study found that 3.7 percent of American adults adhere to these minority religions. Similarly "Other Religions" account for 4 percent of Harvard's 2000 Social Capital Survey Benchmark Survey of 3,000 respondents. This same percentage figure also consistently appears in the religion schedules of the annual General Social Surveys of the National Opinion Research Center (NORC) at the University of Chicago.[9]

In 1991, the Princeton Religious Research Center, using accumulated Gallup Polls, attempted to verify the NSRI figures and similar findings in other surveys. Their analysts reported that they too found only 0.2 percent of Americans were then Muslims. They concluded that enthusiastic Muslim supporters and leaders, as well as those who opposed or feared the growth of Islam, had put into circulation greatly inflated numbers.[10]

Religious Affiliation and Switching

According to the 2000 National Congregational Survey (NCS) carried out by Hartford Seminary there were 1,209 mosques in the United States. ARIS found that 62 percent of Muslim respondents claimed they or somebody in their household belonged to a mosque. This suggests—using the population range outlined above—that somewhere between 600,000 and 1.2 million adults are involved with a mosque giving 600 to 1,000 members per mosque. The Islamic section of the NCS project estimated that around 2 million people (including children) were religiously involved with mosques and that 411,000 worshippers attend the weekly Friday *Jum'ah* prayers.[11]

This report also showed that two-thirds of the 19,000 converts per year to Islam are men and that 14,000 are African-Americans. The ARIS findings, which are very tentative given the small sample involved, tend to support this portrait of religious conversion. They show that over the course of their lifetimes 183,000 people have converted to Islam. However, in addition, ARIS also counted people who *leave* the faith. They were estimated to number 98,000.

Sociodemographic Characteristics

The demographic characteristics of the affiliated Muslim population provided by Bagby, Mamiya, and Nimer's report are quite similar to the ARIS findings reported in Figure 15.1. Both reports portray a predominantly young, male, unmarried population.

Mosque attendees were also overwhelmingly male (78 percent), while half were under 35 years of age. Bagby also reported that 30 percent of mosque attendees were African American—a figure which is almost exactly in line with the ARIS findings. Figure 15.1 shows that 27 percent of all Muslim adherents reported their race as black. This means that although Muslims only accounted for 0.5 to 1.0 per-

Figure 15.1

Demographic Characteristics of U.S. Muslim Adults (18 and over)

DEMOGRAPHIC VARIABLE	U.S. POPULATION	MUSLIMS		
		ALL	WHITE/ASIAN/ OTHER	BLACK
Total	**208,000,000**			
ARIS weighted estimate		1,104,000	800,000	300,000
Upper range estimate		2,200,000	NA	NA
Median age (years)	43	28	27	32
Female	52%	38%	43%	27%
Married	59	49	59	14
College graduate	33	46	52	25
Employed full-time	55	55	53	60
Registered to vote	80	44	35	70
Political preference				
Democrat	31%	35%		
Republican	31	19		
Independent	30	39		
Other/None	8	7		
Percent of total in 10 selected states				
New York	7%	24%	26%	22%
Illinois	4	10	10	14
California	12	9	10	2
Texas	7	9	12	1
Michigan	4	6	4	13
New Jersey	3	5	2	9
Ohio	4	4	3	9
Maryland	2	4	3	8
Georgia	3	4	3	9
Virginia	3	4	4	2

cent of Americans of all racial backgrounds, they comprised approximately 2 percent of the total African-American population, and 5 percent among those who report themselves as Asians.

The geographical distribution reported in Figure 15.1 was in accordance with expected patterns of residence. Muslim Americans tended to be heavily concentrated in New York, Chicago, Los Angeles, Detroit, and the major metropolitan areas of Texas.

In the political arena Muslims had only half the national rate of voter registration. Their party preferences in mid-2001 before 9/11 showed that 35 percent favored the Democratic Party and 19 percent the Republican, while 39 percent declared themselves to be independent.

Figure 15.2

Socioeconomic Characteristics of U.S. Muslim Households

DEMOGRAPHIC VARIABLE	U.S. POPULATION	HOUSEHOLDS WITH AT LEAST ONE MUSLIM ADULT		
		ALL	WHITE/ASIAN/ OTHER	BLACK
Total	**105,000,000**			
ARIS weighted estimate		486,000	360,000	126,000
Upper range estimate		975,000	NA	NA
Average no. of persons per household	2.6	3.4	3.5	3.0
Average no. of adults per household	2.0	2.4	2.5	2.2
Percent who own their homes	71%	38%	41%	31%
Income categories *(in percent)*				
Under $25,000	27%	42%	36%	54%
$25,000-49,999	27	26	28	23
$50,000-74,999	20	11	11	5
$75,000-99,999	12	8	9	10
$100,000 or over	14	13	16	8

Figure 15.2 shows that Muslim households were larger than the national average, a figure which reflects the younger than average median age of the population (28 years of age; see Figure 15.1). In terms of income, Muslim households were more polarized than average: there were relatively fewer middle-income families.

In addition, ARIS asked about the religion of spouses and partners, so it is now possible to report that 27 percent of Muslims with a spouse or partner lived in mixed religious families. Thus, in relation to Figure 15.2, it is relevant to note that not every member of a "Muslim household" was an adherent of Islam, a logical outcome given the preponderance of males among the adherents.

Reflections

This case study of the Muslim population has reiterated themes and issues that we first raised in Chapter 2 of this book. Given the fact that the U.S. Constitution precludes any national census from investigating the religious preferences and characteristics of American citizens, it is impossible to obtain an accurate number for the size of the many small religious groups in the United States. Likewise, it is not feasible for any independent body to conduct an investigation with the reach and depth of the U.S. Census. Religious researchers are therefore limited to two possibilities. They can investigate the places of worship and religious institutions themselves. Or they can survey a representative national sample as with ARIS 2001.

To be sure, the counting of attendees at places of worship and formal members of a religious group obviously does not usually include the full range of adherents, particularly the occasional worshipper and those who only attend for life-cycle events such as marriage and funerals. On the other hand, some people may attend or even join more than a single congregation and so be counted more than once. For this reason, religious leaders' observations and their administrative records are neither comprehensive nor scientifically reliable as to the religious self-identification of the total U.S. population. Depending on their membership criteria and overall religious outlook, it is possible for religious groups to inflate—or deflate—the size of their prospective constituencies. Consequently, there will always be a gap between the view of the religious institutions as to the size and range of their potential constituency and that provided by the members of the public themselves.

Notes

1. "Studies Suggest Lower Count for Number of U.S. Muslims," *The New York Times*, October 25, 2001.
2. Tom W. Smith, *Estimating the Muslim Population in the United States*, New York, The American Jewish Committee, October 2001.
3. Barry A. Kosmin and Seymour Lachman, *One Nation Under God: Religion in Contemporary American Society*, New York, Harmony Books, 1993.
4. "Why the Census of 2000 Failed to Count Arabs," *The Wall Street Journal*, September 28, 2001.

5. Angela Billingham and G. Patricia de la Cruz, *We the People of Arab Ancestry in the United States*, Washington D.C., U.S. Bureau of the Census, 2005.

6. "Arab Americans," *The Economist*, September 22, 2001.

7. Examples include non-ownership of telephone, and language and cultural barriers.

8. Richard Nadeau, Richard G. Niemi, and Jeffrey Levine, "Innumeracy about Minority Populations," *Public Opinion Quarterly*, 1993, 57: 332-347.

9. Tom W. Smith, Intergroup Relations in a Diverse America: Data from the 2000 General Social Survey, New York, The American Jewish Committee, 2001.

10. "Where are the Muslims in the United States?" *Emerging Trends*, September 1991.

11. Ihsan Bagby, Lawrence Mamiya, and Mohamed Nimer, *The Mosque in America: A National Portrait*, Council on American-Islamic Relations, Washington DC, 2001.

SIXTEEN

Current and Future Trends

W
HAT is the place of religion in American society today, and
where is it heading? We have attempted to address these
questions in the preceding chapters. Now it is time to syn-
thesize the evidence, project today's trends forward, and suggest
directions for future research.

Let us begin by reviewing the fundamental conception of this
book—that the United States truly merits the "free market" appella-
tion of the title. As a hotbed of free-market capitalism and as a
democracy that guarantees freedom of religious expression, it invites
competition between religious groups for adherents. This is every bit
as vigorous as the competition between companies for customers.

Religious expression continues to flower in the United States
despite theories that the capitalist pursuit of financial gain is some-
how inconsistent with spiritual life. Our book demonstrates that
religion—far from being Marx's "opiate of the masses"—plays a vital
role in the lives of Americans of all socioeconomic groups.

The great Scottish economist Adam Smith correctly observed that
in the religious sphere, competing sects generate a ferment of activity and increased level of belief, whereas state churches or controlled
and highly regulated religious markets produce indifference. We
find, in the tradition of "rational choice theory" scholars, that the
competition for "market share" in a religious free market seems to
strengthen all of the competitors. Religiosity is far stronger in the
U.S. than in nations such as Russia and China, where organized religion was or is suppressed. It is also stronger than in Western Europe,
which has a long history of state religions.

The free market analogy is an apt description of the American
religious sphere because our data show that American religion is
indeed a sophisticated market system. The religious landscape is

dynamic and constantly in flux. Some people are lifetime participants or "investors;" others enter for only a short time or never. There is constant change in the pattern of supply and the volume of demand. New religious "firms" are constantly being founded, while others merge and some fail and disappear.

Of course, not all Americans avail themselves of freedom of religious choice. Only one in six Americans reported a change in their religious identification over their lifetimes. When religious switching occurs, it is generally into a "neighboring" faith. And regional differences persist despite increased migration.

Another problematic issue concerns the pricing of the product both in dollar terms and perhaps more so in psychological or emotional terms. Financial and economic issues obviously intrude into this market. Is the rise of the mega-church with its wide array of product offerings a social phenomenon, an organizational device, or just the result of the benefits of economies of scale? Or does it owe its success to the long-standing religious phenomena of charisma, the appeal of the accomplished preacher? How do we explain non-member identifiers and episodic involvement? Is this the "free rider" phenomenon?

Less or More Religious?

As in any complex market such as Wall Street, different market sectors, trends, and cycles can be observed. The ARIS data suggest the overall trajectory of American religion is towards polarization and diversity, though both tendencies can be overstated.

Increasingly the media ask if our data suggest the country is becoming more religious or less religious. In fact the answer is yes to both options, as both can and have happened simultaneously. The transcendental majority is deepening its religious commitment even while the irreligious minority is growing in numbers giving the impression of contradictory processes.

For instance, the intensity of religious consumption and demand in the Evangelical Christian sector has been much touted and studied of late. Estimating its size is more difficult because there are no clear theological criteria and institutional ties. Nevertheless the admitted vitality and expansion in that sector of the market has not prevented the simultaneous rise of a secularized population, the "None" phenomenon, "the free-thinkers of the free market nation." This is in effect a withdrawal from the market which is particularly marked among young and West Coast Americans. One result, or even perhaps one cause, of this situation has been the erosion of the middle ground, which is exemplified by the declining market share of the "liberal" Christian churches.

The future of religion in the U.S. is of interest not only to local social analysts and clergy but also to most of the world. This is because foreigners increasingly tend to explain the direction and idiosyncrasies of American politics and foreign policy as due to the influence of "religion." Let us again highlight some of our main findings and discuss their implications.

America remains primarily a Christian society at the beginning of the 21st century. However, the share of the population that self-identified with a Christian faith tradition declined abruptly from 86.2 percent in 1990 to 76.5 percent in 2001. Only a small part of the decrease in self-identified Christians can be attributed to a greater unwillingness among respondents to answer survey questions.

The Rise of the No Religion Population

The most significant trend over this decade was the sharp rise in the proportion of the population in the No Religion category who did not identify with any religious group. Their share rose from 8.2 percent in 1990 to 14.1 percent of American adults in 2001. The rapid increase in absolute numbers of adults who did not subscribe to any religious identification was such that their number more than doubled from 14.3 million in 1990 to 29.4 million in 2001 (see Chapter 2, Figure 2.1). This finding on the sudden and rapid increase in the No Religion group was at first received with a lot of skepticism, yet it has since been confirmed by other surveys including those carried out by the National Opinion Research Center (NORC) and the General Social Survey.

One reason why this powerful trend went below the radar was that the No Religion group is not organized and issues no press releases for the media to disseminate and comment upon. The root causes of the movement towards irreligion are debatable but it appears that polarization is taking place in the religious market. An analogy with a law of physics—that for every action there is an equal and opposite reaction—would suggest that to some extent the increased political power and prominence of evangelical and conservative Christianity and its activist agenda may have alienated other people from religion altogether. Certainly our data shows that the middle ground—the so-called liberal traditions—particularly the Mainline Christians and Jews have lost ground in recent years.

However, the No Religion group had some distinct demographic characteristics. They were more likely to be young, male, single and to be Asian. To illustrate, almost one in every four males aged 18 to 34 professed no religion in 2001. This is more than double the proportion among males aged 65 and over. There were nearly as many Nones as Catholics in this cohort of young males (Chapter 5, Figure 5.4). Single people who never married were also more likely to profess no religion. Furthermore, among cohabiting men, the Nones surpassed Catholics. A research question that remains to be resolved is whether the prevalence of Nones among cohabiters reflects their position in the life cycle, or is a characteristic of those who choose to cohabit.

The implications of a substantial and growing segment of the adult population who profess no religion could have enormous ramifications for the nation's political, social, and even economic life. The increase in the population without any religious identification has economic dimensions because it has particular lifestyles and patterns of consumption and is highly geographically concentrated. States such as Oregon, Washington, California, Colorado, Vermont and Delaware are distinctly more irreligious than others. Yet as we show in different parts of this book, the "Nones," like most very large groups are not homogeneous. Only small proportions are die-hard atheists or agnostics; most are simply disengaged from organized religion. Indeed 45 percent of them "strongly agree" that God exists and 22 percent "somewhat agree."

Political implications

In the civic realm we demonstrated how adults who profess no religion have distinct political patterns. They have a strong tendency to be politically independent. Thus their reluctance to join or identify with any institution holds for both religious affiliation and political party. If the young cohorts maintain their religious preferences as they get older it could have major consequences for societal and political issues which are at the heart of current debates within the U.S. society. Since there is more consensus today on economic issues as regards the virtues of a capitalist economy than there was for instance in the 1930s and 1940s, there is nowadays less class politics. As a result "values" are the new battlefield and the religious divide is more central to politics. This is particularly so where ethical or moral issues are involved such as on stem-cell research, science teaching, assisted suicide, homosexual marriage, the death penalty, and gun control.

One example of a "culture war" divide between the more secularized and more religious forces is the issue of support for stem-cell research. According to a survey conducted in August 2004 by the Pew Research Center for the People & the Press, "white Evangelicals" and "seculars" were the most polarized groups on the importance of conducting stem-cell research. Whereas only 33 percent of "white Evangelicals" said that it was more important to conduct stem-cell research than to destroy embryos, 68 percent of "seculars" expressed this view. Interestingly there was little movement in either group's opinions. A similar survey conducted earlier in March 2002 had found 26 percent versus 66 percent respectively.

Growth in Non-Christian Religions

Looking at the non-Christian religions we found that their share of the population remained small and their share of the national population rose only very slightly from 3.3 percent in 1990 to 3.7 percent in 2001. Yet their absolute numbers grew at an impressive pace rising 31 percent to 7.6 million adults in 2001 from 5.8 million in 1990. As their numbers grew, so did their visibility. Temples and mosques mushroomed around the country. Moreover, specific groups tend to cluster in some states or regions. As shown in Chapter 15, 24 percent of U.S. Muslim adults reside in New York and 10 percent in Illinois.

A shift in labels

Another important finding of ARIS that provides an insight into the current religious climate is the shifts in generic labels: a rise in the "Christian" label and a decline in the "Protestant" label. The number of adults who self-identified as unspecified "Christian" rose from 8.1 million in 1990 to 14.2 million in 2001, while the number of unspecified "Protestants" declined precipitously from 17.2 million to 4.7 million during that period. The increase in the Christian labeling can be partially explained by the recent popularity of fundamentalist and evangelical movements which favor the label "Christian." Though we do not have specific information we should assume that for most respondents this tendency was "symbolic" and was limited to putting a new label on themselves rather than implying a major change in their lifestyle or behavior. But again this is a finding that requires further research. In 2001 we asked respondents to the survey who initially gave these unspecified labels to be more specific, by asking, "What denomination is that?" Yet still the Christian label persisted. If this trend continues, whereby the unspecified "Protestant" continues to diminish while the unspecified "Christian" continues to grow, then further probing of this response category will be required. Obviously we need to better understand these classifications and perhaps ask explicitly if they mean "evangelical Christian."

The decline in the "Protestant" label could also be partially explained by linkage to the decline in the proportion of the population identifying with mainline and liberal Protestant groups (see Chapter 2, Figure 2.1). In Chapter 5 we showed the declining attraction of the Mainline Christian tradition among young cohorts for both men and women. This was similar to what was found in the 1990 survey. The question is whether these young people, who have been exposed to different influences, will or will not return to their family's denominational loyalties as they age. A follow-up survey will help better understand these shifts and even determine in which directions they are heading.

Migration, Immigration, and Homogeneity

Our analysis showed that despite social trends such as high levels of migration over the past decade that might have been thought to encourage homogeneity across the nation, wide regional and state differences in religious composition still persist. A Bible Belt and a secular West can still be differentiated from other regions. Cultural heartlands or regions dominated by particular religious traditions and groups in effect create local social, consumer, and political markets that have special needs and require special treatment.

In contrast a force that might have been expected to dramatically increase religious diversity and change the religious balance of the nation, the recent high rate of immigration, does not seem to have had this effect. Even the especially large number of Latino immigrants failed to increase the proportion of Catholics. Other minority religions such as Islam (see Chapter 15), Hinduism, and Buddhism have grown but not by as much as their "boosters" and some commentators claim. In part this is because the religious free market is dominated by the "Christian brand" which has the best organized and best resourced firms. Conservative Christian churches in particular have a large and enthusiastic sales force. Moreover, in the eyes of many aspiring New Americans from Asia and Latin America to be American is to be Christian and even a Protestant of some type.

Others take advantage of their new freedom to disavow religious ties altogether. American Judaism, despite a minority tendency to bolster tradition, has been eroded by defections to No Religion and high rates of interfaith marriages from which only a minority of the offspring are raised as Jews. And compared with the 1970s and 1980s ,the appeal of cults and New Religious Movements seemed to wane in the 1990s. Neo-pagans have expanded their numbers and become more visible but their recruits cannot compare with the vast legions of new Born Again Christians.

Racial and ethnic religious choices

One historic legacy that persists in the religious market is racial differentiation. Americans of different racial and ethnic backgrounds have different aggregate religious profiles; they favor different brands. Yet interestingly the minorities are as distinct from one another as they are from the white majority. For example, African-Americans are the most religious while Asians are the least religious on a number of measures. We are able to state this categorically because with ARIS we were able to offer for the first time representative national data on the smaller Native American and Asian populations. Yet within the religious traditions race is cancelled out by the religious factor so that Catholics, Baptists or Pentecostals of any race are similar on most key indicators even if they pray separately at the congregational level.

Religious vs. Secular Outlook

In the study of American religion, ARIS introduced and explored a unique concept, religious versus secular outlook. The concept of outlook or worldview correlates with religious belief and belonging yet goes beyond them. In contemporary American society the debates over policy issues intertwine with religious versus secular values. Although ARIS 2001 did not ask about specific social attitudes, other surveys, such as polls conducted by the Pew Forum and the Pew Research Center for the People & the Press, reveal that more religious people also tend to hold more conservative opinions on issues such as the death penalty, gay marriage, social welfare, and religious education in public schools. For example according to a July 2005 survey by these polls, Americans who hold a high level of religious commitment oppose gay marriage 74 percent to 18 percent. Seculars, on the other hand, favor gay marriage 61 percent to 27 percent.

Religious-secular outlook and political attitudes and affiliations are strongly linked. Among adults who describe their outlook as "religious" there is a clear plurality of Republicans over Democrats, 41 percent to 28 percent. Among those with a "secular" outlook of some kind, independent political preference is the strongest, at 43 percent, while Democrat preference at 32 percent exceeds Republican preference at 19 percent (see Chapter 13).

The political gaps between religious and secular Americans help explain the intensity of the culture wars over such issues as abortion, and evolution versus intelligent design. There is, however, a large "bridge group"—those who describe themselves as "somewhat religious." In 2001, approximately 80 million adults were in this category, even more than the roughly 76 million who described their outlook as religious. Among the "somewhat religious," Democrats slightly outnumber Republicans, 34 percent to 29 percent, with independents a strong second at 31 percent. It's also important to note that there are many religious Americans who hold views that might be described as liberal—such as opposition to the death penalty—as well as many seculars who take conservative stances on issues such as assisted suicide.

Religious-secular outlook relates to demography similarly to the way professing a religion does. We found that females and older people tend to describe their outlook as "religious." As we pointed out earlier, females and older people are less likely to be Nones and in general tend more than young men to profess a religion. Religious versus secular outlook scores also vary greatly by religious group. For example, Evangelicals, Pentecostals and Mormons are far more likely to consider themselves as "religious" than Jews or Buddhists.

Members and Potential Members

Next we turn from expressions of religious belief to the issue of belonging. Figures on membership originating from religious bodies are a problem area. There are wide variations in approach to the issue across the groups and so a lack of uniform criteria. ARIS again relied on self-reporting, which has the merit of standardization. Only half of the ARIS survey respondents resided in households where either they themselves or someone else currently belonged to a religious institution. Thus, whereas for many people religious belief is strong, the compulsion to belong to a religious congregation seems to be substantially weaker. Membership varies by religious group. Respondents who identified as Evangelical/Born Again were most affiliated with 83 percent currently reporting household membership, followed by 78 percent among the Assemblies of God and 75 percent among Mormons. At the lower end of the household congregational membership scale were the Buddhists with 28 percent, Protestants with 45 percent and Jews with 53 percent. The household income data by religious group does not correlate well with these rank orderings so we can assume that considerations beyond economics, such as psychological and cultural factors, are at play in determining religious affiliation behavior.

Switching religions

Turning to an area of religious behavior directly concerned with market outcomes, we found in 2001 that more than 33 million American adults, or almost 16 percent of the total adult population, had switched religious identification at some point in their lives. What does it mean to switch out of a religious identification? When does it occur and why? These questions were not part of the ARIS survey but they should be included in any similar future survey. This cultural phenomenon was described by the sociologist Wade Clark Roof as "religious seeking."

The theory goes that in a consumer society, people pick and choose to satisfy their spiritual needs. ARIS 2001, however, discovered that many of the switchers could hardly be described as spiritually hungry: The biggest gainer from religious switching was the "no religion" group. Namely, 6.6 million adults who used to profess a religion opted to switch out of any religious identification. One of the most interesting findings was that a plurality (43 percent) of the "new Nones" previously self-identified as Catholic. True, Catholicism is the largest religious group, making it a natural source, but this is a considerable over-representation. However, it is interesting to note that most Catholics, who decided to switch did not become Baptist, Episcopalian, or Pentecostal; rather they decided to distance themselves from any organized form of religion and found it more acceptable to switch to the No Religion category.

Religious switching as well as waves of immigration is reshaping the landscape of American religion but as we have noted, not always in the directions claimed by those experts who lack access to reliable national statistics. The major increase in the No Religion group is partially explained by the 2.6 million "former Catholics" who opted for the No Religion category. Since a majority of the Hispanic population is Catholic not surprisingly similar shifts occurred. Catholics lost market share in this fast-expanding population from 66 percent in 1990 to 57 percent of the adult Hispanic population in 2001. At the same time the share of the No Religion group among Hispanics increased from 6 percent to 13 percent.

This switching out of a religion might be described as the secularization of the population. It remains to be seen whether this trend will continue. Any further increase in the No Religion segment of the national population will lead the U.S. population in the path of other more secular Western societies especially those in Europe. But as researchers, our immediate goal should be to learn more about the timing and reasons for religious switching generally. We need to add specific questions on when the switching occurred by year and in the life cycle, how many times and how frequently people switch, and whether it was associated with marriage, geographical relocation, or any other reason.

Mixed-Religion Households

The contemporary United States is a mobile and pluralistic society. One consequence of growing tolerance and social mixing in society is increased rates of marriage across social, cultural and ethnic boundaries. ARIS is a unique source for this data as it inquired into the religion of both adult partners in a relationship. Intermarriages were defined as when the religious identifications of the respondent and the spouse or partner were different.

Intermarriages produce either mixed-religion families or add to the rate of switching as one partner tries to accommodate to the other's religious preference. There are differences in the current rate of intermarriage by religious group—from 42 percent of Episcopalians to only 12 percent of Mormons. Who marries whom is of special interest but learning more detail about this trend will require an even larger sample than ARIS. A critical question will be to probe the characteristics of people who switch their religion as a result of or for the purposes of marriage. Do they consider themselves as "intermarried?"

The complexity of intermarried families is apparent with the difficult decision about the religious upbringing of children. The decision about how to raise the children falls on the parents, but it has long-lasting consequences for the attributes of the next generation and the health of the larger religious community. Generally, intermarried families are smaller than same-religious group families. Interestingly, only a fraction (14 percent) of children in intermarried families is raised with no religion. This is a default option, which in theory does not alienate either parent. Yet, it appears that since women are usually more religious than men and because mothers typically are assigned the task of making decisions as to how to raise the children, they are more likely to decide against the "None" option. We need to conduct further studies on the roles of mothers and fathers in order to better understand the process of decision-making with regard to the religious upbringing of children in the growing number of inter-religious families.

Women's Participation in Religion

Religion strongly correlates with demographics. Generally women, more than men, have a "religious," rather than a "secular," outlook. Women also are more likely than men to profess a religion of some type. As women move from the domestic sphere into the labor force and as they acquire higher educational levels shifts in gender roles may occur. Among the younger age cohorts the gender gaps in religious attitudes and behavior appear to have narrowed. Will the gaps disappear entirely? Participation in religious activities adds another task and pressure onto women's busy schedules with family and work. Will they drop or reduce their involvement as they advance their careers? These are crucial issues that need to be explored by religious groups because they are highly dependent on women volunteers.

Across the religious groups there are major socioeconomic gaps reflecting differences in cultural norms regarding appropriate gender roles and levels of social restrictions imposed on women. Religious groups differ widely in full-time employment rates for women and the proportion of homemakers. The most active women in the paid labor force were those in the New Religious Movements. Sixty percent worked full-time compared with only 20 percent of Muslim women.

What is the meaning of our finding that the gaps in women's labor participation were wider than the gaps in educational attainment? For example, almost one-quarter of Mormon women graduated from college, but only one-third work full-time. Mormon women seem to achieve some higher education, yet they do not seem to be encouraged or motivated to be economically active and participate in the labor force. This could be explained by their demanding duties at home and their large families. Women in some religious groups have greater control over their own lives while others lack personal autonomy. Thus religious values affect women's economic participation and living standards not only directly, but indirectly via demographic processes.

The overall conclusion to be drawn from the data presented on gender patterns in education and employment is that religious orientation plays some role in the socioeconomic position of women, which in turn has wider manifestation for the social status of the particular religious groups. This feature is easier to observe among small and homogeneous groups. The Muslims emerged as the most patriarchal group since their gender balance on educational and employment indicators showed most male dominance. The Mormons exhibited a pronounced gender imbalance favoring men in employment but not in education. By contrast the Nones and the Other Religions/NRMs were clearly the most egalitarian groups on the indicators examined, reflecting their more liberal, emancipated attitudes.

Challenges for Religious Leaders

The ARIS survey poses some challenges for religious leaders. The Catholic adherents' behavior challenges the Catholic doctrine on the sacrament of marriage and disallowing divorce. We discovered that Catholic men and women were no more likely to be separated than other groups where divorce was not an issue. In fact, Catholic proportions of "separated" people were similar to the national average. Could we infer from these findings that Catholic teaching is losing its authority on the divorce question? On another family issue we documented more single mothers raising their children without fathers among Pentecostal/Charismatic, Baptist, and Catholic populations than among the No Religion. What do these gaps between religious groups imply? Often, divorce is associated with a breakup of the family and economic privation. Single motherhood is well known to be associated with higher poverty levels. Will children being raised in homes with no male role model or those whose parents live out of wedlock go on to reject religious teachings and values which uphold the sanctity of the traditional family but conflict with their own experience?

ARIS educational data as well as the College Board SAT scores showed how "liberal intellectual elites" are nourished among Unitarians, Jews, Mainline Christians, and Eastern Religions, which were ranked at the top of the educational achievement leagues. These religious groups seem to embrace secular education and science more than do other groups. Even if we set aside the argument of causation, it is hard to overlook the socioeconomic advantages and opportunities that are accessible to such high achievers.

One interesting exception that contradicts the tendency of liberal and secular people to dominate in educational attainment is a small but growing group that identifies religiously as "Evangelical or Born Again." Since our switching data indicate that few were born into this category this may well indicate some defections from "liberalism" among the elites. This emerging group may challenge these intellectual elites when it comes to crucial public debates such as whether to teach the subject of "intelligent design" in science classes. It is also interesting that these Evangelicals, like Jews, were most adept at leveraging their educational advantage into high income, since both groups stood higher on the income index than the educational one. The Evangelicals, while being religiously conservative, have advanced up the economic ladder and emerged as a high status group. Our analysis of socioeconomic rankings placed them as number three above Lutheran and Jews. Becoming an affluent group may very well help them compete for prestige positions in society. This social and political influence could then facilitate the advancement of their religious views.

A unique feature of the ARIS data was that it provided insights into household consumption of modern technologies by adherents of various religious groups. We hardly ever find systematic information on subscription to satellite TV, home entertainment such as DVD or video game system, as well as PC ownership and internet access in relation to belief and religious observance. Rather there are anecdotal stories about what is allowed and what is forbidden religiously. The inclusion of the CENTRIS omnibus data within ARIS provided evidence that allows us to rebuff the common assumption that use of modern technologies is widely regarded by conservative religious groups as immoral. In fact, ARIS findings show that there is no religious factor or bias in the consumption of modern technologies. Both people who self-identify with more conservative faiths and those who identify with no religion share similar patterns.

We learn from these results that the leaders of conservative groups have now realized that it is futile to fight against the modern technological tide. More likely religious leaders from all across the spectrum have recognized the potential of modern devices and mass media to promote their ideas. Whether in mega-churches or in smaller congregations, religious leaders use modern technologies for religious purposes so as to better deliver their own messages and communicate with their members. Therefore, in the future we can expect even greater use of modern technologies in order to facilitate communication between members and religious leaders. As more and more households own PCs and have access to the internet, religious institutions will use these media to disseminate educational materials to children, young people, and older members.

Membership and education

Another unique ARIS finding with important consequences relates to household congregational membership. We showed that in the aggregate congregational membership increases with educational level. To reiterate, post-graduate education was associated with a household membership rate of 63 percent, which was above the national level. Conversely a lower educational level, less than high school, was associated with a membership rate of only 45 percent. This linear relationship is somewhat surprising and indicates that higher education does not appear to alienate people from involvement with organized religion. True, congregational membership inevitably costs money. And this correlation between educational level and religious belonging reflects income level as well. Yet one implication for congregations that wish to boost membership is that reducing financial calls on members might be beneficial in the long run.

We alluded to the differences between religious identification as a state of heart and mind versus religious affiliation as a social condition. The "nominals," those who self-identify with a religious group but are not presently members or active participants, are a crucial population to understand. Why one decides not to join a religious institution is a largely unstudied question. Many additional questions need further exploration. For instance, does identifying with a religion, or belonging to a congregation, mean different things to different people in different cultural and religious traditions, social classes, or at different stages in the lifecycle?

Future Research

Knowing why people switch their religion or why they do not identify with any religion would be enlightening. Such an exercise requires qualitative research modules, which can be done in focus groups or web-based online sessions. These exercises would enrich our knowledge and explain some of the telephone survey findings. This qualitative data-gathering should not replace quantitative data-gathering, but rather accompany it. Since the study of public attitudes towards religion seems to require an integrated design using both types of research methodology, one could conclude that it is a complex operation that requires more resources than other areas of social research. It also requires researchers who have both qualitative and quantitative skills.

Consideration should be given also as to how to continue to research American religion on a national basis in the future so that full justice can be done to small groups and sufficient coverage at the state level and for the major metropolitan areas can be guaranteed. We need to think how such research could be improved next time; hopefully simultaneously with the decennial U.S. Census in 2010. We recommend that the data collected should be geared for the needs of a wide range of consumers of religious data including academics, foundations, religious leaders, clergy, politicians, market researchers, as well as city or local planners. This means that it is essential to replicate the methodology used in NSRI 1990 and ARIS 2001 by gathering data on the whole population and not just members of religious congregations and institutions. This approach would continue to provide vital time series and trend data on religious identification in relation to all the topics covered in this book—basic counts, demography, geography, socioeconomics, politics, membership and minority populations.

To better understand the religious landscape of U.S. society, we also need to improve the coverage of new immigrants, so the next national survey should offer multiple languages, including Spanish and Chinese. Learning from our ARIS 2001 experience suggests that future surveys need to be even larger than ARIS in terms of sample size. While ARIS collected information about religious identification from about 50,000 respondents, it had only 17,000 respondents for questions about religious belief, belonging, and behavior. The next survey should have at least 50,000 respondents for these questions as well. All these recommendations are expensive but given the importance of this topic to social science and its significance to the nation, a consortium of the interests set out above should be able to provide the financial funding. Only in this way will it be possible to continue to properly monitor changes and evaluate trends in the religious marketplace of the future.

We hope that any future research will place religion even more firmly in its wider social and market context. What are its competitors for resources, especially in terms of time? Are they recreation, sports, and entertainment? Can American religion continue to be a whole family activity largely focused around Sunday mornings and the home? How are new lifestyle choices and ever greater reliance on technology likely to change the situation? Considering the rapid changes occurring in society few can confidently predict what a new study would reveal. Predictions are not always wise or safe. The important thing to realize is that religion in America is dynamic, creative, and relevant, and continuously developing and changing in response to the changing national environment in the marketplace.

Methodological Appendix*

Introduction

THE 2001 *American Religious Identification Survey* (ARIS) was designed to replicate, as closely as possible, the methodology used for the 1990 *National Survey of Religious Identification* (NSRI) which took place under the auspices of the Graduate Center of the City University of New York. Wherever appropriate, reference will be made to the similarities and differences between ARIS and the effort of 10 years earlier.

In total, over 50,000 respondents were interviewed over a span of approximately 4 months. The sample was based on a series of national random digit dialing (RDD) surveys conducted through International Communications Research (ICR) as part of the EXCEL and ACCESS national telephone omnibus services. The data from each of the approximately 50 independent surveys were aggregated and weighted to reflect current estimates of the U.S. adult population by age, gender, race/ethnicity, education and geographic components of the 48 contiguous States.

As the reader will note, the data resulting from the survey instruments can be examined within the context of households or individual members (population) or both. Consequently, the data sets contain weighting factors developed for each unit of analysis and for making projections to each on a national or other basis.

Sample Design

The inherent nature of commercial omnibus surveys provides both advantages and disadvantages from the perspective of preferred survey research practices. Omnibus surveys provide a means of reaching and interviewing extremely large household samples in relatively short periods of time while taking advantage of the shared nature of the high costs of survey research. The economic advantage is offset somewhat by the periodic nature of these surveys and the relatively short field periods. The need for minimal geographic sample stratification and controls necessary to insure minimum sample sizes among population subgroups within those strata tend to depress response rates somewhat.

---

* Written with Dale Kulp, President & CEO, Marketing Systems Group, Inc.

A brief description of each of these omnibus services will aid in understanding these issues:

- EXCEL is the research industry's largest telephone omnibus service. It has been in continuous operation for over 15 years. EXCEL surveys are fielded at least twice each week, with each survey having a minimum of 1,000 interviews. Approximately one-half of these are male and one-half female. The sample employs basic geographic stratification at the Census Division level, with target sample sizes allocated proportionately. Although there is some flexibility in terms of final sample size, it is necessary to adhere fairly closely to the established targets of 50 percent male/female within geographic stratum. Respondents are randomly designated using the "last birthday selection" method. The RDD sample used is provided by GENESYS Sampling Systems. The field period for each survey is five days—one wave of EXCEL runs Tuesday through Sunday each week, the other Friday through Tuesday, so both include weekends and the call rule is an original, plus four attempts.

- ACCESS has a more restricted set of question topics than does the more general and varied EXCEL. ACCESS was designed as primarily an omnibus vehicle focusing on residential telecommunications, entertainment, and technology. Both are national in representation, although ACCESS targets only about 1,000 completed interviews per week. The other major difference between the two omnibus surveys is in the execution of data collection. ACCESS is an ongoing survey as opposed to periodic, with flexible daily and more rigid weekly sample size targets identical to those of EXCEL. The everyday, ongoing nature of the data collection provides the ability to use a single large replicated sample, with additional replicates added as required. Sample stratification and respondent selection procedures are handled identically. Similarly, the RDD sample was supplied by GENESYS Sampling Systems.

In summary, both of the telephone omnibus programs utilize national RDD samples. They were designed by the same research group and are operated and overseen by ICR personnel. Moreover, EXCEL was the vehicle used in the 1990 NSRI and GENESYS also provided the sample in that survey effort. In addition, the demographic battery embedded within the two omnibus surveys are virtually identical and both incorporate questions to determine the number of voice lines each residence maintains in order to develop probability of selection adjustments to the individual sample household records.

The underlying RDD samples used in both omnibus programs are provided by GENESYS Sampling Systems. These *equal probability selection mechanism* (epsem) RDD samples are designed using the latest list-assisted methods and are identical to those used almost exclusively by governmental (e.g., the Census Bureau and CDC), social science, and academic researchers. The GENESYS RDD sample frame is completely redefined and rebuilt every quarter and incorporates a precisely defined, extremely fine implicit stratification that underlies every individual sample selection, thus minimizing sample variance. The sample frame was consistently defined as two-digit working blocks in residential exchanges (NPA-NXXs) containing two or more directory listed telephone households.

Survey Components and Data Collection

The survey and data collection incorporated three phases corresponding to the gathering of information for distinct sub-samples and questionnaire segments:

1. The overall effort was fielded from February 2, 2001 through June 7, 2001. During this five month period a total of 34,295 interviews were conducted in the EXCEL omnibus and 15,987 were conducted through ACCESS. All respondents were screened to determine their religious affiliation, and the affiliation of their spouse if any.

2. Between April 19 and June 7, the Comparative Belief/Secularity (CB/S) battery was administered to a total of 14,155 non-Catholics.

3. From April 19 to May 16, the CB/S component was administered to 2,043 self-identified Catholic respondents.

The individual sub-samples and corresponding questionnaire segments were designed so they can be combined in a straightforward manner. The sample of Catholic respondents is a representative subset of all those asked the CB/S questions and the sub-sample asked the CB/S questions is representative of the entire sample. The following section describes the process of combining these samples and the manner in which each subset can be used analytically.

Weighting and Estimation

As in most surveys designed to fulfill multiple objectives, the research team found it necessary to make a series of trade-offs. In this case, there were two critical components of the research design. First was the overall sample of Religious Affiliation identified as part of that overall screening process. Second was the sample of respondents to whom the CB/S questions were administered, which was comprised of a sub-sample of Catholics, with all other respondents being sampled at 100 percent. This was actually a very straightforward design with the corresponding weighting and estimation being carried out in a few simple steps.

The initial phase of the estimation process dealt with the entire sample of 50,282 respondents. One of the primary objectives of this survey was to provide estimates of the population by religious affiliation. Consequently it was deemed desirable to reduce the role of geographic variation in these estimates, as many adherents to specific religions are highly concentrated geographically. To accomplish this the data set was post-stratified into the following geographic components:

- The largest 77 MSAs/PMSAs by central city and non-central city—this resulted in a total of 153 county defined strata (note: Nassau-Suffolk PMSA contains no central city).

- Forty-eight strata, each comprising the residual geography of individual States not defined as part of the MSA/PMSA strata.

For each of the 201 geographic strata, estimates of demographic distributions were then derived from CLARITAS for the following categories: 1) age within sex, 2) race/ethnicity, 3) and household income. In addition, estimates of total households and the population aged 18 older and were also secured for each of the geographic strata.

An initial household weight for each respondent was computed based on the number of voice lines serving his or her household. This weight is actually the inverse of the number of phone lines as it adjusts for the greater probability of selecting a household with two, three or more phone lines, relative to a household with just one line. (One can easily envision that a sample of random telephone numbers will result in twice the number of households with two lines as one would reasonably expect, as this class has twice the probability of selection.)

A second weight, corresponding to the selection of the adult member is then computed: a household with one adult has weight of 1.0; two adults, 2.0 and so on.

With these initial weights computed, the interviews were segregated into the 201 post-strata and a sample balancing (i.e., raking) routine was conducted within each stratum. This is an iterative process that uses the marginal distributions of each of the target demographic variables and the corresponding weighted sample variable categories to compute adjustment factors, which bring the sample and population demographic distributions into close alignment. The final step in this process is the calculation of simple expansion factors to bring the weighted sample totals within each of the 201 strata to the total household and population aged 18 and older estimates derived previously. Following this process each respondent record contains two weights: one for household estimates, the other for estimates of the adult population.

The next phase in the weighting process involved adjusting for the sub-sampling of all respondents for the CB/S comparative study. One simple alternative here would have been to simply treat these sub-samples as an independent survey, and replicate the weighting process used for the full survey. Although straightforward given that the process and procedures were already in place, the result would have produced estimates of religious groups and demographic distributions at variance with the total sample.

Although the comparative study sample was a random subset of the larger, it would have also been subject to sampling variance. It was decided that this was a complication that should be avoided.

It was decided that a better approach would be to use the larger sample to produce estimates to which the sub-sample could then be adjusted; this would also enable one to treat the Catholic sub-sample directly. The full sample and the CB/S sub-sample were post-stratified into 17 groups based on religious affiliation as determined in the questionnaire. These strata included the largest religious groups individually (Baptist, Catholic, Lutheran, etc.) as well as categories corresponding to None, Refused, etc. Based on the total sample, weighted estimates of household and population totals for each religion stratum were created as well as distributions of age, gender, income, race and ethnicity, census region and metropolitan status.

These estimates as well as the CB/S sub-samples were used as input to a similar sample balancing routine as used for the full sample. However, in this case, the input weight for each record corresponded to the final weight developed during the full sample weighting process. The process was repeated for each of the seventeen strata created based on religious affiliation. As noted above, the post stratification process treated the Catholic sub-sample directly and independently, correcting for the intended undersampling.

The final data record for each respondent includes population and household weights in the full sample file. For those included in the smaller CB/S comparative study, the data file also includes a set of household and population weights developed to produce estimates of totals and distributions. For reference purposes the approximate relative sampling rates for the CB/S study are as follows: non-Catholic households, 40 percent; and Catholic households, 20 percent.

Use of the Weighting Factors

The correct application of household and population weights can be confusing. The choice of one or the other may be determined by the question or variable under consideration, or by the analytic intent. Just a few guidelines and examples may be instructive.

The population weights produce estimates of people—specifically, people over 18 years of age. In the CB/S comparative study a question is asked to determine the length of time respondents have been married. Using the population weight will produce an estimate of the number of people married for any given length of time. However, this is not the same as the number of couples, which would be produced by using the households weight.

Similarly, the number of adults with a specific religious affiliation can be computed by applying the population weight. However, there are theoretical problems with using the household weight in combination with religious affiliation because that is a respondent variable. Using the household weight in this case would be the equivalent of classifying a household based solely on the gender of the respondent and ignoring the fact that households can be mixed religions as most contain both males and females.

Demographics present similar difficulties. Income is a household level variable and intuitively one would use the household weight to produce a distribution of household incomes. But one could use the population weight to show the distribution of adults with certain household incomes. These will not be the same because household income is not perfectly correlated with household size.

Classifying the sample into subgroups by using a household level variable (e.g., number of children) does not mean that one then needs to use the household weight to examine religious affiliation. By using the population weight one could then produce estimates of the religious affiliation of adults in households with none, one, two, or more children.

In summary, it is critical to explore the relationship between the context of the variable, or variable being used and the resultant base produced by a given weight.

Survey Errors

Surveys are subject to a wide variety of errors. Some of these are related to the sampling process itself and the inherent variation one expects from the process of selecting samples of households at random—two samples are never identical, but one can predict the distribution of differences one can reasonably expect.

Other errors are of a non-sampling nature: limitations in the sampling frame, non-response biases, etc. These are generally more difficult to quantify since the difference due to non-response, for example, is only directly quantifiable if one has interviewed the non-respondents.

During the weighting and estimation phase one attempts to incorporate and compensate for biases in the sample selection and data collection phases. In some cases, this is fairly straightforward as in the case of households with multiple telephone lines—those with fewer lines are under represented relative to those with more lines. Of course, this does not directly address the issue as to whether the proportions of single line, two-line, etc., households in the resultant weighted sample are the exact proportion as exist in the general population. In other words, there may be secondary bias contributions because in the data collection process itself it may be more difficult to reach households with a single voice line because these households tend to have fewer adults.

One would hope that the weighting and estimation process compensates for both sampling and non-sampling errors. The difference one finds in a sample distribution from what one might expect—say the number of interviews completed in a given state can be a result of either sampling error or non-sampling errors. One can easily correct for the variation, but to the extent that the shortfall is due to a failure to complete interviews among a distinct subgroup within the state, there remains a risk of potential bias in the overall results.

The combined final sample disposition for all weeks of the survey effort is shown below. It should be understood that the total number of sample records used is substantially understated due to the pre-screening of the RDD sample prior to the actual field period. Although the actual number of non-residential sample records eliminated is unavailable, based on the expected eliminations, it can be estimated that the original sample total was approximately 910,000.

Figure A.1

Combined Sample Disposition for ACCESS and EXCEL Omnibus

	SAMPLE	PERCENT	PERCENT	PERCENT	PERCENT
Total	**732,887**	**100.0%**			
Total Non-residental	**413,239**	**56.4**			
Not working/disconnected*	181,196	24.7			
Commercial/non-residental	63,547	8.7			
Undetermined estimated non-residental	168,496	23.0			
Total Residental	**319,648**	**43.6**	**100.0%**		
Not Eligable**	**37,562**	**5.1**	**11.8**		
Ineligible	6,081	0.8	1.9		
Language barrier	12,594	1.7	3.9		
Not available for duration***	10,197	1.4	3.2		
Privacy manager/call blocking	8,690	1.2	2.7		
Eligible to be interviewed	**282,086**	**38.5**	**88.2**	**100.0%**	
Undetermined estimated non-residental	47,534	6.5	14.9	16.9	
Refused screening	119,327	16.3	37.3	42.3	
Callback	55,545	7.6	17.4	19.7	
Started interview	**59,680**	**8.1**	**18.7**	**21.2**	**100.0%**
Refused during/incomplete	8,210	1.1	2.6	2.9	13.8
Complete	51,470	7.0	16.1	18.2	86.2

Notes:

* "No answers" were estimated to be 78 percent not working/unassigned, and 22 percent residential.

** "Not eligibles" include: language barrier (non-English speaking), hard of hearing, and no one in household aged 18 or older.

*** "Not available for duration" are callbacks for respondents unavailable until after the interviewing period.

This disposition has been constructed to take into account the limitations of field period omnibus surveys by placing callbacks beyond the interviewing period into the not-eligible category. Using the most conservative approach, with a base of all residences, the estimated response rate is 16.1 percent. Eliminating households deemed not eligible, raises the response rate somewhat to 18.2 percent.

We have taken care here to insure that the final weighted sample is accurately proportioned across critical geographic and demographic variables, but the risk of response and other biases can not be fully reflected in a simple estimate of sampling variability.

Sampling Variability

All sample surveys are subject to sampling errors. Samples always differ from what one would expect if one had measured the entire population. The expected size of that error is a function of both the sample design and the ultimate sample size. The size of this error is also influenced by the specific weighting process and variation in resultant weights designed to compensate for non-sampling errors such as non-response.

In addition, we have two samples here: one of approximately 50,000 and one of about 17,000. The accompanying standard error tables provide estimates of the sample variability for each data set along with instructions on constructing confidence intervals based on the estimate and the size of the subgroup being examined. These estimates were computed from the weighted sample itself using a balanced replication routine (BRR) across a number of survey variables. Any such table of standard errors is a compromise and an estimate since each survey variable theoretically has its own specific error of measurement and variability.

By examining a range of variables however, one is able to produce an average error, which is then used to produce the accompanying Figure A.2.

Figure A.2

Estimates of Survey Standard Errors

n = 17,000

N =	100	200	300	400	500	1000	2500	5000	10000	15000	17000
1% or 99%	1.26	0.89	0.73	0.63	0.57	0.40	0.25	0.18	0.13	0.10	0.10
5% or 95%	2.77	1.96	1.60	1.38	1.24	0.88	0.55	0.39	0.28	0.23	0.21
10% or 90%	3.81	2.69	2.20	1.91	1.70	1.20	0.76	0.54	0.38	0.31	0.29
20% or 80%	5.08	3.59	2.93	2.54	2.27	1.61	1.02	0.72	0.51	0.41	0.39
30% or 70%	5.82	4.12	3.36	2.91	2.60	1.84	1.16	0.82	0.58	0.48	0.45
40% or 60%	6.22	4.40	3.59	3.11	2.78	1.97	1.24	0.88	0.62	0.51	0.48
50%	6.35	4.49	3.67	3.18	2.84	2.01	1.27	0.90	0.64	0.52	0.49

n = 50,000

N =	100	200	300	400	500	1000	2500	5000	10000	15000	25000	35000	50000
1% or 99%	1.22	0.86	0.70	0.61	0.54	0.38	0.24	0.17	0.12	0.10	0.08	0.06	0.05
5% or 95%	2.66	1.88	1.54	1.33	1.19	0.84	0.53	0.38	0.27	0.22	0.17	0.14	0.12
10% or 90%	3.67	2.59	2.12	1.83	1.64	1.16	0.73	0.52	0.37	0.30	0.23	0.20	0.16
20% or 80%	4.89	3.46	2.82	2.44	2.19	1.55	0.98	0.69	0.49	0.40	0.31	0.26	0.22
30% or 70%	5.60	3.96	3.23	2.80	2.50	1.77	1.12	0.79	0.56	0.46	0.35	0.30	0.25
40% or 60%	5.99	4.23	3.46	2.99	2.68	1.89	1.20	0.85	0.60	0.49	0.38	0.32	0.27
50%	6.11	4.32	3.53	3.05	2.73	1.93	1.22	0.86	0.61	0.50	0.39	0.33	0.27

Note: The standard errors in the above tables are expressed as percentage values. If one were looking for the standard error of a survey estimate of 10 percent with a base size of 5,000, the standard error from the full, 50,000 sample is 0.52 percent, or 10 percent +/- 0.52 percent. From the 17,000 sub-sample, the standard error is 0.54 percent.

A 95 percent confidence interval can be constructed by multiplying the standard error by 1.96; construct a 90 percent interval by multiplying by 1.645; and 80 percent, by 1.282. So, a 95 percent confidence interval for the 10 percent estimate would be 10 percent +/- 1.02 percent, or approximately 9 percent to 11 percent.

Index

References to denominations are limited to places where there is a significant discussion.
Most tables (see list at the front of the book) include data and discussion of the largest denominations.

About the Authors

BARRY A. KOSMIN is research professor in public policy and law and founding director of the Institute for the Study of Secularism in Society and Culture at Trinity College in Hartford, Connecticut. Principal investigator of the CUNY Graduate Center's *American Religious Identification Survey* 2001 and the *National Survey of Religious Identification* 1990, he is co-author of *One Nation Under God: Religion in Contemporary American Society*.

ARIELA KEYSAR, a demographer, is associate research professor in public policy and law and the associate director of the Institute for the Study of Secularism in Society and Culture at Trinity College in Hartford, Connecticut. She was the study director of the *American Religious Identification Survey* 2001 and is co-author of *The Next Generation: Jewish Children and Adolescents*.